From the library of

Beverly Markham

Dollmaker's Workshop

Dollmaker's Workshop

Vera P. Guild

HEARST BOOKS
NEW YORK

Acknowledgments

Special thanks are due to the following individuals for their editorial and artistic help in the preparation of this book: Mary Johnson McLaren, former Senior Editor, Good Housekeeping *Needlecraft* magazine; Marcia Evans; Stephanie Wargo; and Betsy Berger. Thanks also to Leon McCann for his design of the Kitchen Witch.

Assistance provided by the following companies is also gratefully acknowledged: The Elder Craftsmen; Coats and Clark; and Wright's Bias Fold Tape Co.

Book Design: Lynn Yost
Illustrations: Marilyn MacGregor
Photography: David Arky, except for page 16, Myron Miller,
            and page 123, *Good Housekeeping*

Library of Congress Cataloging in Publication Data

Guild, Vera P.
  Dollmaker's workshop.

  1. Dollmaking. I. Title.
TT175.G84   745.592'21   81-4132
ISBN 0-87851-049-4   AACR2

Type set by Fisher Composition, Inc.
Text 11/13, 9/10 Memphis Light and
8/9 Helvetica Light; heads Bookman Contour

Printed in U.S.A.

Contents

Introduction

In nearly every corner of the globe, dolls have always been a cherished part of childhood. They may be put together from a few scraps of fabric lovingly assembled by a mother, or in the hands of an artist, they can be intricately constructed, elaborately costumed works of art. Given a name and cradled in a child's arms, however, any doll can come to life as it develops into a beloved companion with its own magical personality.

Images people make of themselves—or of animals—exert a strange power on the imaginaton, and children, perhaps more than older folk, respond deeply to that power. Dollmakers, too, are usually bewitched by their own creations; indeed, the process of crafting so meaningful an object is one of deep personal involvement, at once fascinating and rewarding.

It is in this spirit of creative involvement that *Dollmaker's Workshop* has been prepared. There are humorous dolls, such as the Swiss Grandma, whose sculpted face never fails to bring forth a smile. The international dolls, from China to Peru to Ireland, make the faraway and strange seem near and friendly. The old-fashioned rag dolls, made of everyday materials in simple designs, are all the more prized by their owners for the love the dollmaker contributed to their creation. The needlework dolls offer a different kind of creative opportunity to those with knitting and crocheting skills. And the dolls made from socks offer the perfect way for the beginning dollmaker to discover hidden talents and let loose artistic imagination.

Comprehensive, step-by-step instructions and drawings simplify the creation of all these dolls. Some of them are very easy to make; others entail more time and dedication, but all are universally appealing. Most of the techniques required to make the dolls are spelled out in the instructions for each project, but basic sewing and needlework stitches, as well as general information and additional designs for faces and hair styles can be found at the back of the book on pages 150 through 160. In most cases, a sewing machine will expedite the work, but any of these projects can be completed entirely by hand.

Ingenious dollmakers may wish to modify the basic designs given by choosing different fabrics or creating new facial expressions or other hair styles. Doll-supply stores and mail-order catalogues offer a wide assortment of accessories, from hair and hats and shoes to tennis racquets and roller skates.

A knowing poet once wrote, "He who gives a child a treat makes joy-bells ring on heaven's street." A doll is a gift of love; make one for a child and reap the rewards.

In the dollmaker's workshop, a quiet corner at home, familiar materials—scraps of fabric, buttons, embroidery floss—lie waiting for skill and imagination to transform them into treasures.

The Sock Dolls *(clockwise from left):* (1) Girl with a Pocket Doll, (2) Muggs Monkey, (3) Eskimo Boy, (4) Twins in a Bunting, (5) Snow Baby.

Sock Dolls

In all likelihood, the ancestor of the charming collection of sock dolls shown at left is the classic colonial-American rag doll. Dolls made from socks have long been in favor, and the reasons for their popularity are easily understood. The basic material, a pair of plain—even old—socks, is inexpensive and readily available in a variety of colors, sizes, and textures. Furthermore, the stretchiness of socks makes them easy to work with and stuff to form the shapes necessary for crafting the doll's body, head, arms, and legs, just as it makes the doll wonderfully soft and cuddly.

Even babies' socks may be used for tiny dolls that fit comfortably in small hands and little pockets. And large, heavy, textured men's socks make wonderful huggable, woolly toys for a larger child.

If you've never made a doll before, it might be a good idea to start with the sock variety. Give a nice old sock a second life and brighten the life of a favorite child. You can vary the faces of your creations by consulting the sections on "All about Faces" and "All about Hair" at the back of the book.

What little house player would not be drawn to the smiling, bright-eyed "Girl with a Pocket Doll" (1), a little mother with her own tiny dolly tucked away in the pocket of her patchwork skirt? Both dolls are fabricated from a single pair of flesh-tinted men's white socks.

The goofy grin on button-eyed, jug-eared "Muggs Monkey" (2), sporting topstitched overalls and a jaunty handkerchief, is guaranteed to brighten the eyes of any child. Muggs requires a pair of men's brown socks.

Rows of red, white, and blue rickrack and bright red overalls enliven the outfit of the almond-eyed "Eskimo Boy" (3), whose gray "fur" coat, felt boots, and fur-trimmed hood are meant to withstand any Arctic blast. This appealing fellow needs a pair of men's beige socks for his body.

And why not double the pleasure of the old nursery rhyme by wrapping two sleepy "Twins in a Bunting" (4) made of flannelette? The flaxen-haired babies are made from pale-pink socks and clad in similar pajamas—blue-and-white checked gingham for the boy and pink-and-white for the girl.

The cuddly "Snow Baby" (5) with the snow-white body and warm-looking snowsuit is particularly easy to make with a pair of child's white anklets and blue brushed tube socks.

Complete directions for each doll begin overleaf, but you may wish to use your imagination to vary the style of the clothes or the expression or materials of the features, especially if you want a doll that is completely washable.

Girl with a Pocket Doll

Materials

- 1 pair medium-heavy men's white socks, size 13, about 22" (55.9 cm) long
- A 2-foot (61-cm) length of white string
- 1 package peach or flesh-colored all-purpose dye
- Polyester fiber for stuffing
- Sewing thread: peach, white, brown, 2 spools red
- 3 strands each of 6-strand embroidery floss: red, white, brown, pink, and black
- A scrap of pink felt
- A 6" × 7" (15.2 × 17.8-cm) piece of black felt
- Lipstick (optional)
- 1 ball of brown rug yarn

- ½ yard (45.7 cm) of ¼"-wide (6-mm) red ribbon
- A 10" × 44" (25.4 × 111.8-cm) piece of medium-weight muslin
- 12 scraps, at least 2" (5 cm) across, of different colored fabrics in small patterns
- Seam binding
- A 15" (38.1-cm) square of printed cotton
- 4 small snaps
- ½ yard (45.7 cm) organdy
- 2 yards (1.83 m) of ¼"-wide (6-mm) lace edging
- 1 yard (.91 m) of ¼"-wide (6-mm) white elastic
- A 4" (10.2-cm) length of double-fold bias tape

The large doll's body

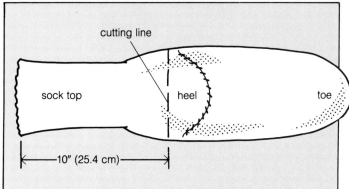

1. The Torso. Dye the socks and string peach or flesh color. When the socks are dry, slip one sock over a hand, press the heel flat toward the toe end, and stitch it to the sole of the sock. Lay the sock flat. Measure 10" (25.4 cm) from the sock top, and mark the distance with a line across the front and back.

Stuff the toe section of the sock to the line with polyester fiber until the sock is almost firm. Cut the sock in two along the line, fold under the cut edges of the stuffed end, and sew the end shut, centering the heel at the back.

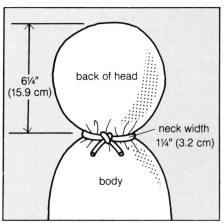

2. The Head. Separate the stuffing in the torso by working it up and down with your fingers, about 6¼" (15.9 cm) from the toe end of the sock. Tie the neck off with the dyed string to a diameter of 1¼" (3.2 cm) with the knot at the back.

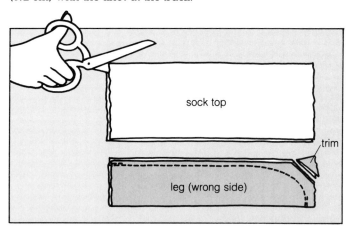

3. Cutting the Legs. Lay the top of the sock flat, and cut along each side to form two equal pieces. Fold each piece in half lengthwise, wrong side out, and stitch a narrow seam along the open edges of the side and ribbed end, rounding off the corner. Trim the corner outside the seam.

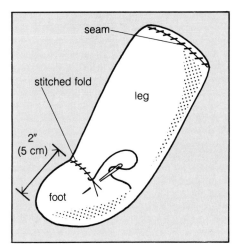

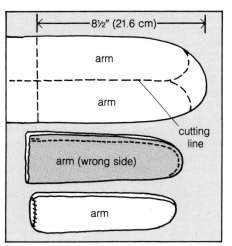

4. Finishing the Legs. Turn each section right side out, stuff it, turn under the open edge, and sew up the opening, centering the seam at the back.

Form the feet by stitching under a fold across the top of each leg 2″ (5 cm) from the ribbed end. Then, with seams turned to the back, stitch the legs to the body, across the entire top of each leg.

5. The Arms. Measure 8½″ (21.6 cm) from the toe of the second sock, mark a line across the sock at that point, and cut the sock in two along the line. Now, cut the toe end in two through both layers (see illustration).

To finish each arm, fold a section in half lengthwise, wrong side out. Stitch the long, open edges together. Turn the arm right side out, stuff it, turn under the open edge, and stitch the end shut.

Attach the arms to the sides of the doll's body, with the seams turned to the back, about 1¼″ (3.2 cm) below the neck.

The large doll's features and hair

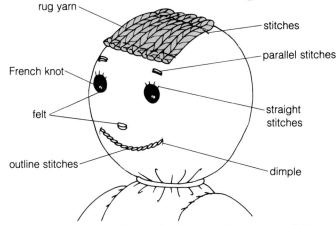

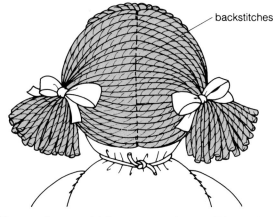

1. The Features. To make the mouth, sew a 1″-long (2.5-cm) curved row of outline stitches about 1¼″ (3.2 cm) above the center of the neck using doubled red floss. Stitch through the back of the head to begin and end the row of stitches. Then, starting and ending at the back of the head again, form dimples by making an invisible stitch with peach thread at each corner of the mouth, running the thread through the sock from one corner of the mouth to the other and pulling tightly on the thread after making each stitch.

The nose. Stitch a ³⁄₁₆″ (5-mm) circle of pink felt to the face with peach thread ½″ (13 mm) above the mouth.

The eyes. Tack two ½″ (13-mm) circles of black felt to the the face 1¾″ (4.4 cm) above the mouth and 2¼″ (5.7 cm) apart. Using black thread, make the eyelashes with single, straight ⅛″-long (3-mm) stitches, about ¹⁄₁₆″ (1.5 mm) apart. Then, with white embroidery floss, make a French knot (page 000) for the pupil of each eye, placing it slightly off center toward the corner of the eye.

The eyebrows. Make two or three ¼″-long (6-mm) parallel horizontal stitches with brown embroidery floss, ½″ (13 mm) above each eye.

If you wish, rouge the cheeks lightly with lipstick.

2. The Hair. To make the bangs, cut about ten 4″-long (10.2-cm) strips of rug yarn. Fold the strips in half, and, one by one, stitch them through the fold in a 2″ (5-cm) line across the top of the head. Arrange the ends of yarn to frame the face, and trim them slightly to round the bangs. Anchor the yarn with a row of stitches about ½″ (13 mm) from the ends.

Make the remaining hair by cutting thirty-six 12″ (30.5-cm) lengths of rug yarn. Starting about ⅓″ (8 mm) from the top end of the bangs, so the hair slightly overlaps the bangs, begin to attach the strips of yarn. One by one, lay the strips from side to side in parallel rows across the doll's head, and attach them at the center of the head with backstitches (page 000). Tie the loose ends of hair to each side of the head with bows of red ribbon.

The large doll's clothes

1. The Pants. Cut two 6″ × 12″ (15.2 × 30.5-cm) pieces of organdy. Turn up one long edge of each piece ⅛″ (3 mm) and press. Stitch a row of narrow lace along the right side of each folded edge. Attach a second row of lace ½″ (13 mm) above the first one.

To attach elastic for the cuffs, make a row of gathering stitches ½″ (13 mm) above the second row of lace. Draw the thread up to gather the fabric loosely. On the wrong side, attach a band of elastic over the gathering stitches, stretching it as you stitch.

Pin the ends of the two pant pieces together wrong side out, and stitch them with 4½″ (11.4-cm) seams, starting at the top edge. Clip the seam allowance at the end of each seam. Press the seams open.

Align the two seams and the edges of the leg ends and stitch them together. Turn under the top edge of the pants ½″ (13 mm), and stitch it close to the cut edge, leaving a small opening. Thread an 8″-long (20.3-cm) strip of elastic through the opening and around the waist. Stitch the ends of the elastic together and close the opening.

2. The Skirt of the Dress. Spread the muslin flat. Cut the small print scraps into various shapes, and arrange them on the muslin so they overlap slightly. Pin the pieces in place, and sew the edges down with zigzag stitching (A), using thread of a becoming accent color. Trim the edges of the outside patches even with the muslin. Then finish the ends of the patchwork with zigzag stitching.

Stitch bias hem tape along one long edge of the patchwork strip on the right side of the fabric.

As shown in drawing B, fold the patchwork strip in half, short sides together and muslin side out. Stitch the sides shut, starting at the hem edge and leaving a 3″-long (7.6-cm) opening at the top. Press the seam open. Slipstitch the seam allowances above the opening to the muslin backing.

Turn up the skirt hem 1¼″ (3.2 cm), pin, and slipstitch.

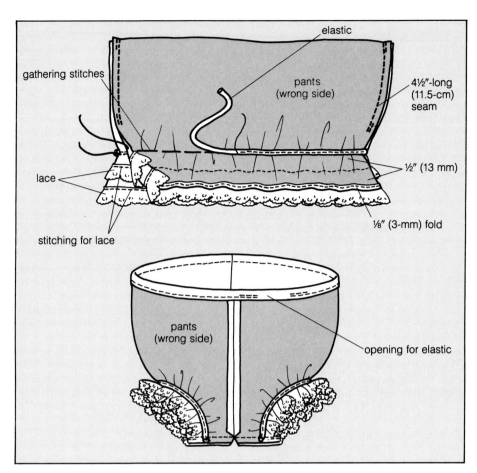

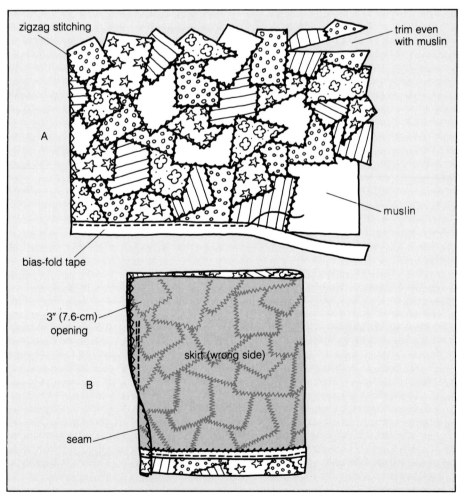

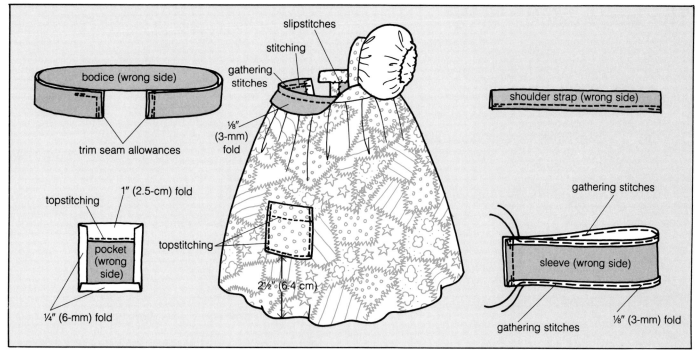

3. Finishing the Dress.

3. Finishing the Dress. Cut the large piece of printed cotton fabric into one 2″ × 11½″ (5 × 29.2-cm) strip for the bodice, two 2″ × 6½″ (5 × 16.5-cm) strips for the shoulder straps, and one 3½″ × 4″ (8.9 × 10.2-cm) piece for the pocket.

The bodice. Fold the bodice strip in half, long sides together and wrong side out. Seam the ends and 1″ (2.5 cm) along the remaining open edges at one end of the strip. Trim the end seams, and turn the bodice strip right side out.

Make a row of gathering stitches ¼″ (6 mm) below the top edge of the skirt. Gather the skirt evenly along the thread to a length of 10″ (25.4 cm).

Pin one edge of the bodice strip even with the top of the skirt, right sides together, with the closed portion of the bodice strip overlapping one end of the skirt. Stitch the edges together just below the gathering stitches in the skirt.

Turn the bodice strip right side out so it encases the top of the skirt. Turn the free edge under about ⅛″ (3 mm) and slipstitch it to the inside of the skirt.

The pocket. Turn under one short edge of the pocket piece 1″ (2.5 cm), and topstitch it along the edge. Turn under the remaining side and bottom edges ¼″ (6 mm), and press.

Pin the pocket to the left side of the skirt front (the seam should be at the back) 2½″ (6.4 cm) above the hem. Topstitch the pocket to the skirt along the side and bottom edges.

The shoulder straps. Fold the two fabric strips (cut earlier) in half, long sides together and wrong side out. Stitch the long edges together, and turn the strips right side out.

Slip the dress on the doll so the bodice reaches the armpits. Pin the back shut. Then pin the shoulder straps in place at the front and back of the bodice, with the seam centered on the underside and the ends to the inside. Stitch the straps to the bodice by hand and attach a snap to secure the bodice at the back.

The sleeves. Cut two 3″ × 12″ (7.6 × 30.5-cm) sections of organdy. Turn under the long edges of the two strips ⅛″ (3 mm), press, and make a row of gathering stitches, stopping short of each end.

Fold the ends of each strip together wrong side out, and seam them. One sleeve at a time, pull the loose ends of thread on one side, gathering the fabric evenly so it will fit comfortably around the doll's arm, and knot the thread. Gather the other side of the sleeve loosely. Slip a sleeve on each arm, loose side first and with the seam under the arm. Slipstitch the upper edge of the sleeve to the bodice and shoulder straps around the entire armhole.

4. The Shoes. Trace the actual-size pattern at left and cut it out. Align the fold line of the pattern on the folded edge of a piece of black felt, pin it in place, and cut out the shoe. Repeat for the second shoe. Stitch just inside the top edges of each shoe, as indicated, then seam the bottom edges together. Trim the seam allowances, turn the shoes inside out, and slip them onto the doll's feet. If the straps are too long, cut each one at the end on the outer side of the foot, overlap it the desired length, and attach it to the shoe with a snap.

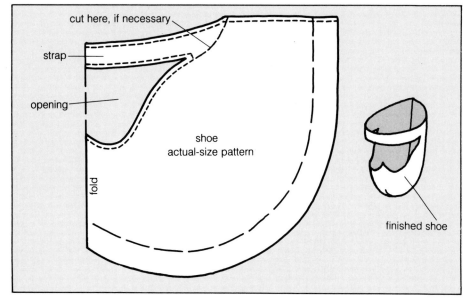

The pocket doll's body

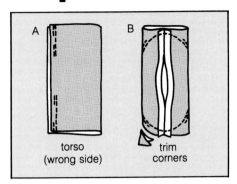

A

B

torso (wrong side)

trim corners

1. The Torso. Cut a 3" (7.6-cm) square and a 1½" × 7½" (3.9 × 19.1-cm) strip from the toe portion of the second sock on the lengthwise grain. Fold the square in half, wrong side out, along the lengthwise grain. Stitch the long edges closed, leaving a 1" (2.5-cm) hole at the center of the seam (A).

Roll the fabric so the seam is at the center, facing up, and stitch a semicircular line at the top and bottom edges to close the ends, as shown in drawing B. Trim off the corners.

The head. Turn the torso section right side out through the opening, and stuff it with polyester fiber until it is almost firm. Stitch the opening shut.

Tie off the neck of the pocket doll with pink floss, as you did for the large doll, about 1¼" (3.2 cm) from the seamless end of the torso section.

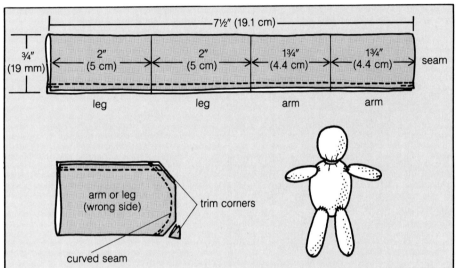

7½" (19.1 cm)

¾" (19 mm)

2" (5 cm) leg

2" (5 cm) leg

1¾" (4.4 cm) arm

1¾" (4.4 cm) arm

seam

arm or leg (wrong side)

trim corners

curved seam

2. The Arms and Legs. Fold the 7½"-long (1.91-cm) strip (cut in Step 1) in half wrong side out, and stitch the long edges together. Cut the strip into two 2"-long (5-cm) pieces for the legs and two 1¾"-long (4.4 cm) pieces for the arms. Stitch one end of each piece shut in a semicircular line, and trim the corners.

Turn each section to the right side, and, as for the large doll, stuff it and sew it shut. Stitch the leg and arm sections to the body at the appropriate places.

The pocket doll's features and hair

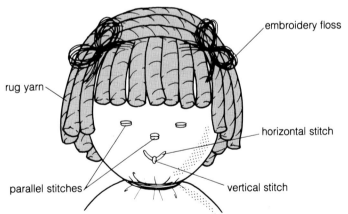

embroidery floss

rug yarn

horizontal stitch

parallel stitches

vertical stitch

stitches

1. The Features. To make the features, use embroidery floss, beginning and ending the thread at the back of the head.

The eyes. Make two parallel horizontal stitches with black floss for each eye halfway down the face and about ½" (13 mm) apart.

The nose. Make two or three tiny horizontal stitches, using white embroidery floss, at the center of the face just below the eyes.

The mouth. Make a ³⁄₁₆"-long (5-mm) horizontal stitch of red floss about ³⁄₁₆" (5 mm) below the nose. Then make a tiny vertical stitch over it from below, pulling the horizon-

tal stitch into a V shape, as shown. If you wish, rouge the cheeks with lipstick.

2. The Hair. Cut eleven 2¾"-long (7-cm) pieces of rug yarn. Lay seven strips across the head from front to back so that one end forms the bangs, and stitch them in place across the top of the head, from side to side. Make a second row of stitches across the back hair, about ¼" (6 mm) from the ends. Lay the remaining four strands of yarn across the head from side to side and secure them with random stitches. Trim the ends of yarn to shape them evenly. Make two small bows of red or pink floss, and attach one to each side of the head.

The pocket doll's clothes

1. Cutting the Fabric. From the organdy, cut two 1¼" × 4" (3.2 × 10.2-cm) sections for the sleeves, a 1¼" × 4" (3.2 × 10.2-cm) piece for the pants, and a 2½" × 12" (6.4 × 30.5-cm) strip for the skirt. Cut two ¾" × 2½" (1.9 × 6.4-cm) strips of black felt for the shoes.

2. Assembling the Clothes. Because the skirt joins the **sleeves** and covers the pants, starting with the sleeves is best.

The sleeves. Turn under the long edges of each sleeve section ⅛" (3 mm), and make a row of gathering stitches. Seam the ends of each piece of fabric together wrong side out, as you did for the large doll. Draw the loose ends of thread at the bottom and top edges together, leaving an opening large enough for the doll's arm, and knot them. Turn the sleeves right side out, slip one on each of the doll's arms, and tack them to the body.

The pants. Stitch three rows of narrow lace ¼" (6 mm) apart across the length of one long side of the pants fabric, starting close to the bottom edge. Turn under the opposite edge ⅛" (3 mm), and make a row of gathering stitches. Stitch the ends of the strip together wrong side out. Turn the band of organdy right side out; slip it onto the doll, lace edge down and seam to the back. Pull in the thread along the gathering stitches until the pants fit the waist, and knot the thread. Stitch the front and back of the pants together between the legs.

The skirt. Cut small patches of fabric, arrange them in overlapping fashion on the organdy, and sew the edges in place with zigzag stitching. Trim even with the organdy, and finish one long edge and the ends of the patchwork with a row of zigzag stitching.

Fold the ends of the patchwork together wrong side out, and seam them to within ½" (13 mm) of the top. Make a row of gathering stitches along the top edge of the skirt and gather it on the thread. Attach a 4" (10.2-cm) length of folded bias tape to the top of the skirt, as you did for the bodice of the other dress. Slip the skirt on the doll, and secure the back with a snap.

The shoes. Fold each shoe strip in half, mark an opening on the folded edge the size of the one shown at right and, keeping the fabric folded, cut it out. Unfold the strip and make two rows of stitching along the top edges of the shoe, the strap, and the opening.

Wrap each shoe piece around the pocket doll's feet. Stitch the ends together along the back of the doll's leg and feet. Trim the excess fabric outside the stitching lines, turn the shoes inside out, and tack them to the doll's feet.

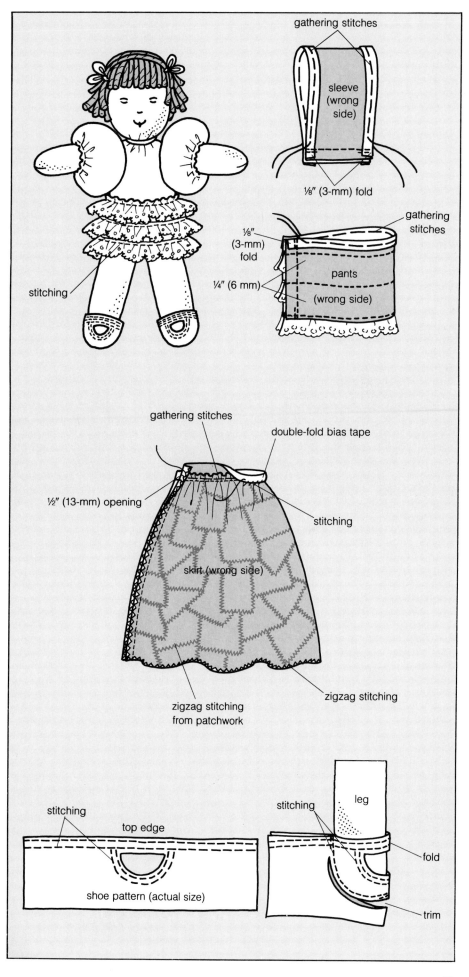

Twins in a Bunting

Materials

1 pair pale-pink flat-knit cotton/synthetic-blend socks, size 7½, with an ankle section that measures at least 5½″ long (14 cm) from the top and 2½″ (6.4 cm) across

Polyester fiber for stuffing

Embroidery floss: pale pink and red

Sewing thread: pink, black, and white

A scrap of pink felt or flannel

1 yard (91.4 cm) of 1″-wide (2.5-cm) yellow cotton braid with fringe

A 4″ (10.2-cm) length of ½″-wide (13-mm) white satin ribbon

An 8″ × 12″ (20.3 × 30.5-cm) piece of pink-and-white checked gingham cotton/synthetic-blend fabric

An 8″ × 12″ (20.3 × 30.5-cm) piece of blue-and-white checked gingham cotton/synthetic-blend fabric

½ yard (45.7 cm) of ½″-wide (13-mm) lace or embroidered edging

2½ yards (2.3 meters) of 1″-wide (2.5-cm) white satin ribbon

A 12″ × 15″ (30.5 × 38.1-cm) piece of white double-faced fabric such as flannelette

Note: It is easy to make the twins identical if you do each step at the same time for both dolls.

The dolls' bodies

1. Cutting the Socks. Draw a cutting line with chalk across each sock 2¾″ (7 cm) from the top. Draw a second line 2¼″ (5.7 cm) below and parallel to the first line. Draw a third line down the middle of each sock, dividing it in half, from the top to the lower line. Then measure and mark a spot 1″ (2.5 cm) from the end of the heel along the sole of the foot and another spot 1″ (2.5 cm) in toward the toe from the center of the back edge of the heel. Draw a curved line connecting the two marks, and continue the line in a curve to the edge of the instep. Cut each sock along all four chalk lines and discard the heel remnants. Trim each arm and leg section, if necessary, to a width of 2½″ (6.4 cm) along the grain of the ribbing.

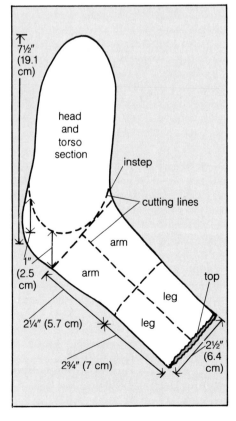

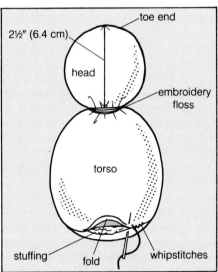

2. The Torsos and Heads. To form the **head** on each doll, mark the neckline 2½″ (6.4 cm) from the toe end of the sock. Stuff the sock firmly to the mark with polyester fiber and tie off the neckline tightly with several loops of pale pink embroidery floss.

The torsos. Stuff the rest of each sock firmly, fold the open edge under, and whipstitch the opening shut.

3. Assembling the Bodies. Fold each leg piece wrong side out, aligning the long edges, and stitch the long edges together, leaving a ⅛″ (3-mm) seam allowance. Center the seam on one side of the leg, and press open the seam allowances. Stitch one end of the leg shut in a curved line. Trim the corners outside the stitching. Turn the legs right side out, stuff them firmly, and whipstitch them shut as you did the torso, but center the lengthwise seam at the middle of the line of whipstitches. Slipstitch a pair of legs about ½″ (13 mm) apart to the bottom of each torso, with the seams facing the doll's back.

The arms. Make the arms exactly as you did the legs, but keep the lengthwise seam at one end of the whipstitches. Attach the arms at the appropriate places on each torso, about ⅜″ (9.5 mm) below the neck.

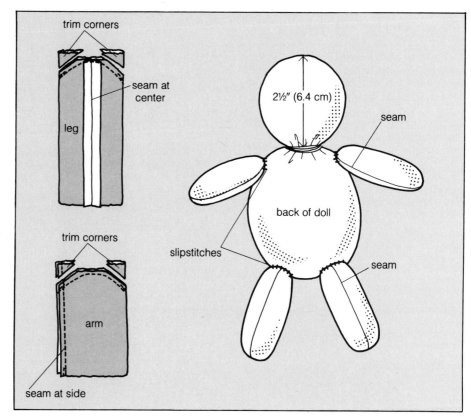

The features and hair

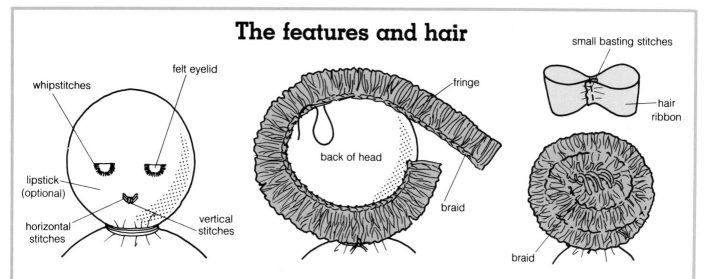

1. The Features. Sew through the head from the back to begin the stitches for making the dolls' features and end the thread at the back of the head.

The mouths. Make each mouth by first making two ¼″-long (6-mm) horizontal stitches with red floss about ¾″ (19 mm) up from the center front of the neckline. Then make two small vertical stitches over the center of the mouth from below to give the mouth a V shape.

The eyes. For each doll, cut two half circles of pink felt or flannel ¼″ (6 mm) across and ¼″ (6 mm) deep for eyelids. Mark two dots on the face ½″ (13 mm) above the mouth and 1″ (2.5 cm) apart. Place an eyelid over each dot, curved side down, and using black thread, attach the curved edge of the eyelid to the face with small, closely spaced whipstitches.

If you like, rub a little lipstick on each cheek.

2. The Hair. Cut the yellow fringed braid in half; each half will make the hair for one doll. Tack one end of a piece of braid to the side of a doll's head at eye level, with the braided side toward the center of the head and the fringe facing out. Slipstitch the braid around the doll's head working in a circle from the outside of the hairline inward and covering the braided part as much as possible with each successive row of fringe. Trim off the excess braid, and whipstitch the cut end to the doll's head. Fluff up the fringe around the braid that shows at the crown of the head and stitch some strands in place to cover it.

The girl's hair ribbon. Fold the ½″-wide (13-mm) white satin ribbon right side out so that it makes a flat loop 1¾″ (4.4 cm) wide, and the edges overlap by ⅛″ (3 mm) at the center. Sew across the middle of the loop, catching the cut ends, with small basting stitches, and gather the center of the loop tightly along the thread to form a bow. Knot the thread but do not cut it. Using the same thread, secure the bow to the top of the doll's head with several backstitches.

The dolls' clothes

1. Cutting the Pajamas. Enlarge the pattern for the pajamas to the scale indicated and cut it out following the directions on page 155.

Fold one piece of gingham in half long edges together, then crosswise. Pin the pattern to the fabric with the center and shoulder edges aligned on the folded edges of the fabric. Cut along all the edges of the pattern that are not directly on folds. Repeat with the second piece of gingham.

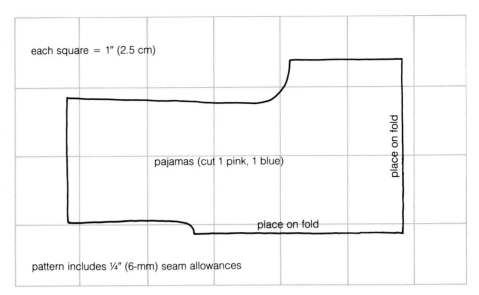

each square = 1" (2.5 cm)

pajamas (cut 1 pink, 1 blue)

place on fold

place on fold

pattern includes ¼" (6-mm) seam allowances

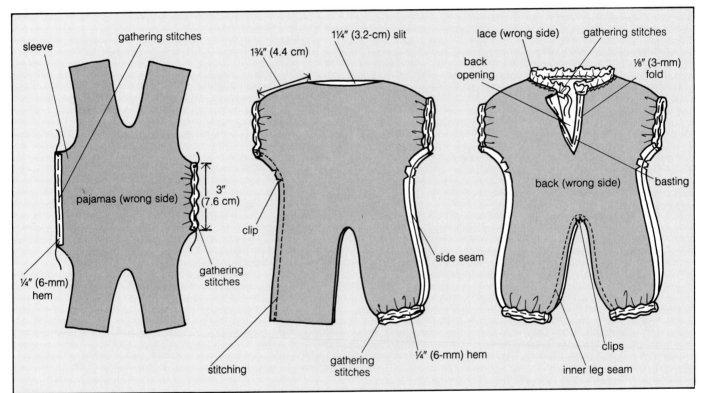

sleeve

gathering stitches

1¾" (4.4 cm)

1¼" (3.2-cm) slit

lace (wrong side)

gathering stitches

back opening

⅛" (3-mm) fold

pajamas (wrong side)

3" (7.6 cm)

clip

gathering stitches

¼" (6-mm) hem

back (wrong side)

basting

stitching

gathering stitches

¼" (6-mm) hem

side seam

clips

inner leg seam

2. Sewing the Pajamas. To sew each pair of pajamas, first open the fabric and turn it wrong side up.

The sleeves. Turn up and baste a ¼" (6-mm) hem along the edge of each sleeve. Gather the edge of each sleeve along the basting thread to a length of 3" (7.6 cm) and knot the thread.

Fold the pajama fabric in half at the shoulders, wrong side out, and align the side edges carefully. Pin and stitch the sides together, and press open the seam allowances.

The legs. Turn up and baste a ¼" (6-mm) hem along the bottom of each leg. Gather the hem along the thread to a length of 3¼" (8.3 cm), and knot the thread.

Align the inside edges of the legs, pin, and stitch them together from the end of

one leg to the end of the other. Clip the seam allowances at the curve.

The neckline. Cut a slit along the neck fold, centered 1¾" (4.4 cm) from the end of each sleeve. Cut a 1¼" (3.2 cm) opening down the top of the center back. Turn under the edges of the back opening ⅛" (3 mm) and baste.

The collar. Cut the lace or embroidered edging in half, and baste along the top edge. Gather the collar along the basting thread until it fits the neckline opening, and knot the thread.

Pin the collar right side up to the wrong side of the fabric around the neck of the pajamas, overlapping the edge by ⅛" (3 mm) and adjusting the gathers evenly. Turn under the ends of the collar at the center back, and backstitch it to the neck edge. Turn the pajamas right

side out, and slip the pink ones on the doll with the bow in its hair and the blue ones on her twin. Slightly overlap the edges of the back opening and sew them together with small running stitches, and remove the basting. Fold each collar over the outside, covering the neckline seam, and catch it to the pajamas with tiny stitches.

The bunting

1. Making the Bunting. Cut a 22" (55.9-cm) length of 1"-wide (2.5-cm) white satin ribbon and put it aside for the ties. Fold the remaining ribbon in half lengthwise right side out, aligning the edges, and press it with a warm iron.

The pocket. Cut a 16" (40.6-cm) length of the folded ribbon, slip it over one 15" (38.1-cm) side of the flannelette, and pin. Sew the ribbon to the blanket ⅛" (3 mm) from the ribbon edges. Fold up the bound edge 3½" (8.9 cm), making a deep pocket, and pin. Stitch the ends of the pocket shut ⅛" (3 mm) from the edges. With a few backstitches, tack the top edge of the pocket to the back of the bunting 4½" (11.4 cm) from each side.

Binding the bunting. Pin the remaining folded ribbon over the side and top edges of the bunting, starting at the bottom of one side with the end of the ribbon turned under and finishing at the bottom of the opposite side in the same fashion. Miter the ribbon at the corners. Stitch the ribbon to the bunting ⅛" (3 mm) from the ribbon edges.

Attaching the ties. Cut the 22" length (55.9-cm) of ribbon into two equal lengths. Turn the bunting pocket side down, fold under one end of a tie, align it at the side edge with the top of the pocket, and pin it in place. Stitch across the folded edge of the ribbon ⅛" (3 mm) from the fold. Cut a deep notch in the loose end. Repeat for the other tie.

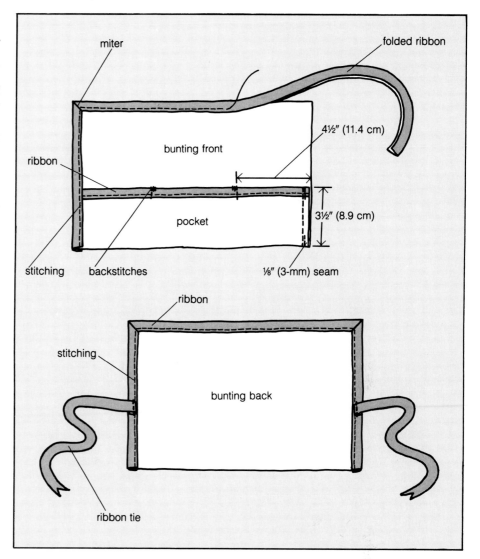

2. Wrapping the Twins. Turn the bunting over, pocket side up. Place the twins side by side in the center pocket. Fold the outer edges to the center, and tie the ribbons in a bow. Fold back the top corners of the bunting diagonally to show the twins' faces.

Eskimo Boy

Materials

1 pair medium-weight cotton/synthetic-
  blend men's beige socks, size 10
Sewing thread: beige, red, black, white,
  gray, and blue
Polyester fiber for stuffing
A 6″ (15.2-cm) length of fine string
Scraps of white and black iron-on tape
¼ yard (22.9 cm) red corduroy
Embroidery floss: black
Cardboard
20 yards (18.20 m black rug yarn
¼ yard (22.9 cm) gray fake-fur fabric
A 5″ × 26″ (12.7 × 66-cm) length of gray
  felt
A 6″ × 24″ (15.2 × 61-cm) length of white
  cotton

¼ yard (22.9 cm) red-and-blue plaid
  gingham
1 yard (91.4 cm) red-and-white patterned
  bias-fold tape
4 feet (1.22 m) medium-sized blue
  rickrack
4 feet (1.22 m) medium-sized white
  rickrack
5½ feet (1.67 m) medium-sized red
  rickrack
A 9″ (22.9-cm) length of gray bias tape
Five ¼″ (6-mm) snaps
Three ⁵⁄₁₆″ (8-mm) snaps
½ yard (45.7 cm) of ½″-wide (13-mm) gray
  grosgrain ribbon

The doll's body

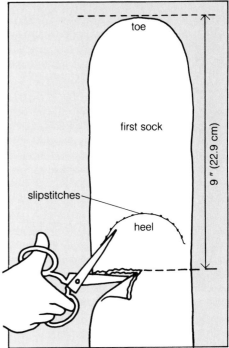

1. Cutting the First Sock. Place a hand
in one of the socks, fold the heel flat
toward the toe, and slipstitch it in place.

Lay the sock flat with the heel centered. Measure 9″ (22.9 cm) from the toe,
mark a line across the sock at that point,
and cut the sock in two along the line.

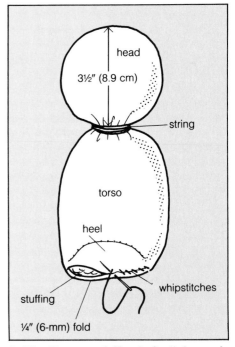

2. The Torso and Head. Stuff the sock
firmly with polyester fiber, turn the cut
edge under ¼″ (6 mm), and whipstitch
the opening, rounding the ends.

Form the head by tightly winding a
piece of fine string two or three times
around the stuffed section, 3½″ (8.9 cm)
from the toe, or seamless, end. Tie the
string securely and trim the ends.

3. The Arms and Legs. Lay the second sock flat with the heel centered. Measure 4¾″ (12.1 cm) down from the toe and mark a cutting line at that point. Mark a similar cutting line 5¼″ (13.3 cm) from the top of the sock. Then mark a line dividing each section in half lengthwise. Cut the sock through both thicknesses along all four lines.

Fold each arm and leg section lengthwise wrong side out, aligning the edges, and stitch the long edges together. Also stitch across the cut end of the sections from the sock tops. Turn the arms and legs right side out, stuff them, turn the open edges under ¼″ (6 mm), and whipstitch the openings. Whipstitch the arms to the sides of the body, 1½″ (3.8 cm) below the neck, with the lengthwise seams facing forward. Whipstitch the legs side by side to the bottom of the body, keeping the lengthwise seams facing the back of the doll.

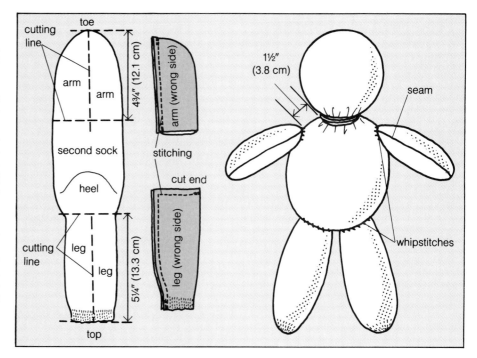

The features and hair

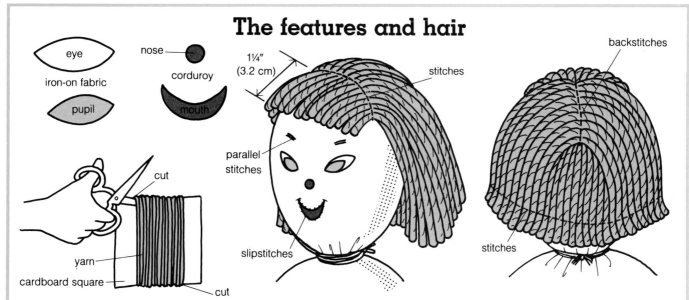

1. The Features. Trace the actual-size patterns (top left) for the features. Then cut out the tracings and use them as patterns to cut two large white eyes and two smaller black pupils from iron-on tape and a mouth and nose from the red corduroy fabric for the pants.

The mouth. With doubled thread and a long needle, slipstitch the mouth to the face 1¼″ (3.2 cm) above the center of the neck. Starting and ending the thread at the back of the head, form dimples by making an invisible stitch at each corner of the mouth, running the thread through the sock just behind the mouth from one corner of the mouth to the other, and pulling tightly on the thread after making each stitch.

The nose. In a similar fashion stitch the nose on ½″ (13 mm) above the mouth.

The eyes. Place the eyes about ¼″ (6 mm) higher than the nose and 1½″ (3.8 cm) apart. First, iron on the white eye pieces so that the outside corner of each eye turns up slightly. Overlap the inner left and outer right of each white piece with a black pupil set at a similar angle, and iron them in place.

The eyebrows. Sew three or four ⅜″-long (9.5-mm) parallel stitches close together ⅝″ (16 mm) above each eye with black embroidery floss, setting them at the same angle as the eyes.

2. The Hair. Cut a 7″ (17.8-cm) square of cardboard. Wind the black rug yarn around the cardboard twenty times, keeping the strands of yarn close together, and cut through the yarn along both edges of the cardboard.

Lay the strands of yarn in parallel rows from front to back across the doll's head, so the ends of yarn frame the face like bangs in front. Stitch the yarn in place in a line from one side of the head to the other, 1¼″ (3.2 cm) from the end of the bangs. Now cut an 8¼″ (20.9-cm) square of cardboard. Wind rug yarn around the cardboard twenty-five times, and cut it as before, along both edges of the cardboard. Attach the yarn, laying it from side to side across the doll's head and backstitching through the middle of the yarn down the center of the head for about 3″ (7.6 cm), starting at the top of the bangs. Trim the hair to a pleasing length around the head, and anchor the yarn with a row of stitches about 1″ (2.5 cm) from the ends.

The doll's clothes

1. Cutting the Fabric. Enlarge the patterns for the shirt, overalls, coat, hood, and boots to the scale indicated and cut them out, following the instructions on page 155. Fold each piece of fabric in half crosswise. Using the patterns and aligning the arrows on the lengthwise grain of the fabric where indicated, cut out the following: *fake fur*—two sections for the back of the jacket and one on the fold for the front; *gray felt*—two strips on the fold for the center of the boots, four boot sides, and one hood; *white cotton*—two sections for the back and one on the fold for the front of the shirt; *plaid gingham*—same as for the coat (for the lining); *red corduroy*—two pieces, one for each side of the overalls. Also, cut an 8″ × 16″ (20.3 × 40.6-cm) piece of fake fur for the hood.

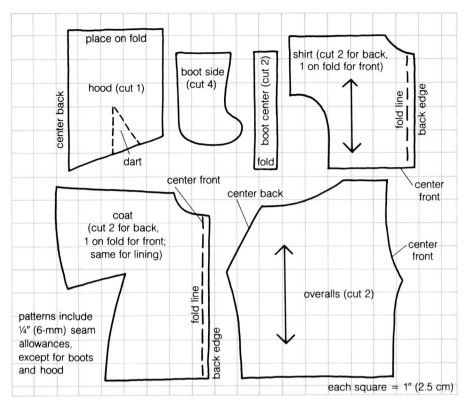

2. The Shirt. Pin the shirt front to the two back pieces, right sides together, at the shoulders. Stitch the shoulder seams, and press them open. Encase the neck and sleeve edges with the patterned bias-fold tape, and stitch the tape in place, overlapping the ends by about ¼″ (6 mm).

Fold the shirt in half across the shoulders, align the side edges, and stitch them together. Clip the seam allowances along the curves, and press them open. Turn under ¼″ (6 mm) along both edges of the back opening and along the bottom edge, and press. Turn under another ¼″ (6 mm) on these edges and stitch. Sew three small snap fasteners at the top, center, and bottom of the back opening.

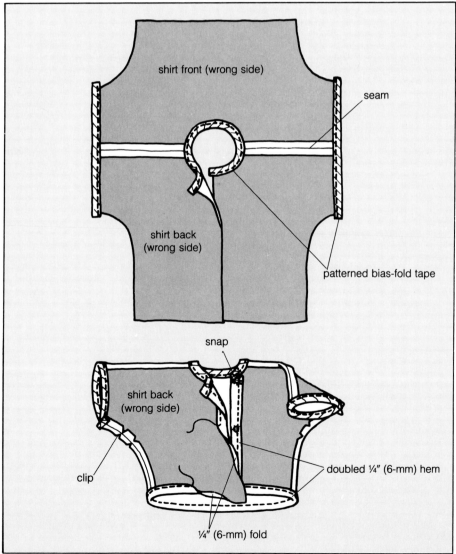

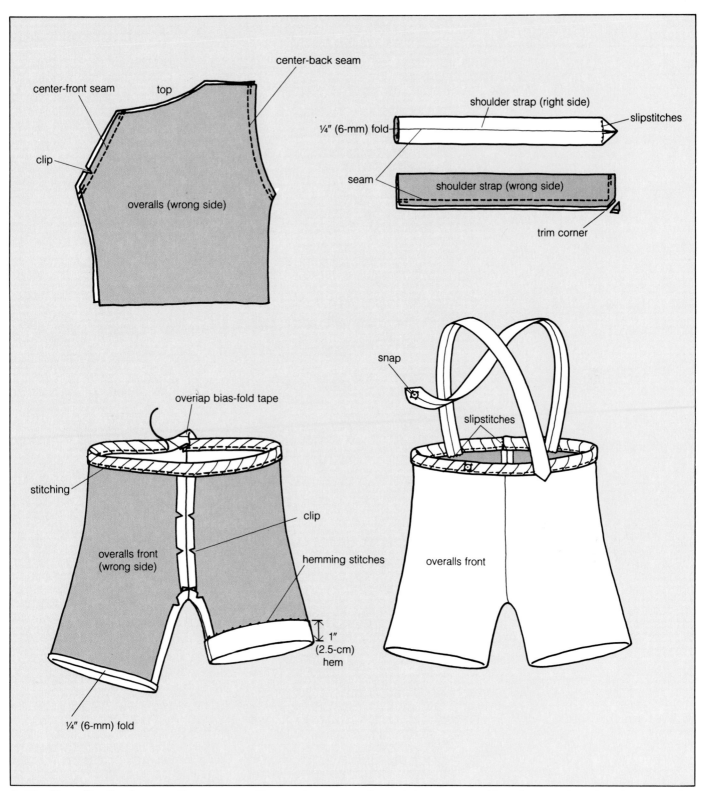

center-front seam
top
center-back seam

clip

overalls (wrong side)

shoulder strap (right side)
slipstitches
¼" (6-mm) fold

seam
shoulder strap (wrong side)

trim corner

overlap bias-fold tape

snap

stitching

slipstitches

overalls front
(wrong side)

clip

hemming stitches

overalls front

1"
(2.5-cm)
hem

¼" (6-mm) fold

3. The Overalls. Pin the overall pieces, right sides together, along the center front and center back seams. Stitch them together, clip the seam allowances along the curves, and press them open.

Align the center front and back seams, pin the inner edges of the legs, right sides together, and stitch. Clip the seam allowances at the curve, and press them open.

Turn up ¼" (6 mm) along the bottom edges of the legs, then turn up a 1" (2.5-cm) hem and slipstitch it in place.

Encase the upper edges of the pants with the patterned bias-fold tape, leaving ¼" (6 mm) of excess tape at each end. Overlap the tape ends at the center back, and slipstitch the tape in place.

The shoulder straps. Fold each strap in half lengthwise, right sides together. Stitch the edges of the long side and one end together, and trim the corner. Turn the straps right side out, center the seam on one side, and press. Turn under the corners at the finished end to form a point, and slipstitch them in place.

Turn the cut edge of each strap to the inside about ¼" (6 mm). Pin the cut end of one strap to the top of the overalls 1½" (3.8 cm) from the center back, seam side down, and stitch it in place. Likewise, sew the other strap to the back of the pants an equal distance from the center-back seam. Cross the straps at the back, and fasten each one to the opposite side at the front with a small snap at the top of the curve in the pants.

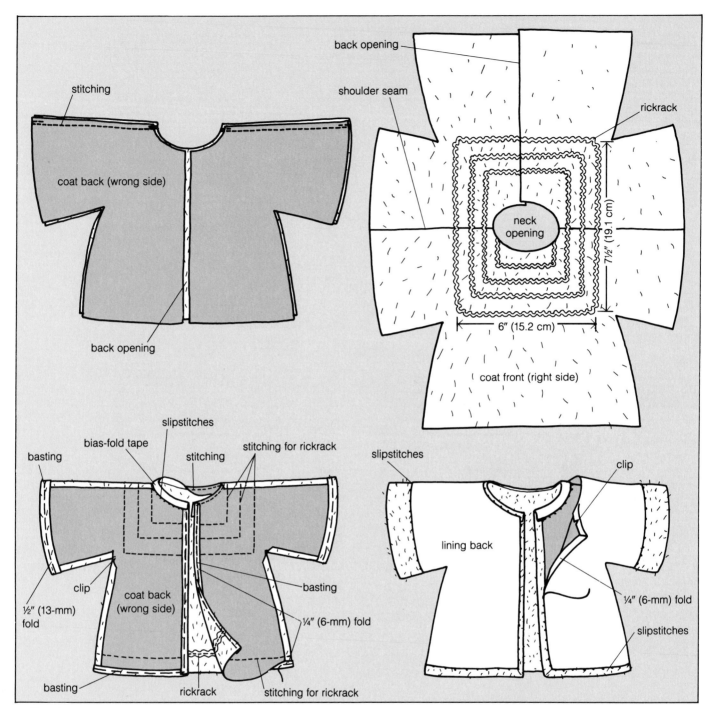

4. The Coat. Pin the edges of the coat sections, right sides together, along the shoulders, and stitch the shoulder seams.

Spread the coat open right side up, and center a 6″ × 7½″ (15.2 × 19.1-cm) rectangle of blue rickrack around the neck opening, with the long sides of the rectangle going from front to back across the shoulders. Stitch the rickrack in place with matching thread, turning the ends under at the back opening and anchoring them on the wrong side of the coat. In similar fashion, sew a row of red rickrack ¼″ (6 mm) inside the blue and a row of white rickrack ¼″ (6 mm) inside the red. Sew a final row of blue rickrack ¼″ (6 mm) inside the white row on the front of the coat only, anchoring the

ends on the wrong side of the neck opening.

Fold the coat in half along the shoulder seam right sides together, align the side edges, and stitch the side seams. Clip the seam allowances at the curves.

Stitch a row of red rickrack to the right side of the coat 1″ (2.5 cm) above the bottom edge.

Turn under ½″ (13 mm) of fabric along the edges of the sleeves, and baste. Turn under ¼″ (6 mm) of fabric along the edges of the back opening and bottom of the coat and baste.

Stitch one edge of the gray bias-fold tape around the neck edge, right sides together, so the tape extends ¼″ (6 mm) beyond the neck opening at each end. Clip the seam allowances at intervals

along the curve, turn under the ends of the tape, and turn the tape to the inside of the neck edge, covering the seam allowances. Slipstitch the edge of the tape in place.

The coat lining. Trim ½″ (13 mm) from the lower edge of the lining sleeves. Stitch the shoulder and underarm seams of the lining, right sides together. Clip the seam allowances at the curves, and press them open. Press under ¼″ (6 mm) on all the cut edges of the lining, clipping the edge slightly, as necessary in the curved areas.

Slip the lining over the coat, wrong sides together, matching the seams. Slipstitch the lining to the coat. Fasten the back opening by sewing on three ⁵⁄₁₆″ (8-mm) snaps.

5. The Hood and Boots. Align the broken pattern lines together on the wrong side of one felt **hood** piece, and pin. Stitch along the line on one side of the resulting fold to form the dart. Align the edges of the center back and whipstitch them, wrong sides together.

Fold the band of fake fur in half lengthwise, right sides together, and stitch the ends shut.

Turn the band right side out, and pin one long edge to the front edge of the hood, right sides together. Stitch the band to the hat. Turn under ¼" (6 mm) of the remaining free edge of the fur band, turn the band over the seam allowances to the inside of the cap, and slipstitch it in place along the fold.

The ties. Cut two 9" (22.9-cm) lengths of ½"-wide (13-mm) gray ribbon for the ties. Turn under one end of each tie, and sew a tie through the fold to the bottom of the fur band at each side of the hat.

The boots. Align the side sections of the boot with the center section, and whip the edges together with closely spaced stitches. Stitch four rows of rickrack—white, blue, red, and white—about ⅛" (3 mm) apart around the top of the boot, lapping the ends at one back seam. Stuff the toes of the boots with polyester fiber and slip the boots on the doll over the pant legs.

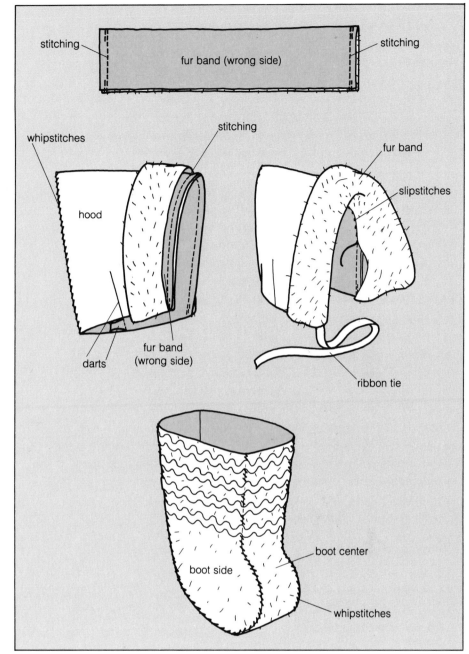

Snow Baby

Materials

1 pair white nylon stretch anklets, girls'
   size 6 to 8½
1 pair pale-blue brushed tube socks,
   size 9 to 11
Sewing thread: to match socks
Polyester fiber for stuffing
Embroidery floss: blue, pink, and black
Yarn, approximately 10 yards (9 m)
   each: pale pink and pale blue
Pink chalk

The doll's body

1. Shaping the First Sock. To form the doll's head, stuff the toe of one anklet with polyester fiber, and tie it off with two wraps of doubled thread about 2½″ (6.4 cm) below the toe seam to make the neckline. Stuff the next 4″ (10.2 cm) of the sock about three quarters full.

The legs. Cut the ribbed leg section of the anklet in two up the middle, and continue ¼″ (6 mm) past the ribbing. Turn under ⅛″ (3 mm) of fabric along the cut edges, and whipstitch the front and back edges together, forming the inner leg seam, as shown. Sew a row of gathering stitches around the end of each leg as close to the bottom edge as possible. Stuff the rest of the body and the legs. Pull each leg end tight along the gathering thread, and knot the thread securely.

The feet. Tie the ankles with doubled thread ¾″ (13 mm) above the end of the foot. Make a bend in each leg by backstitching partway through the body and the stuffing, starting at the crotch and ending 1″ (2.5 cm) higher at each side of the body, as shown.

2. The Arms. To make the arms, cut off the toe section of the second anklet 3″ (7.6 cm) from the end. Turn it inside out. Mark a line up the center, then sew a

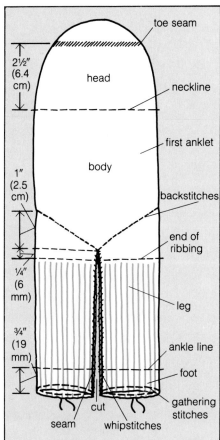

line of stitching ¼″ to each side of the mark, rounding off the top end of the stitching to the nearest side. Cut the toe section in half along the center mark to separate the arms. Turn each arm right side out and stuff it with polyester fiber. Tie off each arm 1″ (2.5 cm) from the closed end to make the wrist and hands.

Turn the edge of each arm under around the opening so the arms are about 1⅜″ (3.5 cm) long, then whipstitch an arm to each side of the body 1″ (2.5 cm) below the neck.

Tie one strand each of pink and blue yarn together around the neck, wrists, and ankles. Knot the yarn and tie a bow at each place.

3. The Features. To make the nose, find the midpoint of the face; this will be the center of the nose. Starting the thread at the back of the head, make a small backstitch about 3/16″ (5 mm) below the center. With your fingertips, pinch up a bit of stuffing about 3/8″ (9.5 mm) across, and wind the thread tight enough to hold the stuffing in the nose. Make a second backstitch next to the first one to hold the nose securely. Then, stitching under the nose to hide the thread, catch the thread that is wrapped around the nose with a tiny stitch at each quarter point. Finish at the back of the head.

Using embroidery floss, stitch the eyeballs with blue horizontal stitches, each pupil with a black French knot, and the mouth with a long horizontal pink stitch pulled down by a small vertical stitch, at the center and below it, into the shape of a V. Place the eyes just above the nose and 1″ (2.5 cm) apart, and place the center of the mouth about 1/4″ (6 mm) below the nose. Color the cheeks and nose with soft pink chalk.

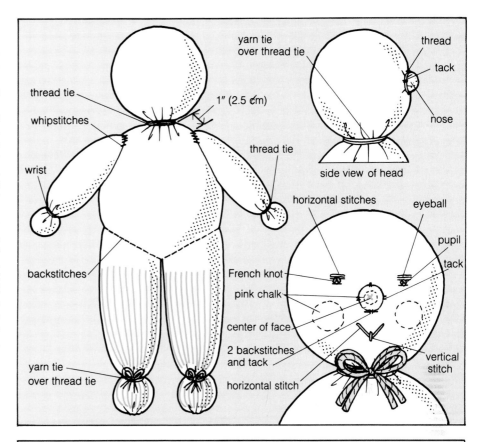

The doll's clothes

l. The Cap. Cut the leg end off the second anklet 1/4″ (6 mm) beyond the ribbing. Turn the section inside out, and sew gathering stitches along the line between the ribbing and the plain knit; gather the sock along the thread very tight, and knot the thread securely. Turn the cap right side out, roll the open edge up twice, 1/4″ (6 mm) the first time and 1/2″ (13 mm) the second.

The tassel. Wrap two strands of blue yarn and one strand of pink yarn around two fingers about fifteen times. Carefully slip the loops off your fingers, holding them together. Tie the loops together tightly with thread, leaving long ends on the thread. Cut the loops opposite the thread tie to make the tassel. Fluff the tassel and trim the ends to about 3/4″ (19 mm). Use the ends of the thread tie to stitch and knot the tassel to the top of the cap. Pull the cap onto the doll's head, covering the toe seam on the forehead by adjusting the brim.

2. The Snowsuit. Lay a blue sock flat, wrong side out, so the toe seam runs from side to side across the top. Make a curving cut 3″ (7.6 cm) long and 1/4″ (6 mm) deep 1/4″ (6 mm) from the end of the toe seam down one side of the sock, cutting through both layers. Do not cut into the toe seam. Turn the edge of the opening under 1/8″ (3 mm), and stitch it in place to finish the hood opening.

The armholes. Rotate the sock so the hood opening is at the center front, facing up. Draw a line from the bottom

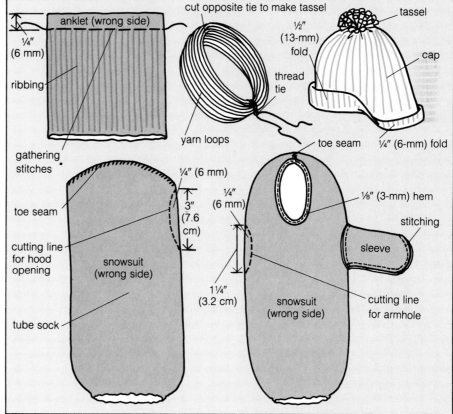

point of the hood opening out to both sides. Measure down 1/4″ (6 mm) from this mark and make a curving cut 1 1/4″ (3.2 cm) long and 1/4″ (6 mm) deep, along both sides toward the bottom.

The sleeves. Cut the toe off the second blue sock 3″ (7.6 cm) from the end. Turn the toe section inside out and stitch

a seam on each side of the center, rounding off the ends as for the doll's arms. Cut between the seams to separate the sleeves. Turn the sleeves right side out and stitch them to the snowsuit around the armholes, right sides together, leaving 1/8″ (3 mm) seam allowances. Slip the snowsuit on the doll.

Muggs Monkey

Materials

⅛ yard (11.4 cm) beige felt
1 pair synthetic-blend men's
  brown socks, size 10 to 13,
  with a 9″ (22.9-cm) leg
  (measured up from the heel)
Polyester fiber for stuffing
Sewing thread: brown, beige,
  bright blue, and orange
Two ½″-diameter (13-mm)
  round dark-brown shank
  buttons

A 48″ (121.9-cm) length of
  brown knitting yarn
⅜ yard (34.4 cm) of 45″-wide
  (114.3-cm) cotton fabric
A 12″-long (30.5-cm) piece of
  ¼″-wide (6-mm) elastic
Two ⁵⁄₁₆″-diameter (8-mm)
  round orange buttons
Two ³⁄₁₆″ (5-mm) snaps
A 2″ (5-cm) square of orange
  print fabric

The monkey's body

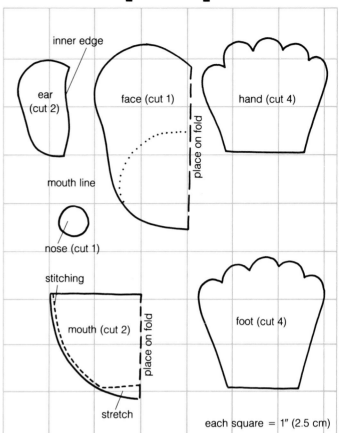

each square = 1″ (2.5 cm)

1. Cutting the Felt Pieces. Enlarge the face, ear, nose, mouth, hand, and foot patterns to the scale indicated and cut them out, following the instructions on page 155.

Using the patterns, cut one face and two mouth sections out of beige felt folded in half, with the center line of each pattern piece placed on the fold. Cut one nose, two ears, and four each of the hand and foot patterns from the felt. Lightly transfer the stitching lines onto the face and mouth fabric.

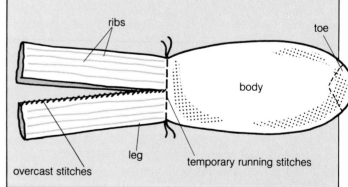

2. Starting the Body. Stuff the unmarked sock compactly up to and including the heel with polyester fiber. Make a row of temporary running stitches along the edge of the stuffing to keep it from slipping.

The legs. Count the ribs (the vertical knitted rows) in the leg section of the sock and mark the center front and back with a chalk line. Cut along each chalk line separately, between two ribs, from the top edge of the sock to the running stitches.

Form the legs by joining the cut edges of each half of the sock top with closely spaced overcast stitches; stop at the running stitches. Remove the running stitches, and firmly stuff the legs. Turn under the open edge of each leg ¼″ (6 mm), and whipstitch the end of the leg closed.

3. Assembling the Body. To form the **head,** wind a doubled length of matching thread several times around the body section 4½″ (11.4 cm) down from the top, draw it tight, and knot it at the back.

The arms. Cut off the leg section of the second sock. Mark and cut along the center front and back, just as you did for the legs on the first sock. Align the cut edges of each half wrong side out; join the long edges, and close one end of each arm with closely spaced overcast stitches.

Turn the arms right side out and stuff them. Turn under about ¼″ (6 mm) at the open (shoulder) end, center the lengthwise seam down the middle of one side of the arm, and close the end with whipstitches. With the lengthwise seam of the arm turned down toward the body, stitch an arm, across the shoulder end, to each side of the body, about 1″ (2.5 cm) down from the neck.

The hands and feet. Whipstitch the edges of matching pieces together in pairs, leaving the straight wrist and ankle edges open. Lightly stuff the hands and feet, including the fingers and toes. Slip the hands over the ends of the arms and the feet over the legs as far as possible, and slipstitch them in place. Bend the feet up, and sew them to the front of the legs with a row of small whipstitches, as shown at right.

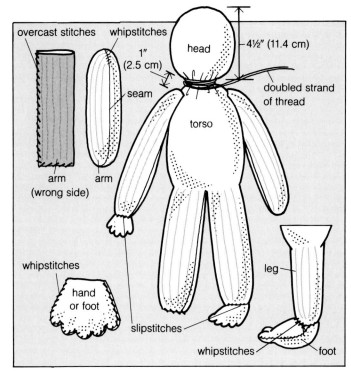

The features and hair

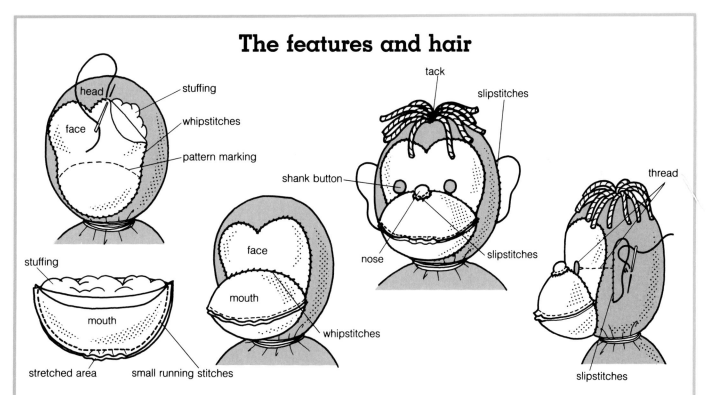

1. The Features and Hair. Pin, and then begin sewing the face section to the head with tiny ⅛″-long (3-mm) whipstitches. From time to time, as you sew, insert a small amount of stuffing under the face to pad it lightly.

The mouth. With your fingers, stretch the center of each curved edge of the mouth section to pucker the mouth. Align the mouth sections along the curved edges, and join them with a row of tiny running stitches along the line transferred from the pattern. Stuff the mouth firmly; then pin and whipstitch it to the face, joining the upper edge along the pattern marking and the lower and side edges to the corresponding edges of the face.

The nose. Make a row of running stitches around the edge of the nose section, gather the nose along the thread

to puff it somewhat, and then slipstitch the nose to the center top edge of the mouth.

The ears. Join an ear to each side of the head with slipstitches; align the center of the ear with the nose, and stitch along the inner edge of the ear.

The eyes. Using a long needle, sew a brown shank button to each side of the face, ¾″ (19 mm) from the nose. Make several stitches from each eye through the head to just behind the closest ear and back, pulling the thread tightly each time before finally securing it behind the ear.

The hair. Wind the yarn ten times around three fingers held together, and cut the loops at one end. Tack the strands through the center between the cut ends to the top of the monkey's head.

The overalls

1. Cutting the Fabric. Enlarge the patterns for the pant leg, bib, strap, and pocket to the scale indicated and cut them out, following the directions on page 155. Using the patterns, cut two pant pieces, one bib, two straps, and one pocket from the cotton fabric.

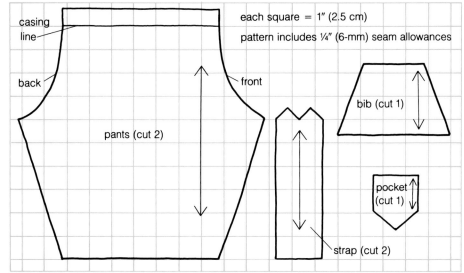

2. The Overalls. To make the overalls, align the center-front edges of the two pant sections right sides together, and seam them. Press open the seam allowances.

The casing for the elastic. Turn the top of the pants under along the casing line and stitch it down ⅛″ (3 mm) from the edge. Cut a 12″-long (30.5-cm) piece of elastic, insert it through the casing, and pin the ends even with the edges of the casing. Stitch the elastic in place ¼″ (6 mm) from each end.

Hemming the cuffs. Press under ¼″ (6 mm) at the lower edge of each leg. With orange thread, topstitch ⅛″ (3 mm) from the fold, and then make a second row of topstitching ⅛″ (3 mm) above the first row.

The pocket. Press under ½″ (13 mm) of fabric at the top and ¼″ (6 mm) along the sides and lower edges of the pocket. Pin the pocket to the front of the left leg 1″ (2.5 cm) below the casing line and 1″ (2.5 cm) to the right of the center-front seam. With orange thread, topstitch close to the side and lower edges of the pocket. Sew a second row of topstitching ⅛″ (3 mm) inside the first row.

The remaining seams. Align the edges of the fabric at the center back of the pants, right sides together, and stitch the center-back seam. Press open the seam allowances. Then align the inside edges of the legs and stitch them together, matching the center-front and -back seams as well as the hems at the lower edges of the legs.

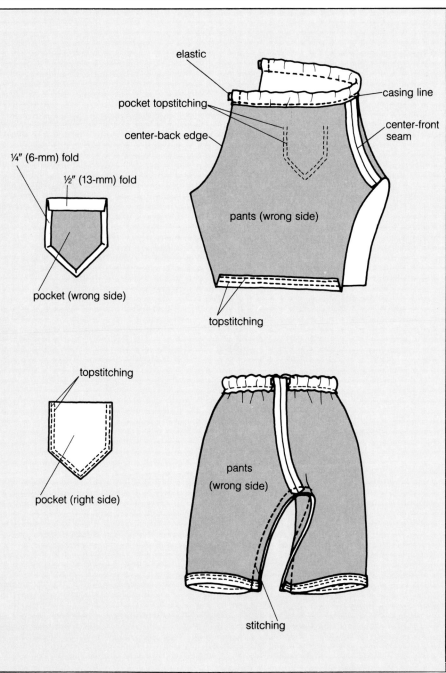

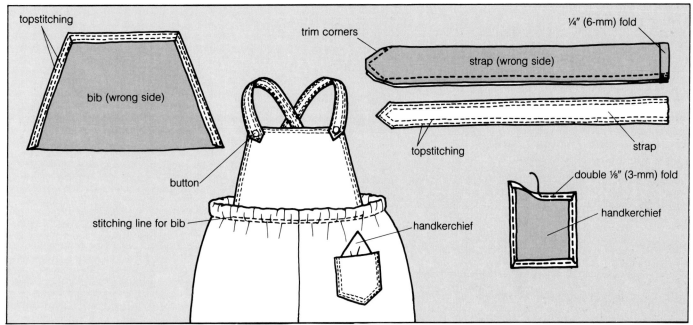

3. Finishing the Overalls. Turn under ¼" (6 mm) of fabric along the top and side edges of the bib, and press.

Topstitch close to the fold with orange thread. Add another row of topstitching ⅛" (3 mm) inside the first. Smooth the fabric along the elastic for about 2" (5 cm) on each side of the center front of the pants. Center the bib, right side out, inside the front of the pants, so the bottom of the bib is 1" (2.5 cm) below the top of the pants. Stitch the bib to the pants along the casing line, using thread that matches the pants.

The straps. Press under ¼" (6 mm) at the straight end of each strap. Fold the strap in half lengthwise wrong side out, and stitch along the open edges, but leave the straight end open. Trim the seam allowances and clip the corners. Turn the straps right side out and press. With orange thread, topstitch around the outside of each strap, close to the edge. Then make a row of topstitching ⅛" (3 mm) inside the first row.

Attach a strap to each top corner of the bib by lapping the pointed end ½" (13 mm) over the top of the bib and sewing a button at the center of each point through both the strap and the bib.

Put the overalls on the monkey. Cross each strap in back, and tuck the ends inside the pants at points equidistant from the center seam. Mark the positions for snaps on the outside of each strap and on the inside of the casing for the elastic at the waist. Sew the snaps in place and secure the straps.

The handkerchief. Cut a 2" (5-cm) square of fabric, turn under and stitch a double ⅛" (3-mm) hem around the edges. Slip the handkerchief into the pocket leaving one point visible.

The Rag Dolls *(clockwise from lower left):* (1) Colonial Lady, (2) Appalachian Mountain Couple, (3) Matilda Mouse, (4) Sandy Sneakers, (5) Waking-Sleeping Girl, (6) Tillie Turtle, (7) Lillie Longstockings, (8) Girl with a Straw Hat, (9) Day of the Week Dolls.

Rag Dolls

The stuffed fabric, or rag, doll is a perennial childhood treasure. Ease of construction and the wide range of materials available have contributed to the popularity of this type, but the reason fabric dolls endure is the fascination they hold for children. Soft, cuddly, and often having an almost human quality, these dolls are many a child's most faithful friend.

The dainty "Colonial Lady" (1) has a captivating painted face. Garbed in pantaloons and a rickracked-edged dress, she wears felt shoes stitched permanently into her leg seams.

Amusing denizens of Dogpatch, the "Appalachian Mountain Couple" (2) typify the hillbilly dolls of the Appalachian region. Made of unbleached muslin or cotton, their expressive, cartoon-like faces are created with stuffed fabric-circle noses and fanciful embroidery. Ma wears a poke bonnet and gingham and carries a broom; barefoot four-toed Pa sports burlap, denim, and a corncob pipe.

"Matilda Mouse" (3), whose imploring eyes are particularly endearing, requires soft synthetic fur and felt. The floppy ears, legs, feet, tail, and button nose are attached with hand stitches.

An all-American imp made of felt, "Sandy Sneakers" (4), with his hand-made sneakers and fringed denim cut-offs, is actually an imaginative adaptation of the classic flat gingerbread man. In fact, if made with brown felt for the body and white felt or embroidery floss for the features, he can be turned into just that. His head, body, and legs are cut and seamed together as one; the arms are attached separately.

The ingenious cotton "Waking-Sleeping Girl" (5) reverses from front to back, and both sides are identical, with one exception. On one side her cornflower-blue eyes are wide open; turn her over, and she is fast asleep. The doll's body requires only two pieces of fabric, seamed all around.

Friendly, all-felt "Tillie Turtle" (6) pokes her head out of a bright-green spotted shell. Whipstitches and machine stitching are used to join her.

Long black cotton legs, long embroidered lashes, and long yarn braids characterize "Lillie Longstockings" (7). Her arms and legs—with front seams that help form feet and hands—are stitched to the torso of this ruffled, eyelet-clad country lass.

The "Girl with a Straw Hat" (8), fetchingly dressed in a ribbon-trimmed frock, features unusual front seams that form a curved head and shaped feet.

Dimpled lasses with thick yarn hair, the "Day of the Week Dolls" (9) are made from a simple pattern in which only the head is separate. A change of skin or hair color and dress fabric expands the design further, making variations limitless.

The doll's body

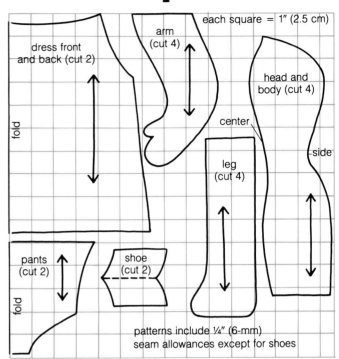

each square = 1" (2.5 cm)

dress front and back (cut 2)

arm (cut 4)

head and body (cut 4)

center

-side

leg (cut 4)

pants (cut 2)

shoe (cut 2)

fold

patterns include ¼" (6-mm) seam allowances except for shoes

1. Cutting the Fabric. Enlarge the patterns for the doll's various body sections, dress, pants, and shoes and cut them out, following the directions on page 155. The arrows on the pattern pieces should be aligned with the lengthwise grain of the fabric.

Using the pattern pieces, cut four each of the arm and leg sections out of the pink or peach cotton fabric. Then cut two of the body section; flop the body section sideways, and cut two more pieces facing in the opposite direction. Cut two pieces each for the dress and pants from the white cotton fabric and two pieces for the shoes from the blue felt. Also, cut two 5" × 12" (12.7 × 30.5-cm) rectangles from the white fabric to be used for the petticoat.

Girl with a Straw Hat

Materials

½ yard (45.7 cm) of 36"-wide (91.4-cm) pink or peach cotton fabric

½ yard (45.7 cm) of 36"-wide (91.4-cm) white cotton fabric

Scraps of light-blue felt

Sewing thread: to match fabric, felt, yarn, and ribbons

Polyester fiber for stuffing

Scraps of dark-blue iron-on tape

Scraps of red iron-on tape

An 8¼" × 6" (20.9 × 15.2-cm) piece of cardboard

Dark-brown knitting worsted

Cellophane tape

A 9" × 1" (22.9 × 2.5-cm) strip of tissue paper

½ yard (45.7 cm) of ½"-wide (13-mm) blue taffeta ribbon

1 yard (91.4 cm) of ½"-wide (13-mm) pregathered white lace

½ yard (45.7 cm) oval elastic cord

1½ yards (137.2 cm) of ½"-wide (13-mm) embroidered ribbon

24 inches (61 cm) of ¼"-wide (6-mm) grosgrain ribbon

A doll's straw hat with a 3¾"-diameter (9.5-cm) head opening

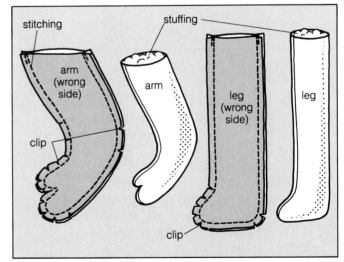

stitching

stuffing

arm (wrong side)

arm

leg (wrong side)

leg

clip

clip

2. The Arms and Legs. Align the edges of two of the arm sections right sides together; pin and stitch, leaving the top open for turning and stuffing. Repeat for the other arm and both legs. Clip the seams along the curves, press the seam allowances open with your fingers, and turn the arms and legs right side out.

Stuff each limb compactly with polyester fiber. Fold under the edge around the opening of each limb about ¼" (6 mm) and set aside.

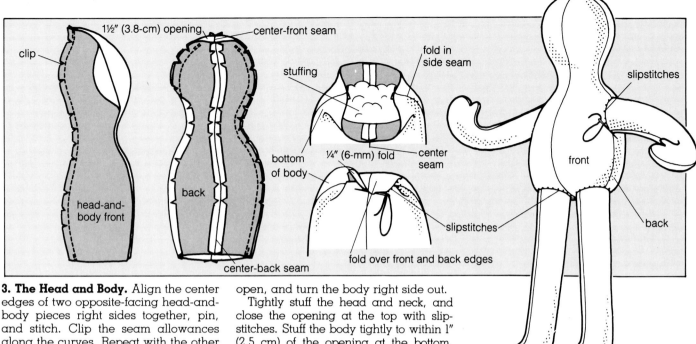

3. The Head and Body.

3. The Head and Body. Align the center edges of two opposite-facing head-and-body pieces right sides together, pin, and stitch. Clip the seam allowances along the curves. Repeat with the other two body pieces.

Pin the front and back head-and-body sections right sides together with the edges aligned, and stitch from one side to the other, leaving a 1½"-long (3.8-cm) opening at the top of the head; do not close the bottom. Clip the seam allowances at the curves, press them open, and turn the body right side out.

Tightly stuff the head and neck, and close the opening at the top with slipstitches. Stuff the body tightly to within 1" (2.5 cm) of the opening at the bottom. Turn the doll upside down with one hand, and press the side seams down over the stuffing as shown. With the other hand, overlap the front and back edges of fabric, tucking under the cut edge on top; pin the opening shut. Slipstitch the folds and the center seam in place.

Pin the arms and legs to the body in the appropriate places, and slipstitch each to the body around the circumference of the opening. (The lengthwise seam of each leg should face front and back; the arm seams face top and bottom, thumbs up.)

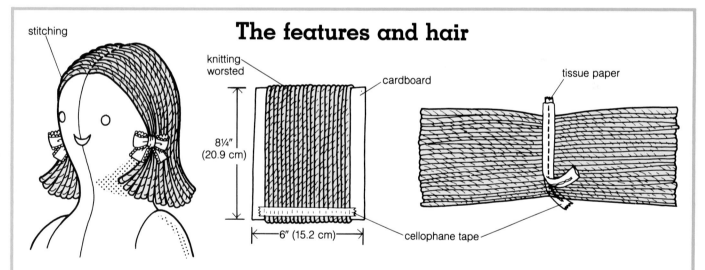

The features and hair

1. The Features. Cut two ⅜"-diameter (9.5-mm) circles for the eyes from dark-blue iron-on tape. With a pencil, mark the positions for the eyes about 2¼" (5.7 cm) apart at the same level as the outermost curves of the head. Iron them in place, following the directions on the package.

The mouth. Cut a ⅝"-long (16-mm) crescent, ⅛" (3 mm) across at the center, from red iron-on tape. Place it over the center seam about ½" (13 mm) lower than the eyes, and iron it to the face.

2. The Hair. Cut an 8¼" × 6" (20.9 × 15.2-cm) rectangle of cardboard. Wind the brown knitting worsted lengthwise around the cardboard, keeping the strands of yarn side by side and close together as you work. Place a strip of cellophane tape across the yarn to hold it in place at one end of the cardboard; then carefully cut through the loops of yarn at the other end with scissors. Remove the cardboard, and lay the strips of yarn flat, tape side down.

Cut a 9" × 1" (22.9 × 2.5-cm) strip of tissue paper. Fold it into thirds lengthwise, and place it across the yarn on top of the tape. Baste the paper to the yarn. Turn the yarn tape side up, and stitch down the center of the tape. Carefully tear the tape and tissue from the yarn.

Attaching the hair. Lay the hair across the head, from side to side, so that the stitches in the hair align with and cover the center front and back seam of the doll, with the hair beginning 1" (2.5 cm) in front of the top of the head. Pin the hair in place; tack it down across the front around the face, and sew a curved row of stitches about 2½" (6.4 cm) from the end of the hair.

Trim the ends of hair neatly. Cut the blue taffeta ribbon in two, and trim the ends. Tie together a few strands of hair at each side of the doll's head with a taffeta bow.

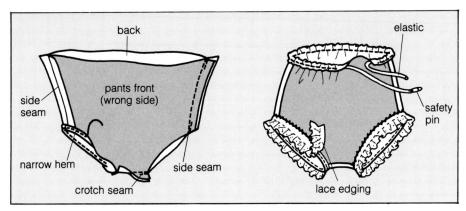

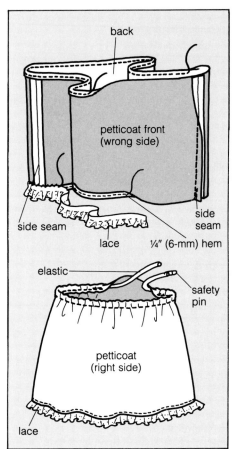

The doll's clothes

1. The Pants. Pin the two pant pieces right sides together, and stitch the side and crotch seams. Press open the seam allowances.

Turn up and stitch a narrow hem around the leg openings. Then stitch a band of pregathered lace around the edge of each hem on the wrong side of the leg opening.

Turn under a ¼" (6-mm) hem at the waist; pin and stitch it in place, leaving a small opening for the elastic cord. Attach a safety pin to one end of the elastic cord, and use it to thread the elastic around the casing at the waist.

Turn the pants right side out, and put them on the doll. Adjust the elastic to fit the waist, and sew the ends together. Stitch the casing for the elastic shut.

2. The Petticoat. Pin the two 5" × 12" (12.7 × 30.5-cm) rectangles of white fabric right sides together. Stitch the side seams (short edges); press open the seam allowances. Stitch ¼" (6-mm) hems along the top and bottom, leaving a small opening at the top for the elastic.

Sew a row of pregathered lace along the bottom edge of the petticoat on the wrong side. Insert elastic in the top casing as before, turn the petticoat right side out, and put it on the doll. Adjust the elastic to fit the waist, and tack the ends securely. Close the casing.

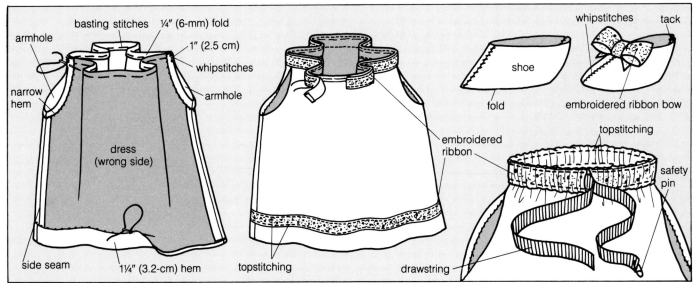

3. The Dress. Place the front and back of the dress right sides together; pin and stitch the side seams, and press open the seam allowances. Turn up a 1¼" (3.2-cm) fold along the bottom edge, and hem it in place. Sew narrow hems around the armholes.

Fold ¼" (6 cm) of fabric around the neck edges over on the right side, and baste in place.

With the dress still turned wrong side out, whipstitch the front and back together for 1" (2.5 cm) along the top of each armhole, starting at the neck edge and working down the armhole.

The trimming. Turn the dress right side out. Pin the embroidered ribbon, right side out, along the neck edge, starting and ending at the center front and hiding the fold of the dress underneath. Tuck under the loose ends of ribbon, until they just meet. Topstitch both edges of ribbon to make a casing for the grosgrain ribbon drawstring.

Topstitch another length of embroidered ribbon to cover the hemline, stitching both edges of the ribbon around the bottom of the skirt on the right side of the fabric.

The drawstring. Press the dress. Attach a safety pin to one end of the grosgrain ribbon; insert it at the center

front of the dress, and work it through the casing until both ends of the ribbon are the same length. Put the dress on the doll; gather the neckline and tie the ends into a small bow. Trim the ends and tack the bow in place.

4. The Shoes and Hat. Fold the fabric for each **shoe** lengthwise, and join the ends together with tiny whipstitches. Tie two tiny bows from the remaining embroidered ribbon, and tack one to the front of each shoe. Slip the shoes onto the doll's feet, and tack them securely to the legs at the back.

The hat. Secure the hat to the back of the doll's head with two small hat pins.

Sandy Sneakers

Materials

½ yard (45.7 cm) of 72"-wide (1.83-m) pale-orange felt

Two 8" × 12" (20.3 × 30.5-cm) pieces of yellow felt

An 8" × 12" (20.3 × 30.5-cm) piece of red felt

Scraps of blue and white felt

Sewing thread: to match the felt and fabrics, plus gold

Polyester fiber for stuffing

A soft brown pencil or eyebrow pencil (optional)

¼ yard (22.9 cm) of 36"-wide (.91-m) blue denim

A ⅜" (9.5-mm) gold button

¼ yard (22.9 cm) of 36"-wide (.91-m) white cotton knit

A ⅛" (3-mm) snap

1 pair white cotton baby socks, smallest size or size 3

1 yard (.91 m) of ¼"-wide (6-mm) twill tape

Cellophane tape

The doll's body

1. Cutting the Fabric. Enlarge the body, arm, and hair patterns to the scale indicated and cut them out, following the instructions on page 155. Cut two body and four arm sections from folded pale-orange felt. From yellow felt, cut one back-hair section using the whole pattern, then cut one front-hair section. Transfer pattern markings to the fabric.

2. The Body and Arms. Stitch the **body** sections together ⅛" (3 mm) from the edges, leaving openings between the dots on the head, shoulders, and feet. Stuff the doll firmly with polyester fiber, and stitch the openings on the head and feet shut with tiny backstitches. Work the stuffing flat along the dotted line above the legs with your fingers, and stitch across the line.

The arms. For each arm, stitch two arm sections together ⅛" (3 mm) from the edges, leaving the straight ends open. Stuff firmly to within ¾" (19 mm) of the openings. Aligning the dots on the arms with the shoulder curves, insert the straight ends into the shoulder openings, and stitch them in place through all thicknesses.

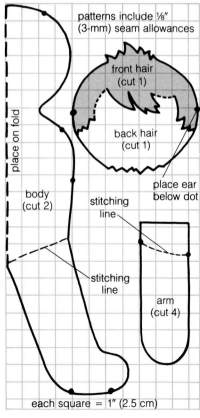

patterns include ⅛" (3-mm) seam allowances

place on fold

front hair (cut 1)

back hair (cut 1)

place ear below dot

body (cut 2)

stitching line

stitching line

arm (cut 4)

each square = 1" (2.5 cm)

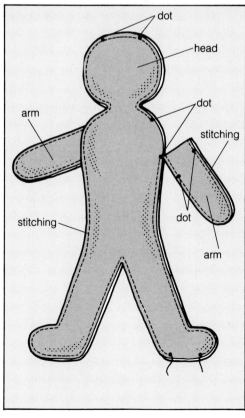

dot

head

arm

dot

stitching

stitching

dot

arm

The features and hair

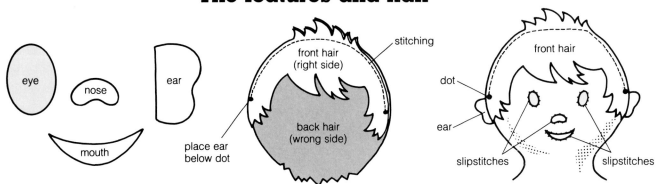

1. Cutting the Fabric. Trace the actual-size patterns for the features given above onto tracing or tissue paper, and cut out the patterns. Using the patterns, cut one nose and one ear from pale-orange felt, two eyes from blue felt, and one mouth from red felt. Turn the ear pattern over sideways on the pale-orange felt and cut a second ear.

2. The Hair and Ears. Align the top edges of the hair pieces, right sides out, and stitch them together ⅛″ (3 mm) from the edge between the dots. Slip the hair over the top of the head, and mark the sides of the head below the dots. Remove the hair. Place the ears along the edges of the back of the head section just below the marks, and sew them in place by hand. Slip the hair in place and tack it at intervals along the hairline, back and front.

3. The Features. Slipstitch the eyes in place 3″ (7.6 cm) from the top of the head and 2″ (5 cm) apart. Slipstitch the nose in place 3¾″ (9.5 cm) and the mouth 4½″ (11.4 cm) from the top of the head. Freckles can be added with a brown soft pencil or eyebrow pencil if desired.

The doll's clothes

1. Cutting the Fabric. Enlarge the patterns for the doll's clothes to the scale indicated and cut them out, following the instructions on page 155. Cut two T-shirt pieces from the white cotton knit, placing the center of the pattern along a lengthwise fold on the fabric; also cut a 1½″ × 10½″ (3.8 × 26.7 cm) horizontal strip of white knit for the neck binding.

With the denim fabric folded in half, cut two fronts, two backs, and two pockets for the jeans. Cut one denim strip 15½″ × 2″ (39.4 × 5 cm) for the waistband. For the shoes, cut four shoe tops and two tongues from red felt; cut four soles from white felt. Cut eight ¼″ × 1¾″ (6-mm × 4.4-cm) strips of blue felt for the racing stripes.

2. The T-Shirt. Pin the front to the back with the right sides together; stitch the left shoulder seam and press it open. On the right shoulder stitch for 1¾″ (4.4 cm) from the sleeve edge.

Beginning at the right shoulder opening, pin the neck binding along the neckline with right sides together, stretching the binding slightly. Stitch them together. Trim the end of the binding even with the edge of the seam allowance of the right shoulder. Press the neck seam allowance toward the binding, then press the right shoulder seam, including the open edge and the neck binding, open. Fold the free edge of the binding to the wrong side, leaving a ½″-deep (13-mm) neckband around the neck opening. Pin and stitch along the lower edge of the binding from the right side and through all layers. Turn under and stitch

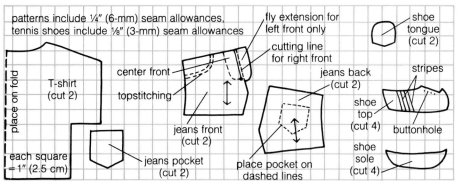

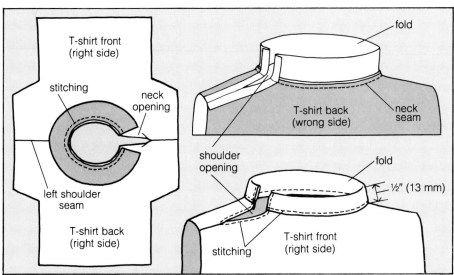

the edges along the shoulder opening.

Fold the shirt in half across the shoulders, right sides together. Align the underarm edges; stitch the lower edges of the sleeves and the sides. Clip the seam allowances at the underarm corners, and press them open. Turn under and

stitch a ¼″ (6-mm) double hem along the lower edge of the shirt. To hem the sleeves, turn under a double ¼″ (6-mm) fold and stitch it in place. Try the shirt on the doll, lap the right front shoulder edge about ½″ (13 mm) over the back, and sew on a snap.

3. The Jeans. Align the two **pants back** pieces, right sides together, and stitch the center-back seam. Press the seam allowances to one side, and from the right side sew a double row of topstitching along the seam and through the seam allowances to imitate a flat felled seam. Press under ¼" (6 mm) on all sides of the pocket pieces. Make a double row of topstitching along the top edge to hold the hem in place (A). Place the pockets right side out on the right side of the jeans back over the pattern markings and stitch along the sides and bottom of the pockets ⅛" (3 mm) in from the edges. Make a ⅜" (9.5-mm) fringe along the bottom of the legs by removing several horizontal threads (B).

The pants front. Place the pants front pieces right sides together, and stitch the center-front seam below the dot. On the left front, fold the fly extension to the wrong side along the center-front line, and sew a curved line of stitching to imitate a fly-front zipper. On the left front, fold the fly extension to the wrong side ½" (13 mm) from the center front line and stitch along the edge. On the pants fronts, make two rows of topstitching along the curved pattern markings to imitate front pockets. Make a ⅜" (9.5-mm) fringe along the bottom of the legs by removing horizontal threads (C).

Joining the front and back. With right sides together, stitch the front of the jeans to the back along the sides. Press the seam allowances to the front and on the right side make a double row of topstitching along the seam and through the seam allowances to imitate a flat felled seam. With right sides together, sew the front to the back along the inside leg seam. Clip the seam allowances at the corner of the inner leg seam and press them open (D).

The waistband. Fold the waistband in half lengthwise, wrong side out, and then turn ¼" (6 mm) of fabric along one long edge to the wrong side. Stitch a seam across each end and trim the corners (E). Turn the waistband right side out, and press it. Align the right side of the unfinished edge of the waistband with the wrong side of the top edge of the jeans and stitch them together. Press the waistband toward the seam allowances, turn the waistband over them and pin the folded edge to the right side of the pants. Stitch along this and the remaining edges of the waistband (F). Make a buttonhole on the left side, and sew a button on the right.

4. The Sneakers and Socks. Pin, then stitch, the blue stripes to the tops of the **sneakers** along the edges, using white thread, and making sure that you flop one of the top pieces for each shoe. Stitch along the dotted line marked on each shoetop and around the curved edge of the tongue. Lap a sole over each shoe top ½" (13 mm); using red

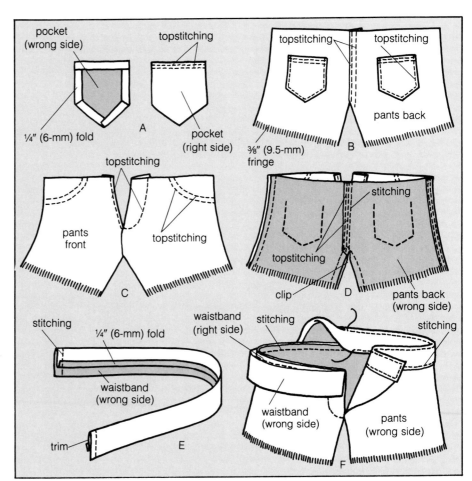

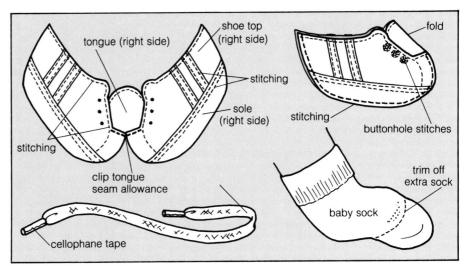

thread, stitch along the top edge of the sole. Make another row of stitching ¼" (6 mm) below the first row. Lap a shoe top ¼" (6 mm) over one half of the bottom and side of the tongue, and stitch along the edge from the row of topstitching to ⅛" (3 mm) from the center-front edge.

Attach the other side (the reverse image) of the shoe to the other half of the bottom and side of the tongue. Clip a V-shaped wedge from the seam allowance of the tongue at the center bottom. Align the edges of the two shoe pieces, and stitch around the outside of the shoe from the bottom of the tongue to the top of the heel.

Work a circle of buttonhole stitches around each dot to reinforce the felt. Using pointed scissors, make a hole through each dot. Cut the 1-yard (.91-m) piece of twill tape in half. Wrap a small piece of cellophane tape around the ends of each piece to resemble shoelaces. Carefully lace them through the holes in the shoes.

The socks. Put the baby socks on the doll so that the tops end about 4½" (11.4 cm) from the bottoms of the feet; trim off any excess sock that does not fit the foot. Turn under the edges and slipstitch them together. Slip the shoes over the socks and tie the laces.

The doll's body

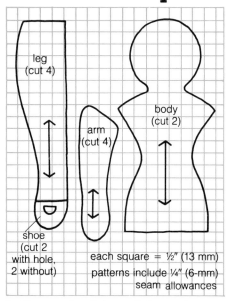

leg
(cut 4)

arm
(cut 4)

body
(cut 2)

shoe
(cut 2
with hole,
2 without)

each square = ½" (13 mm)

patterns include ¼" (6-mm)
seam allowances

1. Cutting the Fabric. Enlarge the patterns to the scale indicated and cut them out, following the instructions on page 155. Placing the arrows of the patterns along the lengthwise grain of the fabric, cut two body, two arm, and two leg sections from the off-white cotton fabric; then flop the arm and leg patterns sideways and cut two more of each.

Trace the lines indicated on the enlarged leg pattern to make a pattern for the shoes. Use the pattern to cut four shoe pieces from brown felt, cutting out the area indicated on two of the pieces for the shoe fronts.

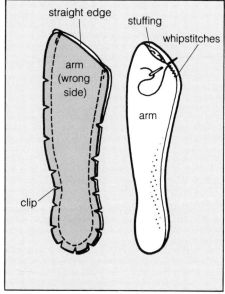

straight edge

stuffing

whipstitches

arm
(wrong
side)

arm

clip

2. The Arms. Stitch two arm sections at a time, right sides together, leaving the straight edge open at the wider end. Clip the seam allowances along the curved areas, and turn the arms right side out. Stuff the arms with polyester fiber, turn the open edge under ¼" (6 mm), and whipstitch the top sides of the arms together from front to back.

Colonial Lady

Materials

¼ yard (22.9 cm) off-white cotton fabric
A scrap of brown felt
Acrylic paint: brown and red
A small acrylic paintbrush
Sewing thread: to match fabrics
Polyester fiber for stuffing
16½ yards (15 m) brown pearl cotton
A 5" (12.7-cm) square of cardboard
A 2"-square (5-cm) scrap of green fabric

⅜ yard (34.4 cm) of 45"-wide (114.3-cm)
  striped or print cotton fabric
⅛ yard (11.4 cm) white cotton fabric
A 10" (25.4 cm) scrap of lace
1¼ yards (114.3 cm) of ⅜" (9.5-mm) rickrack
  to contrast with the striped or print fabric
½ yard (45.7 cm) of ¼"-wide (6-mm) velvet
  ribbon to match the rickrack

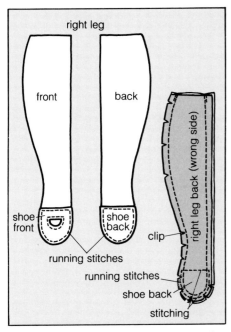

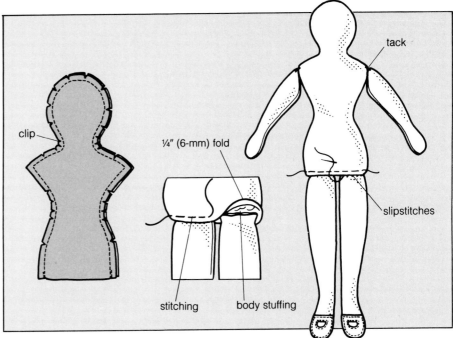

3. The Legs.

3. The Legs. Match two leg pieces for the right leg so that the curved edge will be to the right side of the doll; flop the other two leg pieces so that the curve will be to the left side of the doll. Using tiny running stitches around all the edges, sew a shoe front to the end of each front leg section, and a shoe back to each leg back. Stitch the front and back of each leg, right sides together, around the edges, leaving the top open. Clip the seam allowances along the curved area. Turn the legs right side out with the eraser end of a pencil or an-

other long, blunt object, and stuff them compactly with polyester fiber to within ½″ (13 mm) of the tops. Set the legs aside.

4. Assembling the Body. Stitch the two **body** sections, right sides together, along the edges, leaving the bottom edge open. Clip the seam allowances along the curves of the neck and waist areas. Turn the body right side out and stuff it firmly.

The legs. Turn the bottom edge of the body under ¼″ (6 mm) and stitch the fold. Insert the legs between the front and back sides, flattening the upper

edge of each leg from side to side before pinning it in place. Make sure the legs are on the proper side of the body and that the shoes are facing in the right direction, then baste them in place. Slipstitch the body and legs together securely, from one end of the bottom opening to the other.

The arms. Aligning a shoulder seam of the body with the upper seam of the arm, tack the arms at the center point securely to the body on the appropriate side, leaving the arms some mobility.

The features and hair

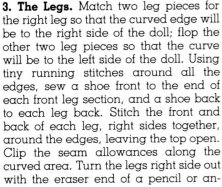

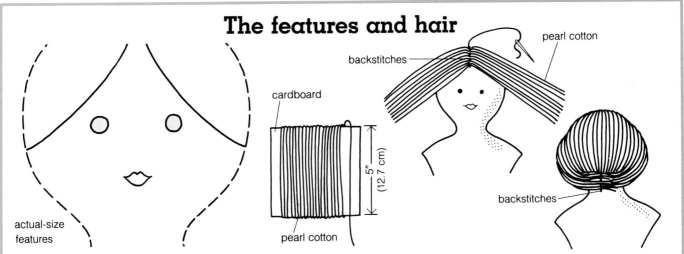

5. The Features. With a soft pencil, trace the actual-size pattern given here on tracing or tissue paper. Turn the paper over and retrace the features, transferring them onto the right side of the body front, aligning the eye markings with those transferred from the pattern for the body.

To paint the features, add a drop of ordinary dishwashing detergent to a small amount each of red and brown acrylic paint. Carefully paint the eyes, using the brown paint; paint the mouth red. Allow the paint to dry before sewing the body pieces together.

6. The Hair. Wrap the brown pearl cotton around the 5″-square (12.7-cm) piece of cardboard about fifty times. Cut the strands along one edge of the cardboard. Lay the strands, a few at a time, in close parallel rows across the doll's head from side to side, and attach them through the center with backstitches of pearl cotton. Begin at the point indicated on the pattern piece and at about the same level on the back of the head. Drape the hair forward on each side of the head, over the brow, and around to the back of the head. Twist the ends of hair around each other and tack them to the head with backstitches.

The doll's clothes

1. Cutting the Fabric. Out of the striped or print fabric, cut a 9½″ × 31″ (24.2 × 78.8-cm) rectangle for the skirt, two 5½″ × 8″ (14 × 20.3-cm) rectangles for the sleeves, and a 3″ × 7″ (7.6 × 17.8-cm) piece for the bodice.

Out of the white fabric, cut two 9½″ × 4½″ (24.2 × 11.4-cm) rectangles for the pantaloons and a 10″ × 4″ (25.4 × 10.2-cm) rectangle for the cap.

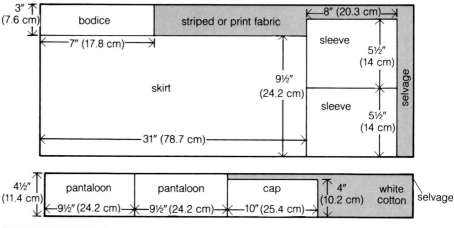

2. The Pantaloons. Fold under ¼″ (6 mm) of fabric along one 4½″-long (11.4-cm) end of each section, and stitch a piece of lace along the folded edge on the right side of the fabric.

Fold each pantaloon section in half lengthwise wrong sides out, and pin the edges together. Beginning 3¾″ (9.5 cm) from the top, or unfinished, end, stitch the leg seam. Clip the seam allowances just below the opening, and press them open.

Turn the leg sections right side out, and fold the top edge down over the legs. Matching the inside leg seams and aligning the free edges of fabric above them, stitch the pantaloon sections together, forming the crotch seam. Slip the pantaloons on the doll, and then make a pleat at each side of the center-front seam toward the hips to make the waist fit.

Pin the pleats in place, and then sew the pantaloons to the doll all the way around the waist with running stitches.

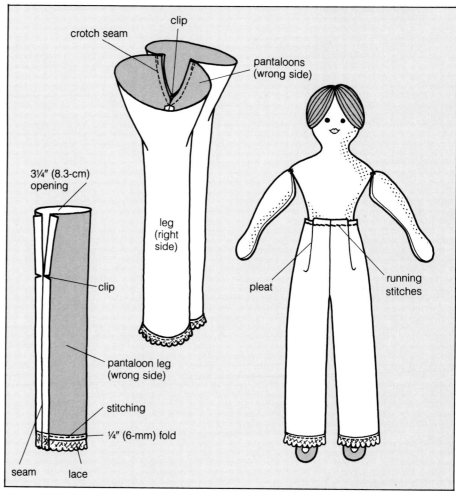

3. The Bodice. Press under ¼″ (6 mm) of fabric along the top and one side edge of the bodice. Make 1½″ (3.8-cm) slashes down from the top fold 1⅞″ (4.7 cm) in from each short edge. Wrap the bodice, long folded side at the top, around the doll so that the slashes fit under the arms and the opening is at the center back. Pin the bodice in place. Sew the bodice to the body around the waist with the running stitches, gathering the waist as you stitch, then sew the folded edges together over each shoulder with whipstitches. Close the back opening with slipstitches, with the folded short edge of the fabric at the center back opening lapped over the unfinished side

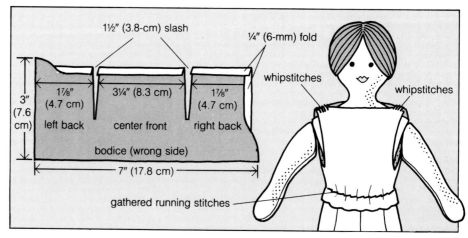

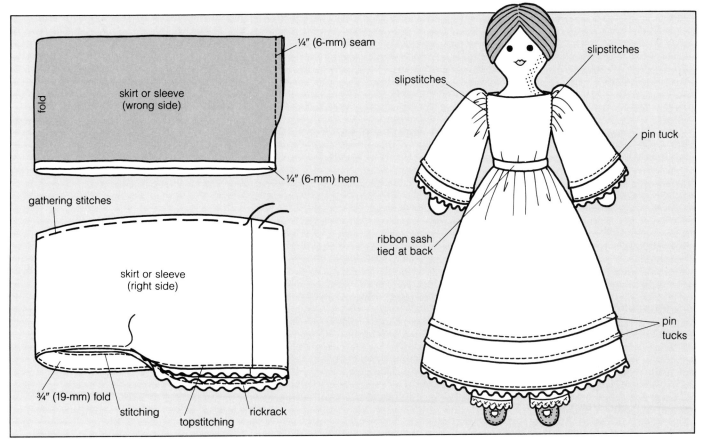

4. Finishing the Dress. Fold the **skirt** piece in half crosswise wrong sides out, and align the short sides and stitch them together. Press open the seam allowances. Turn under a ¼″ (6-mm) hem along the bottom edge. Sew a row of gathering stitches ¼″ (6 mm) from the top edge of the skirt, then turn the skirt right side out.

Pin a row of rickrack along the edge of the hem, so that half of the rickrack shows below the hem. Topstitch along the edge of the fabric to secure the hem and rickrack.

Fold the hem of the skirt ¾″ (19 mm) under, pin, and make a row of stitching on the right side of the fabric a scant ⅛″ (3 mm) from the edge of the fold to form a pin tuck. Make a second pin tuck, in the same fashion, ⅝″ (16 mm) above the first one.

Slip the skirt on the doll, and gather the top to fit her waist. Turn under the fabric along the gathering stitches, and slipstitch the skirt top to the bodice.

The sleeves. Fold the fabric for each sleeve in half wrong side out; align the long edges, and stitch them together. Press open the seam allowances. Turn under a ¼″ (6-mm) hem along the bottom edge, and sew a row of gathering stitches ¼″ (6 mm) from the top edge.

Turn the sleeves right side out, and attach the rickrack along the hem as was done for the skirt. Stitch one pin tuck, as for the skirt, ⅝″ (16 mm) above the hemmed edge.

Slip a sleeve over each of the doll's arms, and gather the top of the sleeves to fit the shoulder, concentrating the gathers at the top. Turn the top edge of each sleeve under along the row of gathering stitches, and then slipstitch the sleeve to the bodice along the fold. Tie a 14″ (35.6-cm) length of ¼″-wide (6-mm) velvet ribbon around the waist, with the bow in the back, for a sash. Neatly trim the ends of the ribbon.

5. The Mob Cap. Fold the cap fabric in half, wrong side out, align the short edges, and stitch them together. Press open the seam allowance. Turn up ⅝″ (16 mm) of fabric along the bottom edge and sew a row of gathering stitches ½″ (13 mm) from the fold. Sew a row of gathering stitches along the unfinished top edge, starting and stopping ¾″ (19 mm) from the seam. Gather the top of the cap to a width of 1½″ (3.8 cm). Anchor the gathers with a row of running stitches just outside the gathering stitches.

Turn the cap right side out, and place it on the doll's head with the seam to the back and the gathers at the center of the head. Gather the stitches around the bottom of the cap to fit the head, and knot the thread. Tack the cap to the doll's head at the center front and back and at the sides. Lift the fabric lying above the bottom row of gathers at the center back to cover the hole at the top of the head, and tack it with slipstitches just above the row of running stitches.

The rosettes. Roll up three 1¼″ (3.2-cm) lengths of velvet ribbon to make a bud shape, and stitch through each one to hold its shape. Using pinking shears,

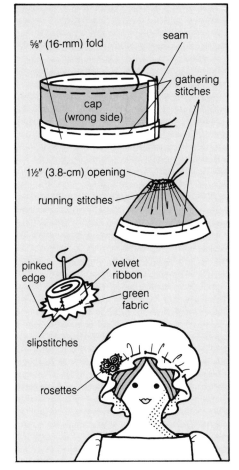

cut three ½″ (13-mm) circles from a scrap of green fabric. Tack a rosette to each of the green circles, and then tack the rosettes in a cluster to the cap.

Tillie Turtle

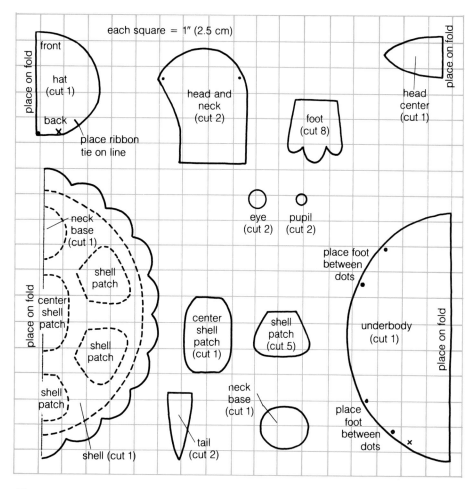

each square = 1" (2.5 cm)

front

place on fold

hat
(cut 1)

back

✗

place ribbon
tie on line

head and
neck
(cut 2)

foot
(cut 8)

head
center
(cut 1)

place on fold

neck
base
(cut 1)

shell
patch

eye
(cut 2)

pupil
(cut 2)

place foot
between
dots

center
shell
patch

place on fold

shell
patch

shell
patch

center
shell
patch
(cut 1)

shell
patch
(cut 5)

underbody
(cut 1)

place on fold

shell
patch

shell (cut 1)

tail
(cut 2)

neck
base
(cut 1)

place
foot
between
dots

✗

1. Cutting the Fabric. Enlarge the patterns to the scale indicated and cut them out, following the directions on page 155. Using the patterns, cut the following pieces from felt, and transfer onto them all the appropriate pattern markings: *bright-green felt*—one shell (upper body), one center head, two head-and-neck sections, and one neck base; *beige felt (or optional beige iron-on fabric patches)*—one underbody, eight foot pieces, two tail sections, one center shell patch, and five outer shell patches; *black felt*—two eye pupils; *white felt*—two eyes; *red felt*—one hat.

Materials

A 12" × 18" (30.5 × 45.7-cm) piece of bright-green felt
A 10" × 23" (25.4 × 58.4-cm) piece of beige felt (or beige iron-on patches, optional)
A few scraps of black and white felt
A 5" × 6" (12.7 × 15.2-cm) piece of red felt
Sewing thread: beige, bright green, red, black, and white
Polyester fiber for stuffing
Embroidery floss: red
½ yard (45.7 cm) of ¼"-wide (6-mm) red ribbon
A few small artificial flowers

The body

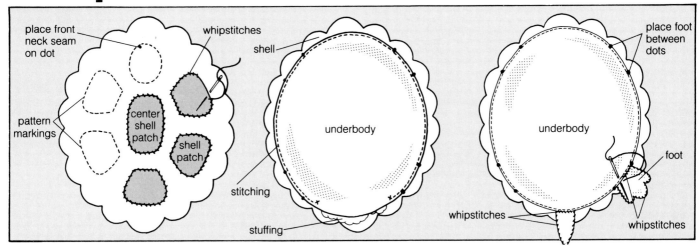

2. The Body. Whipstitch the beige shell patches in position on the shell section, or use iron-on patches, securing them with a few stitches in addition to the ironing, if you wish.

Center the underbody, markings out, on the underside of the shell; pin and then stitch the two sections together just inside the edge of the underbody, leaving an opening between the Xs for stuffing. Stuff firmly with polyester fiber, and stitch the opening closed.

The feet and tail. Align and whipstitch two foot sections together for each foot, leaving the straight end open. Stuff the feet firmly, whipstitch the openings closed, then whipstitch them to the underbody, attaching one foot between each pair of dots.

Whipstitch the turtle's two tail pieces together, sewing around all three sides, then whipstitch the tail to the seam allowance of the underbody section at the center back.

The head and hat

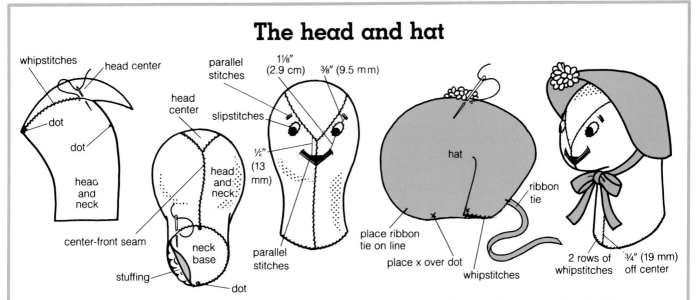

1. The Head. Whipstitch the head center to each head-and-neck piece, between the dots. Whipstitch the center-front and center-back seams of the head-and-neck pieces together. Stuff the head firmly, then whipstitch the neck base around the neck opening, matching the neck seams to the dots on the base.

The eyes. With tiny, almost invisible slipstitches, attach a black pupil over one end of each white eye piece. Slipstitch an eye, pupil to the left and angled slightly down, on each side of Tillie's head 1⅛" (2.9 cm) above the top of the center-front seam and just outside the seam of the center head section.

The eyebrows. Make a few parallel, horizontal stitches, using black thread, about ⅜" (9.5 mm) above each eye, just outside the seam of the center head section.

The mouth. With red embroidery floss, make about twenty ¾" (19-mm) straight stitches for each side of the mouth, starting about ½" (13 mm) below the front end of the head center and angling the stitches up at the outer ends about ⅛" (3 mm). Pull the stitches slightly as you work, to create dimples and accentuate the smile. Fill in the top center of the mouth with ten to twelve ¼" (6-mm) horizontal straight stitches. When you have finished, the mouth should be about ⅛" (3 mm) wide at the ends and somewhat thicker in the middle.

2. Finishing the Head. Pin the base of the neck 1" (2.5 cm) above the seam between the underbody and shell sections at the center front, turning the center-front seam of the neck ¾" (19 mm) to the left to give the head a slight tilt. Whipstitch the base of the neck in place with doubled thread, going around the neck twice.

3. The Hat. Fold the Xs at the back of the hat to the dot at the center back, and whipstitch the resulting inverted pleat in place along the edge. Stitch a 9" (22.9-cm) length of red ribbon to each side of the hat at the mark indicated for the tie, and sew a few flowers under the brim at the front. Tie the hat in place on Tillie's head.

Matilda Mouse

Materials

½ yard (45.7 cm) of 60″-wide (1.5-m)
 gray fake-fur fabric
Scraps of gray, white, and black felt
Sewing thread: gray, white, and black
Polyester fiber for stuffing
Embroidery floss: white, 1 strand
A ½″-diameter (13-mm) black shank
 button
½ yard (45.7 cm) of 36″ (91.4-cm)
 cotton print fabric
1 snap
A 14″ × 14″ × 21″ (35.6 × 35.6 ×
 53.4-cm) triangle of wool fabric

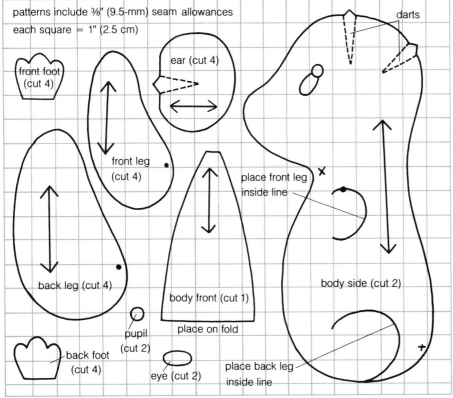

patterns include ⅜″ (9.5-mm) seam allowances

each square = 1″ (2.5 cm)

front foot
(cut 4)

ear (cut 4)

darts

front leg
(cut 4)

place front leg
inside line

back leg (cut 4)

body side (cut 2)

body front (cut 1)

place on fold

pupil
(cut 2)

back foot
(cut 4)

eye (cut 2)

place back leg
inside line

The mouse's body

1. Cutting the Fabric. Enlarge the patterns given here to the scale indicated, and cut them out, following the instructions found on page 155.

Pin the pattern pieces to the wrong side of the fake-fur fabric, with the arrows aligned on the lengthwise grain and the nap running down from the top of each piece. Cut out and transfer the pattern markings for the following: one body side, two ears, two front legs, and two back legs.

Flop the pattern pieces sideways so they face in the opposite direction, repeat marking, and cut out the same number of pieces for each as before.

Align the straight edge of the body front on the fold of a doubled piece of fur fabric and cut it out. Cut a piece of fur fabric 1½″ (3.8 cm) wide and 12″ (30.5 cm) long for the tail.

Using the remaining patterns, cut the following body pieces for the mouse from felt: four gray front feet, four gray back feet, two large white ovals for the eyes, and two small black circles for the pupils of the eyes.

2. The Torso. Stitch the darts on the head area of the body sides, slash them open along the fold, and press open.

Pin the body front and one of the body sides together between the Xs, wrong sides out, smoothing the pile away from the edges. Stitch from the middle of one X to the middle of the other. If some pile gets caught in the seam, gently pull it free with a pin. Attach the second body side to the body front in the same way.

Pin the body sides together, matching the head darts, and seam them between the Xs (around the front of the head and down the back), leaving an opening at the back for stuffing. Clip the seam allowances along the inner curves, and turn the body right side out.

Stuff the body firmly with polyester fiber, and close the back opening with slipstitches.

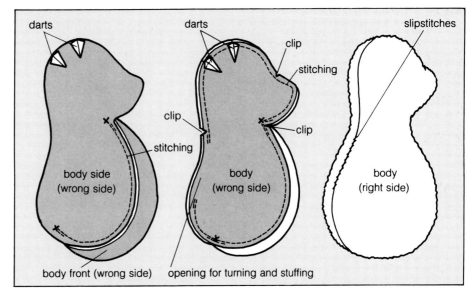

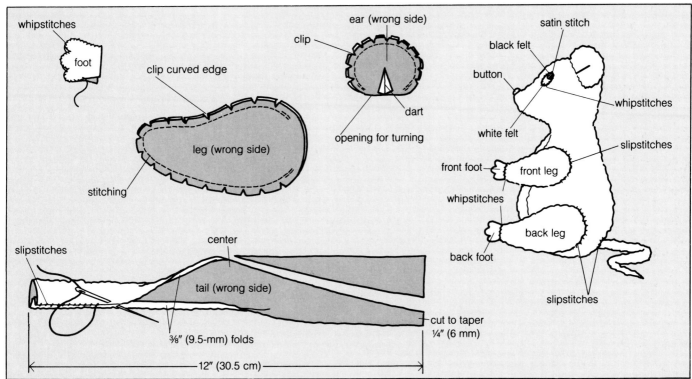

3. Finishing the Body. Use doubled thread for any stitches done by hand to attach and finish all of the body parts and the features.

The legs. Pin two matching pieces together, wrong sides out, for each front and back leg. Stitch around the edge of each leg, leaving an opening at the large curved end. Clip the seam allowances along the curves, and turn the legs right side out.

Stuff the legs softly so that they are fairly flat, and sew them shut with slipstitches. Slipstitch the legs securely to the body at the positions indicated on the pattern.

The feet. Pin two matching felt pieces together for each front and back foot. Whipstitch the edges of each pair together, leaving the straight edges open. Stuff each foot softly with polyester fiber.

Slip the front feet over the ends of the front legs and the back feet over the ends of the back legs, matching the seams. Whipstitch the feet in place, easing them slightly to fit the legs.

The tail. Taper one end of the tail section by cutting, in a slightly curving line, from the middle of the long edges of the fabric to a point ¼" (6 mm) in from the corner on the end to be tapered. Turn under ⅜" (9.5 cm) of fabric on the long edges of the tail; fold the tail in half lengthwise, right side out, and slipstitch the edges together. Sew the wide end of the tail to the body with the seam turned downward.

The ears. Stitch the darts on all four ear pieces, slash them open along the fold, and press open.

To make each ear, align a pair of ear pieces and pin them together, wrong

sides out. Stitch around the ear, leaving the straight edge open. Clip the seam allowances around the curved edges and turn the ear right side out. Slipstitch the openings shut. Pin the ears to the head along the straight edges, facing them forward and about 2" (5 cm) apart, just behind the dart at the top of the head. Slipstitch the ears in place.

The eyes. Whipstitch the ovals of white felt onto the face in the position indicated on the pattern, about 1¼" (3.2 cm) up from the nose and ½" (13 mm) from the head seam. With white embroidery floss, make a satin stitch dot at the center of each black-felt pupil. Then lap one of the pupils over the top of each white eye piece and slipstitch it in place around the edges.

The nose. Sew the black button to the top of the nose.

The mouse's clothes

1. Cutting the Apron. Following the layout, cut the cotton print fabric into three 8¼″ × 16″ (20.9 × 40.6-cm) skirt sections, a 2¾″ × 16½″ (7 × 42-cm) waistband, two 2¾″ × 6¾″ (7 × 17.1-cm) straps, and a 3¾″ × 4½″ (9.5 × 11.4-cm) bib. A ½″ (13-mm) seam allowance is included in all the measurements.

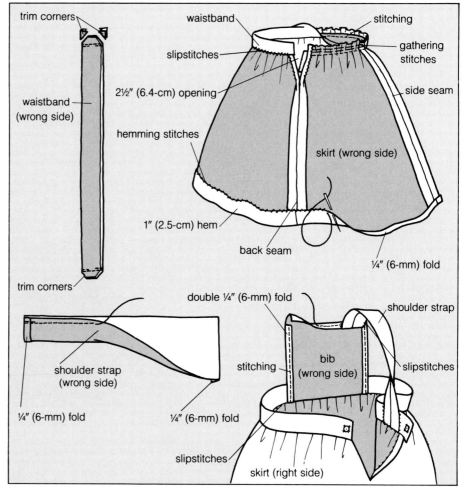

cutting layout for apron

selvage

3¾″ × 4½″
(9.5 × 11.4 cm)

bib

waistband 2¾″ × 16½″ (7 × 42 cm)

straps
2¾″ × 6¾″
(7 × 17.1 cm)

skirt
8¼″ × 16″
(20.9 × 40.6 cm)

skirt
8¼″ × 16″
(20.9 × 40.6 cm)

skirt
8¼″ × 16″
(20.9 × 40.6 cm)

2. The Skirt. Fold the waistband in half lengthwise, wrong side out, and stitch a seam across each end. Clip the corners, turn the waistband right side out, and press.

Pin the short ends of the skirt together, wrong sides out, to form a continuous band, and seam them, leaving a 2½″ (6.4-cm) opening at the end of one seam for the waist. Press all the seams open, and slipstitch a narrow hem along the open edges of the one seam.

Turn up the lower edge of the skirt ¼″ (6 mm) and press, then turn up a 1″ (2.5-cm) hem and slipstitch it in place.

Gathering the skirt. Machine-baste two rows of stitches, one ½″ (13 mm) and the other ⅜″ (9.5 mm) from the top of the skirt, and gather the skirt along the stitches to fit the waistband. Pin one edge of the waistband to the top of the skirt, right sides together, aligning the ends of the waistband with the open edges of the skirt and distributing the fullness evenly. Stitch the waistband to the skirt, just below the gathering stitches, then press it up toward the seam allowances. Turn the waistband over the seam allowances, make a narrow fold along the free edge, and press. Slipstitch the free edge to the wrong side of the skirt along the fold.

3. The Bib. Press under a double ¼″ (6-mm) fold along both short sides and one long side of the bib section. Stitch along the edges of the folds to hem the three sides. Turn up ¼″ (6 mm) of fabric along the unfinished, or lower edge, of the bib, and press it. Center the bib, right side facing out, at the inside of the skirt front (the opening is at the back), aligning the bottom of the bib with the bottom edge of the waistband. Stitch the bib to the waistband along the lower edge of the waistband.

The straps. Press under ¼″ (6 mm) on both ends of each strap. Fold each strap in half lengthwise, wrong side out, and stitch the long edges and one end closed. Turn the straps right side out, and press them so the seams are centered on one side. Pin one end of each strap, seam side down, to one of the top

inside corners of the bib. Pin the other end of the strap to the opposite side of the waistband 1¾″ (4.4 cm) from the center-back opening. Slipstitch the straps in place. Try the apron on the mouse, and sew the snap in place on the waistband so that the apron fits at the waist when the snap is closed.

4. The Shawl. Fringe the two short ends of the triangle of wool by drawing out the threads for ½″ (13 mm). Staystitch just inside the fringe. Make a doubled ¼″ (6-mm) fold on the long edge, press, and hem it in place. Wrap the shawl around the shoulders of the mouse as shown, and tie the ends.

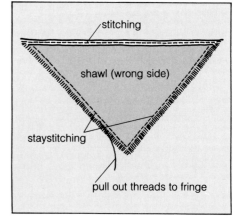

The doll's body

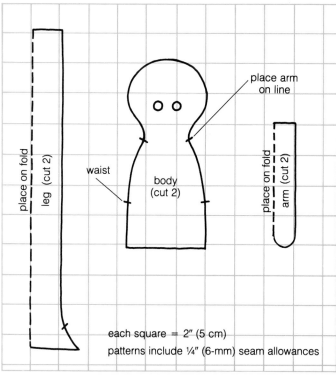

place arm on line

place on fold
leg (cut 2)

waist

body (cut 2)

place on fold
arm (cut 2)

each square = 2" (5 cm)
patterns include ¼" (6-mm) seam allowances

1. Cutting the Body Fabric. Enlarge the body, leg, and arm patterns to the scale indicated and cut them out, following the instructions on page 155. Cut two body and two arm sections from the beige fabric and two legs from the black. Mark the shoulder lines on both body sections and mark the circles for the eyes on the right side of one body piece.

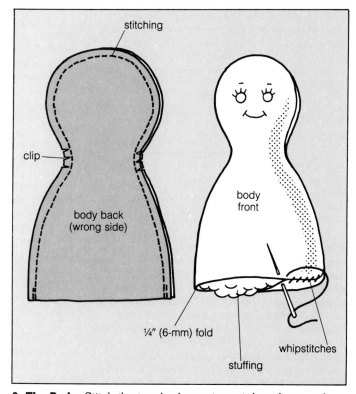

stitching

clip

body back (wrong side)

body front

¼" (6-mm) fold

stuffing

whipstitches

2. The Body. Stitch the two body sections right sides together, leaving the bottom edge open. Clip the seam allowance in the curves of the neck area. Turn the body right side out and stuff it compactly with polyester fiber, then turn the open edge under ¼" (6 mm), and whipstitch it shut.

Lillie Longstockings

Materials

¼ yard (22.9 cm) cream-beige cotton fabric
½ yard (45.7 cm) black cotton fabric
6-strand embroidery floss: bright blue, black, and red
Sewing thread: to match fabrics
Polyester fiber for stuffing

30 yards (27.4 m) rust-orange 4-ply knitting yarn
1 yard (.91 m) of 36"-wide (.91 m) cotton print fabric
3½ yards (3.2 m) of ¾"-wide (19-mm) pregathered white eyelet
1 package ⅜"-wide (5-mm) rickrack, to contrast with the print fabric

49

The arms. Fold each arm section in half lengthwise, right sides together. Seam the side and rounded end, clip the seam allowance along the curved area, turn the arm right side out, stuff it compactly, and stitch it shut as you did the body section. With the seams turned to the back, whipstitch the top of each arm to the body along the appropriate shoulder marking.

The legs. Fold, stitch, stuff, and sew each section shut as for the arms, but center the seam down the front of the leg. Join the legs to the lower edge of the body with whipstitches.

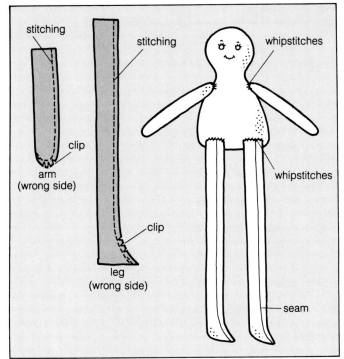

The features and hair

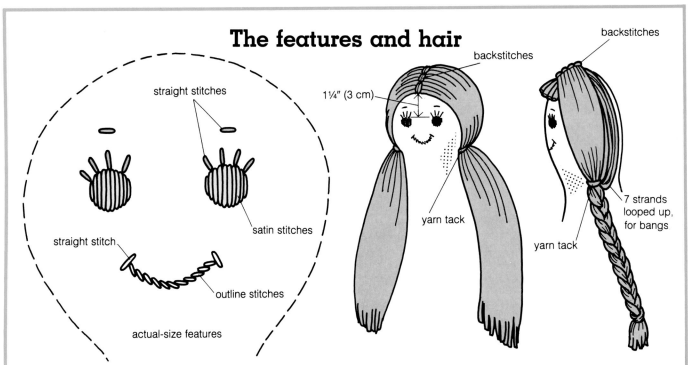

1. The Features. With a soft pencil, trace the actual-size pattern given here on tracing or tissue paper. Turn the paper over, and retrace the features, transferring them onto the right side of the body front, aligning the eye markings.

Stitch the features, using six-strand embroidery floss. Fill in the eyes with vertical satin stitches of blue, and make the lashes and eyebrows with black straight stitches. Make the mouth with red outline stitches.

Double the remaining strand of yarn, and use it to anchor the hair from front to back with a row of ⅜"-long (9.5-mm) backstitches. Smooth the strands so they frame the face and, with the same doubled strand of yarn, tack them down over the seam at the top of the neck area on each side of the head.

2. The Hair. Cut twenty-nine 36"-long (.91- m) strands of four-ply knitting yarn. Center twenty-eight of the strands in parallel rows across the center front of the head, about 1¼" (3 cm) above the eyes.

The bangs. Gather the ends of seven strands of yarn from the back of each cluster of hair at the side of the head, loop them back up to the top of the head, and tack them in place just behind the hairline. Then slip the ends of these strands forward under the other yarn strands, pulling them all the way through; trim the ends to the desired length to make the bangs.

Separate the remaining free ends of yarn into groups of seven and braid firmly. Knot the ends of each braid 8" (20.3 cm) from the head, and trim the ends evenly 1½" (3.8 cm) from the knot.

The doll's clothes

1. Cutting the Clothes Fabric. First enlarge the patterns for the bodice and hat to the scale indicated, following the directions on page 155. Then, cut the print fabric crosswise into two pieces: one 22″ long (56 cm) and the other 14″ long (35.6 cm).

Fold the 14″-long (35.6-cm) piece of fabric in half lengthwise, place the hat and bodice pattern pieces along the fold as indicated, and cut them out. Slash the back section of the bodice piece along the fold line.

Cut the 22″-long (56-cm) piece of fabric lengthwise, with the grain, into an 18″-wide (45.7-cm) section for the skirt and two 7½″-wide (19-cm) sections for the pants.

2. The Pants. Turn under ¼″ (6 mm) along one end of each pants section, and stitch a band of pregathered eyelet to the fold on the wrong side of the fabric. Align the sides of each pants section, wrong side out, and seam them, starting at the trimmed bottom edge and ending 5″ (12.7 cm) from the top edge. Clip each seam allowance at the end of the opening and press it open.

Turn the leg sections right side out, and align the seams and free edges of fabric above them; pin and stitch the pants sections together, forming the crotch seam. Clip at the crotch. Press the seam open.

Turn under ¼″ (6 mm) of fabric at the waist, and stitch the fold in place with a row of gathering stitches. Slip the pants on the doll, gather the fabric evenly along the row of stitches until it fits the waist of the doll, and knot the thread. Stitch the top edge of the pants to the doll's body.

3. The Bodice. Finish the edges of the sleeves with eyelet, as you did for the pants. Stitch around the neck opening ¼″ (6 mm) from the edge, and clip the fabric at ¼″ (6-mm) intervals almost to the stitches.

Turn the fabric under along the row of stitches and press. Sew a row of eyelet around the neck opening on the wrong side of the fabric so the eyelet extends beyond the fabric. Stitch a row of rickrack on the right side over the seam between the eyelet and bodice fabric.

Fold the bodice in half, wrong side out, across the shoulders and sleeves. Seam under the arms and along the sides. Clip the seam allowance at the corners, and press open.

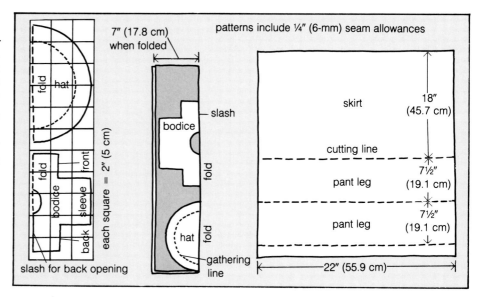

each square = 2″ (5 cm)

slash for back opening

7″ (17.8 cm) when folded

slash

bodice

fold

hat

fold

gathering line

patterns include ¼″ (6-mm) seam allowances

skirt — 18″ (45.7 cm)

cutting line

pant leg — 7½″ (19.1 cm)

pant leg — 7½″ (19.1 cm)

22″ (55.9 cm)

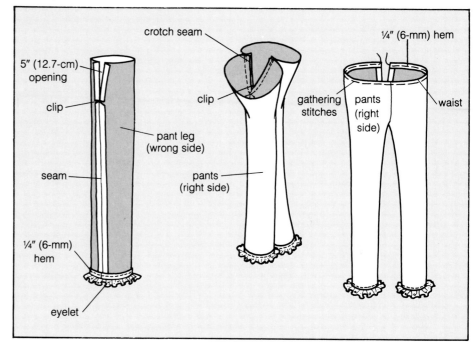

5″ (12.7-cm) opening

clip

seam

¼″ (6-mm) hem

eyelet

pant leg (wrong side)

crotch seam

clip

pants (right side)

¼″ (6-mm) hem

gathering stitches

pants (right side)

waist

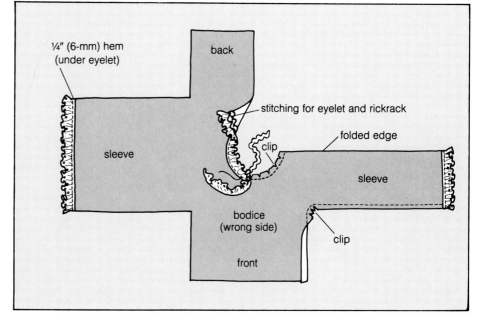

¼″ (6-mm) hem (under eyelet)

back

sleeve

stitching for eyelet and rickrack

clip

folded edge

sleeve

bodice (wrong side)

clip

front

51

4. The Skirt. Stitch a ¼″ (6-mm) hem at one end of the skirt fabric. Attach a row of eyelet along the edge of the hem on the wrong side, and sew another row of eyelet 3″ (7.6 cm) above the first, on the right side of the fabric. Fold the fabric down over the top of the upper row of eyelet, and stitch the fold in place along the edge. Stitch a row of rickrack between the rows of eyelet. Align the sides of the skirt, wrong side out, and stitch them together, ending the seam 1½″ (3.8 cm) from the top edge. Press open the seam allowance. Make a row of gathering stitches around the top of the skirt, and gather the skirt along the thread to fit the waist of the doll, plus ½″ (13 mm). Knot the thread.

5. Assembling the Dress. Pin the waist edges of the skirt and bodice right sides together, aligning them at the center front and distributing the fullness evenly. Stitch the edges together, and press the seam allowances up toward the bodice. Stitch a ¼″ (6-mm) hem along the edges of the back opening, slip the dress on the doll, overlap the back edges, and slipstitch them closed.

6. The Hat. Pin a strip of eyelet, wrong side up and bound edge out, around the edge of the hat fabric. Stitch the eyelet to the hat just inside the bound edge. Turn the eyelet over along the stitching line, and press.

Stitch a row of rickrack over the seam between the eyelet and hat fabric on the underside of the hat, matching the color of the rickrack with the top thread and using white thread in the bobbin.

Sew a row of gathering stitches along the dotted line transferred from the pattern. Gather the hat along the basting thread until it fits the doll's head, distributing the fullness evenly, and knot the thread. Slipstitch the hat to the doll's head along the gathering thread.

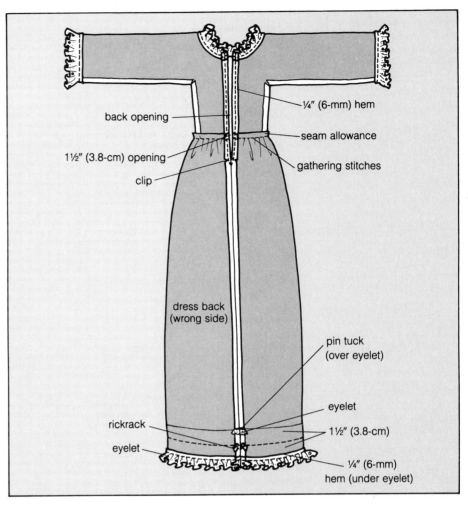

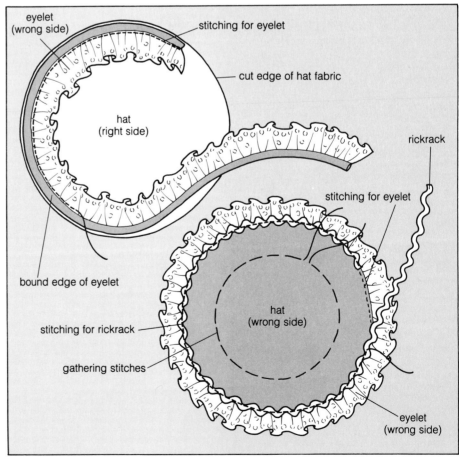

Materials

1 yard (.91 m) of 36"-wide unbleached muslin or flesh-colored fabric

½ yard (45.7 cm) of 36"-wide (.91-m) white fabric

1 yard (.91 m) of 36"-wide (.91-m) red-and-white checked gingham fabric

A 4" × 9" (10.2 × 22.9-cm) piece of nonwoven interfacing

An 8" (20.3-cm) square of black felt

½ yard (45.7 cm) of 36"-wide (.91-m) dark-blue denim

An 8" × 12" (20.3 × 30.5-cm) piece of burlap

½ yard (45.7 cm) of 36"-wide (.91-m) light-blue printed fabric

Sewing thread: to match all fabrics

Polyester fiber for stuffing

Tissue paper

6-strand embroidery floss: black, brown, red, white, and blue

Cardboard

Knitting worsted: dark brown and gray

Cellophane tape

¾ yard (68.6 cm) of ⅛"-wide (3-mm) flat elastic

1 yard (.91 m) of 2"-wide (5-cm) light-blue double-edged embroidered edging

¾ yard (68.6 cm) of ½"-wide (13-mm) flat black lace

A 6" (15.2-cm) length of elastic cord

A small amount of raffia or strawlike yarn

White glue

A 7" (17.8-cm) bamboo stick, ¼" (6 mm) in diameter

1 yard (.91 m) jute or other wrapping cord

A 5" (12.7-cm) bamboo stick, ³⁄₁₆" (5 mm) in diameter

A 2" (5-cm) corncob, ½" (13 mm) in diameter

Note: If no zigzag machine is available, two rows of short, straight stitching ⅛" (3 mm) apart may be used instead of zigzag stitching.

Appalachian Mountain Couple

1. Cutting the Fabric. Enlarge the patterns and cut them out, following the instructions on page 155. Pin the patterns to the fabrics, aligning the arrows with the lengthwise grain, and cut as follows (note that several of the fabrics will be used later to cut pieces for which there are no patterns). Fold the unbleached muslin or flesh-colored fabric along the lengthwise grain, and from it cut the head, body front, body back, woman's leg, man's leg, and man's foot twice each to get four pieces of fabric for each body part; cut the arm pattern four times to get eight pieces. Cut two woman's pant pieces from folded white cotton fabric. From folded red-and-white checked gingham, cut two woman's bodice pieces, two dress sleeves, two bonnet brims, and one bonnet crown. Also cut one woman's bonnet brim from folded nonwoven interfacing. Cut the woman's shoe twice from folded felt to get four pieces. From

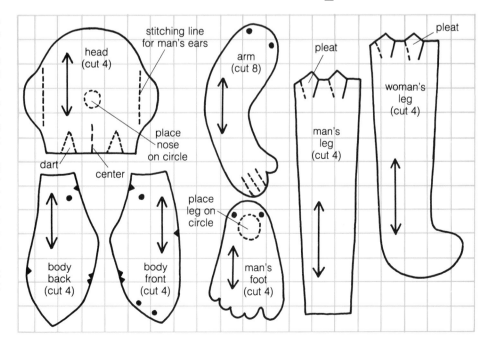

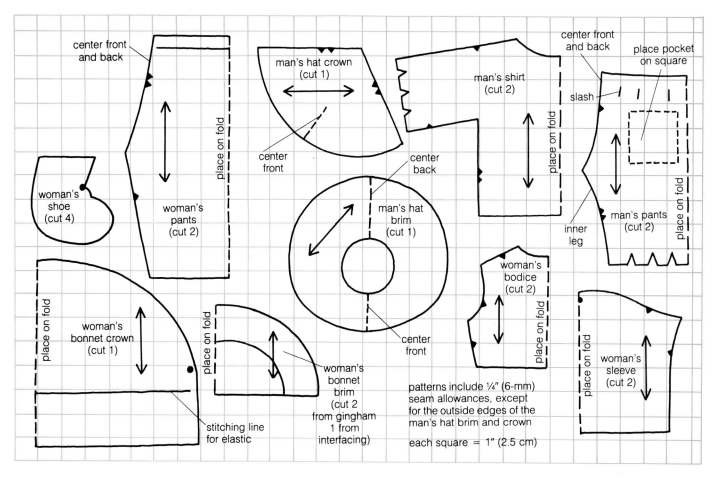

center front and back

man's hat crown (cut 1)

man's shirt (cut 2)

center front and back

place pocket on square

slash

woman's shoe (cut 4)

woman's pants (cut 2)

place on fold

center front

man's hat brim (cut 1)

center back

place on fold

man's pants (cut 2)

inner leg

place on fold

place on fold

woman's bonnet crown (cut 1)

place on fold

center front

woman's bodice (cut 2)

place on fold

woman's sleeve (cut 2)

place on fold

stitching line for elastic

woman's bonnet brim (cut 2 from gingham 1 from interfacing)

patterns include ¼″ (6-mm) seam allowances, except for the outside edges of the man's hat brim and crown

each square = 1″ (2.5 cm)

folded cotton print fabric cut two man's shirt pieces, and from folded denim, cut two man's pant pieces. Cut one man's hat crown and one brim from burlap. Transfer all pattern markings to the fabric pieces.

For the noses, cut two 1¼″ (3.2-cm) circles from the unbleached muslin or flesh-colored fabric. Also, cut an 8½″ × 20″ (21.6 × 50.8-cm) piece of white fabric for the petticoat skirt and a 1½″ × 10½″ (3.8 cm × 26.7-cm) strip for the waistband. For the dress, cut a piece of red-and-white checked gingham fabric 11½″ × 35″ (29.2 × 88.9 cm) for the skirt and a 6½″ × 1¼″ (16.5 × 3.2-cm) piece for the

neckband; also from the red-and-white checked gingham, cut two 1½″ × 11″ (3.8 × 27.9-cm) strips to be used for the bonnet ties. For the woman's apron, cut a piece 7″ × 11″ (17.8 × 27.9 cm) from light-blue printed fabric and a 1½″ × 22″ (3.8 × 55.9-cm) strip for the apron waistband and ties.

The dolls' bodies

2. The Head and Body. For each doll, pin and stitch the darts on the wrong sides of the head front and back, and press them toward the sides. Then pin and stitch the two body-front pieces, right sides together, along the center front edges. Clip the seam allowances at the curve and press them open. Similarly, seam the center of the body back, leaving a 2″ (5-cm) opening at the top for turning and stuffing. Baste the opening closed along the seam line, then clip the seam allowance at the curve and press it open.

Stitch the head front to the body front and the head back to the body back, right sides together, and press the seams open. Then pin the front section to the back, right sides together, matching the center seams. Stitch around the outer edges.

Slit the basting stitches along the back opening and turn the head and body right side out. Stuff firmly with polyester fiber, and slipstitch the opening closed.

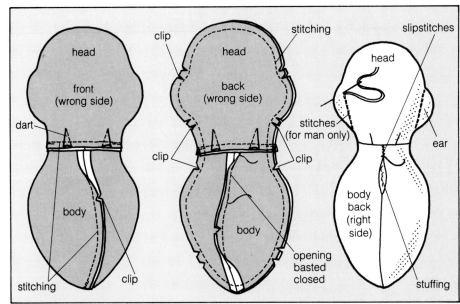

The ears. Stitch the ears on the man as follows (do not stitch ears on the woman): using a needle and doubled matching thread, make small stitches from front to back, then back to front,

along the dotted lines indicated for the ears on the pattern; pull the thread tightly after each stitch to make an indentation along the stitch line. Leave the woman's ears as they are.

3. The Arms and Legs. For each **arm,** pin two sections, right sides together, and stitch around the edges, leaving the spaces between the dots open for turning and stuffing. Clip the seam allowances along the curves and press them open. Turn the arms right side out, and stuff them firmly with polyester fiber; turn the edges of fabric along each opening under ¼″ (6 mm), and slipstitch them closed. To make the fingers, stitch along the lines indicated in the same manner as for the ears.

The man's legs and feet. Pin two leg pieces together, wrong side out, for each leg, and stitch along the edges, leaving the legs open at the top and bottom; press the seam allowances open. Turn under ¼″ (6 mm) at the lower, or smaller, ends, and baste. Turn the legs right side out, and stuff them firmly all the way to the bottom end and to within 1½″ (3.8 cm) of the top.

Join two foot pieces for each foot in the same manner, continuing to stitch along the dotted lines at the inner corners of the toes and leaving an opening between the dots for turning and stuffing. Clip the seam allowance almost to the stitching between the toes. Turn the feet right side out and stuff firmly, using a blunt instrument to push the stuffing into the toes. Turn in the opening edges, and slipstitch them closed.

Pin a leg to each foot in the position marked on the foot, with the back leg seam at the center of the heel; slipstitch the legs to the feet.

The woman's legs. For each leg, join two leg sections, leaving the top open for turning and stuffing. Turn the leg right side out; and stuff it firmly to within 1½″ (3.8 cm) of the top.

4. Finishing the Bodies. Whipstitch the arms securely to the body fronts and backs, matching the dots from the pattern markings.

Make four pleats around the top of each leg, folding the solid lines marked along the pleat allowances over onto the dotted lines; baste the pleat allowances closed. Turn under the top edges of each leg ¼″ (6 mm), and baste; pull two edges together, matching the seams, and slipstitch the leg closed. Whipstitch each pair of legs to the appropriate body, between the dots on the bottom seam, as shown.

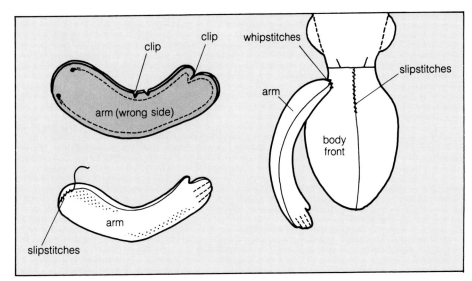

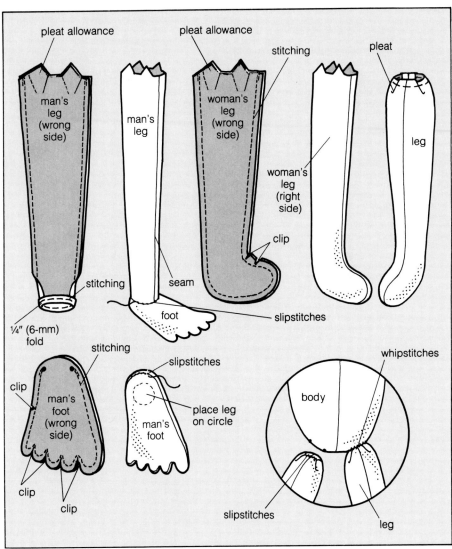

The features and hair

1. The Features. Trace the patterns for each doll's features on tracing or tissue paper with a soft pencil. Turn the paper over and retrace the features on the faces, matching the nose positions.

Use two strands of six-strand embroidery floss for the features. For the **man,** make the eyes and eyebrows with black outline stitches and the mouth with red, beginning and ending with long stitches at the corners of the mouth. Make the pupils with black satin stitches. Make a brown French knot for each freckle, starting and ending each stitch at the back of the head.

For the **woman,** work the eyes and eyebrows in black outline stitches; use white satin stitches for the eyeballs and blue for the irises. Make black French knots for the pupils (again from the back). Work the mouth with red satin stitches, and use outline stitches at the corners of the mouth.

To make the **noses,** sew a row of gathering stitches ⅛" (3 mm) from the edges of each 1¼" (3.2-cm) fabric circle. Gather the fabric to fit the nose position marked on the face, and stuff the nose firmly. Fold the edge under around the stuffing, and slipstitch the nose in position to the face.

2. The Woman's Hair. Cut a piece of cardboard 8" × 6" (20.2 × 15.2 cm). Wind gray yarn fifty times lengthwise around the cardboard, pushing the strands close together as you wind, so they measure 4" (10.2 cm) across. Place a strip of cellophane tape across the yarn at one end of the cardboard, then carefully cut through the yarn at the other end.

Cut a 5" × 1½" (12.7 × 3.8-cm) strip of tissue paper, and fold it lengthwise into thirds. Place the paper across the center of the yarn on the opposite side from the cellophane tape; baste the tape, yarn, and paper along the center of the tissue paper. Turn the yarn tape side up, and stitch along the center of the tape. Remove the tape and tissue paper. Lay the hair across the head from side to side, with the stitching line centered at the top, so the hair starts on the forehead ¾" (19 mm) below the center top seam of the head and runs down the back of the head. Tack the hair in place along the stitching.

Tack the hair with a row of stitches, starting just above the ears and slanting back to the bottom end of the part. Wind additional gray yarn tightly around each half of the hair ½" (13 mm) and 2" (5 cm) from the ends, and tie it securely. Using gray yarn, tack the top windings to the head just below and behind each ear, then turn the pigtails upward and tack the second windings over the back hair as shown in the drawing.

3. The Man's Hair and Beard. For the **hair,** cut thirty 8" (20.3-cm) lengths of dark-brown yarn; tie the lengths together at the center, making sure that the ends are even. Pin the center tie of the yarn to the center back of the head; spread the yarn like spokes to cover the head as shown. To make bangs, tack the ends of the front hair to the forehead with running stitches ¾" (19 mm) below the top head seam, using matching doubled thread. Tack the remaining ends to the back of the head behind the ears with running stitches in a curve from the top of one ear through a point 1½" (3.8 cm) below the center of the back of the head to the top of the other ear.

The beard. Mark the bottom of the face ¾" (19 mm) below the mouth, and make a curved line from the lower end of one ear through the mark to the lower end of the other ear. Cut fifteen 5" (12.7-cm) lengths of yarn and fold them in half; tack the yarn through the folds to the face along the marked line, keeping the strands close together.

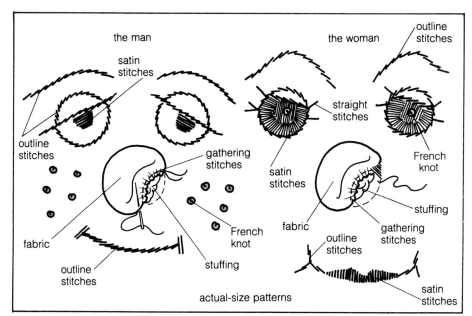

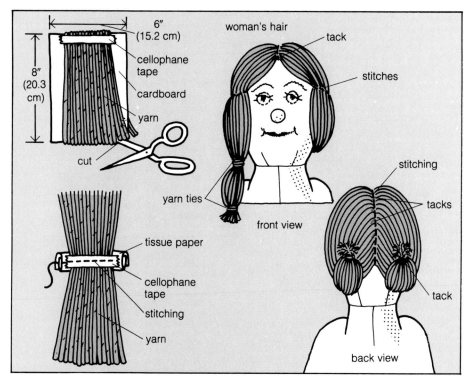

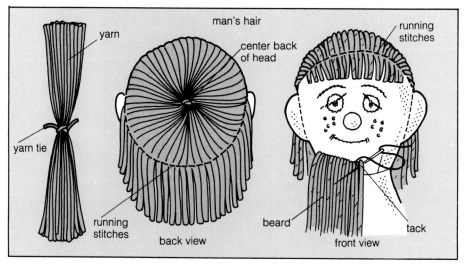

56

The woman's clothes

1. The Pants. Align the two pants pieces, right sides together, then pin and stitch the center front seam. Press open the seam allowances. Turn under ¼" (6 mm) of fabric along the edge of the waist, and baste. Pin the ends of a 7" (17.8-cm) length of ⅛"-wide (3-mm) flat elastic ¼" (6 mm) below the edge of the fold, and sew it in position with zigzag stitching, stretching the elastic to fit flat while stitching. Join the center-back seam, stitching through the elastic twice.

Lap embroidered edging ¼" (6 mm) over the bottom edges of the pants on the right side, and stitch in position. Join the inner leg seams, matching center seams and joining the ends of the edging. Turn the pants right side out.

2. The Petticoat. Lap a 20" (50.8-cm) length of double-edged embroidered edging ¼" (6 mm) over one long edge of the petticoat fabric on the right side, and stitch it in position. Fold the ends of the petticoat together, wrong side out, and stitch them together, leaving a 2½"-long (6.4-cm) opening at the top. Turn under ¼" (6 mm) on each side of the opening, and press. Sew a row of gathering stitches ¼" (6 mm) from the upper edge, and gather the fabric along the thread to a length of 10" (25.4 cm).

Align the right side of the waistband with the wrong side of the upper edge of the petticoat, extending the ends of the waistband ¼" (6 mm) beyond the gathers and distributing the gathers evenly. Pin, and stitch them together. Press the seam allowances toward the waistband. Turn under ¼" (6 mm) on the other three edges of the waistband, press, and fold the waistband over the seam allowances to cover the seam line on the right side of the petticoat. Stitch it in place. Lap the ends of the waistband over each other to fit the doll, and sew on a snap.

3. The Dress and Apron. Pin and seam the dress **bodice** front and back, right sides together, at the shoulders, and press the seam allowances open. Slash the back open down the center line, turn under the back edges ¼" (6 mm), and make a row of zigzag stitching along each fold. Turn under ¼" (6 mm) on the lower edge of each sleeve, and press. Lap the straight edge of the black lace over the right side of the folded edge, and secure it with zigzag stitching.

Cut a 3" (7.6-cm) length of ⅛"-wide (3-mm) flat elastic for each sleeve. Pin the ends to the sleeve seams ¼" (6 mm) above the lower edge on the wrong side; attach the elastic with zigzag stitching, stretching it as you sew so that the fabric lies flat. Sew a row of gathering stitches along the upper edge of the sleeves between the notches. Pin the sleeve to the bodice lining up the dot on

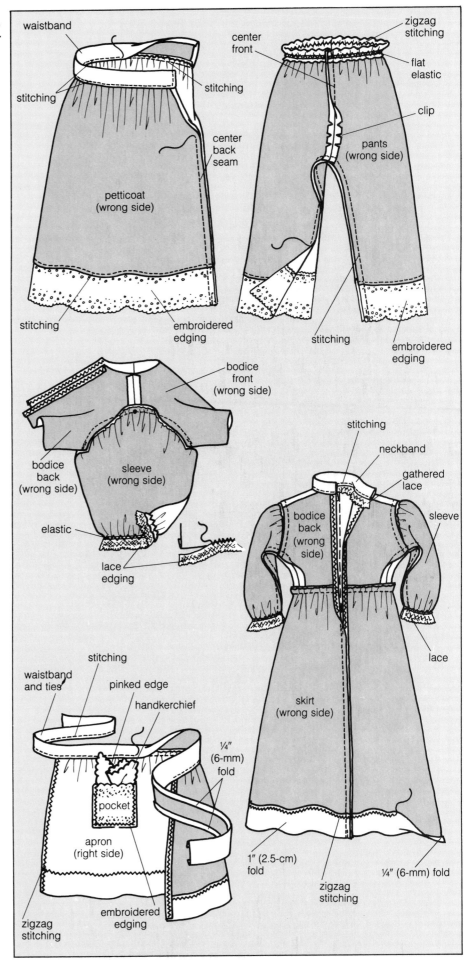

each sleeve with the shoulder seam and drawing the gathers along the thread as evenly as possible to fit. Stitch between the notches, and press the seam allowances toward the sleeve.

Join the underarm seams from the bodice waist to the ends of the sleeves, stitching twice through the ends of the elastic. Clip the seam allowances at the inner corner and the curve on each sleeve, and press them open. Turn the ends of the neckband fabric under ¼" (6 mm), and press. Join one long edge of the neckband to the neck edge of the bodice wrong sides together; clip seam allowances along the edge of the neck along the curves, and press them toward the neckband.

Make a row of gathering stitches along one edge of a 12" (30.5-cm) length of black lace, and gather the lace along the thread to a length of 6" (15.2 cm). Sew the gathered edge to the lower edge of the neckband, distributing the gathers evenly. Turn under ¼" (6 mm) on the other long edge of the neckband, fold it over the neck edge, and stitch it over the gathered edge of the lace on the right side.

The skirt. Turn up one long edge of the skirt fabric ¼" (6 mm), then turn it up 1" (2.5 cm) and press; sew it in place with zigzag stitching. Join the center-back seam of the skirt, leaving a 2¼" (5.7-cm) opening at the waist. Turn under ¼" (6 mm) of fabric along both sides of the opening and press; secure the folds with zigzag stitching. Make a row of gathering stitches ¼" (6 mm) from the upper edge of the skirt. Pin the skirt to the bodice waist, right sides together, at the center fronts and the back openings; gather the skirt evenly along the thread to fit the bodice waist; pin and stitch the skirt to the bodice. Press the seam allowances toward the bodice. Overlap the back opening edges by ½" (13 mm), and sew on snaps at the neck and waist to close the opening.

The apron. Turn under 1" (2.5 cm) along one long edge of the apron fabric, press, and sew it in position with zigzag stitching. Turn under ¼" (6 mm) of fabric on the short ends, press, and secure it with zigzag stitching.

Pin a 2" (5 cm) length of 2"-wide (5-cm) embroidered edging 2" (5 cm) from the right edge and 2½" (6.4 cm) above the lower edge of the apron fabric for a pocket; sew it in place with zigzag stitching around the side and lower edges.

Make a row of gathering stitches ¼" (6 mm) from the upper edge of the apron; gather the fabric along the thread until it measures 7¼" (18.4 cm); knot the thread. Join one long edge of the right side of the waistband-tie to the wrong side of the apron, with the ends extending evenly, and distribute the gathers evenly. Press the seam allowances toward the waistband; turn under ¼" (6 mm) on the lower edges of the ties, and press. Turn under ¼" (6 mm) of fabric on the opposite edge of the waistband and ties, fold the waistband over the top of the skirt, and stitch it over the seam on the right side. Using pinking shears, cut a 2" (5-cm) square of white fabric for a handkerchief. Fold it so the corner points extend in the same direction, and tack the folded end inside the pocket.

4. The Bonnet and Broom. Baste the nonwoven interfacing to the wrong side of one of the **bonnet brim** pieces, matching the edges. Pin the two brim pieces right sides together, and stitch around the curved edge, leaving the straight edge open. Clip the seam allowances, and trim them ⅛" (3 mm) from the stitching. Turn the brim right side out, press, and sew a row of basting stitches along the unstitched edge. Make a row of zigzag stitching along the curved edge of the bonnet brim and along the curved pattern marking.

The crown. Turn under ¼" (6 mm) of fabric on the three straight edges of the

crown between the dots, and secure them with zigzag stitching. Pin a 6" (15.2-cm) length of elastic cord along the line marked from the pattern. Zigzag-stitch the elastic in position, stretching it so that the fabric lies flat while you sew. Make a row of gathering stitches ¼" (6 mm) in from the curved edge of the crown. Join the straight edge of the brim to the crown between the dots, matching the centers and distributing the gathers evenly. Press the seam allowances toward the crown. Turn under ¼" (6 mm) of fabric on the long edges of each tie strip, and press. Fold each tie in half lengthwise, wrong sides together; pin and sew the edges together with zigzag stitching. Stitch one end of each tie securely to the ends of the bonnet brim, on the underside.

The broom. Cut a piece of cardboard 2" × 3" (5 × 7.6 cm). Wrap raffia or strawlike yarn thirty-five times lengthwise around the cardboard. Place a strip of cellophane tape across the raffia at one end of cardboard, and cut the raffia across the other end. Fold the strands in half along the cellophane tape with the tape inside, and wrap the raffia around the 7" (17.8-cm) bamboo stick, holding it in place with additional raffia wound tightly for ½" (13 mm) at the end; fasten the ends. Glue the raffia to secure it. Bend the fingers of the woman's left hand around the broom handle, and tack them securely to the palm.

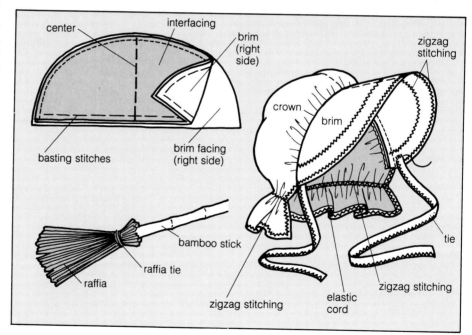

The man's clothes

1. The Shirt. Align the front and back shirt pieces, right sides together, and join the shoulder, underarm, and side edges; clip the seam allowances at the underarm corner. Slash the back open along the center line; turn under ¼"

(6 mm) of fabric around the neck and along the back edges, clipping along the curves; sew the fold with zigzag stitching. Turn the shirt right side out, and overlap the back edges ½" (13 mm); sew on one snap to close the back opening at the neck and another snap 2" (5 cm) below the first.

2. The Pants, Hat, and Pipe. Cut a 2"

(5-cm) square of denim for the pocket of the **pants** and a 2" (5-cm) square of printed fabric for the handkerchief. Pin the side and lower edges of the wrong side of the pocket to the right side of one pants section in the position indicated by the pattern marking. Pleat the handkerchief and tuck it into the pocket with the points extending out; pin. Stitch around all the edges of the pocket, using zigzag stitching and catching the handkerchief with the stitching.

Align the pants pieces, right sides together, and pin and stitch the center-front and center-back seams; clip the seam allowances along the curves, and press them open. Join the inner leg seams in the same manner, matching the center seams. Turn under ¼″ (6 mm) of fabric around the waist, press, and sew the fold with zigzag stitching. Using a razor blade or sharp knife, make small vertical slashes around the waistline below the stitching on the lines indicated. Weave the jute cord through the slashes for a belt, and tie the ends in a bow at the center front.

The hat. Pin the two straight edges of the crown together, and seam them, using zigzag stitching; press the seam allowances to one side. Turn the crown right side out, and lap the lower edge ¼″ over the inner edge of the brim, matching the center front and back; pin and join with zigzag stitching. Make two more rows of zigzag stitching about ½″ (13 mm) and 1″ (2.5 cm) in from the outer edge of the brim to reinforce it and keep it from raveling. Push the point of the crown in about 2″ (5 cm) for the effect shown in the photograph on page 53.

The pipe. Sharpen one end of the 5″ (12.7-cm) bamboo stick, and dip it in white glue. Push the stick into the corncob on an upward angle about ½″ (13 mm) above the lower end, and wipe off any excess glue. Bend the fingers of the left hand around the pipe stem and tack the fingertips securely to the palm.

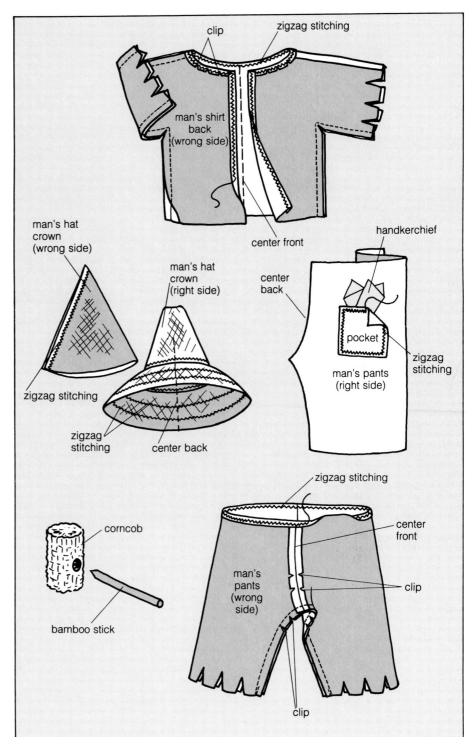

Day of the Week Dolls

Materials

Note: The materials listed are enough to make only one doll. To make more dolls, multiply the materials by the number of dolls for which each will be used.

An 11″ × 22″ (27.9 × 55.8-cm) piece of percale fabric in pink, brown, or off-white, as desired

A 10″ × 18″ (25.4 × 45.7-cm) piece of cotton print fabric

A 3″ × 4″ (7.6 × 10.2-cm) piece of black felt

Scraps of iron-on fabric: navy, red, and white

Lipstick (optional)

25 yards (22.75 m) rug yarn: black, brown, orange, and/or yellow, as desired

A 4¾″ (12.1-cm) length of ½″-wide (13-mm) lace trimming

Sewing thread: to match all fabric, yarn, and ribbon

⅜ yard (11.5 cm) of ¼″-wide (6-mm) satin ribbon, to go with the dress fabric

½ yard (45.7 cm) of elastic cord

2 small snaps

Polyester fiber for stuffing

The dolls' bodies

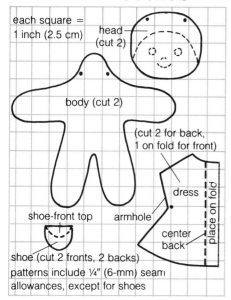

each square = 1 inch (2.5 cm)
head (cut 2)
body (cut 2)
(cut 2 for back, 1 on fold for front)
dress
armhole
place on fold
center back
shoe-front top
shoe (cut 2 fronts, 2 backs)
patterns include ¼″ (6-mm) seam allowances, except for shoes

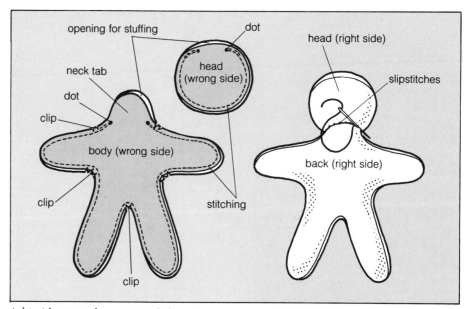

opening for stuffing
dot
head (wrong side)
neck tab
dot
clip
body (wrong side)
head (right side)
slipstitches
clip
stitching
back (right side)
clip

1. Cutting the Fabric. Enlarge the patterns to the scale indicated and cut them out, following the instructions on page 155. Fold the pink, off-white, or brown fabric for each body in half wrong side out, and using the patterns, cut two pieces for each body and head. Transfer all pattern markings onto the pieces.

2. The Bodies. Stitch the body sections, right sides together, around the edges, leaving an opening between the two dots at the neck; backstitch at the dots for reinforcement. Clip the seam allowances at the curves, and press them open with your fingers. Turn each body right side out, and stuff it with polyester fiber. Turn under the edges along the opening ¼″ (6 mm), and slipstitch it closed to form the neck tab.

The heads. Seam the two head pieces for each doll together as for the bodies; turn the head right side out, stuff it, and sew the opening closed with slipstitches.

3. Finishing the Body. Center the machine-stitched edge of the head over the neck tab, and sew the tab securely to the back of the head with slipstitches.

60

The features and hair

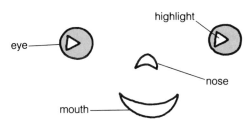

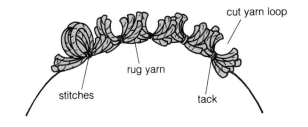

actual-size patterns for features

1. The Faces. Trace the actual-size pattern for the features on tracing or tissue paper with a soft pencil. Turn the paper over and retrace the features, transferring them onto iron-on fabric as follows: for each doll make two navy eyes, two white wedges to highlight the eyes, one red nose, and one red mouth. Cut the pieces out. Place the cutout features on the faces, using the cutting pattern for the head on the opposite page as a guide for positioning, and press them in place with a hot iron.

To form dimples at the corners of the mouth, run a needle with red thread from the back of each head to one corner of the mouth. Make a tiny invisible stitch, then push the needle under the fabric to the other corner of the mouth, and pull the thread tight. Make another small stitch and

run the needle through the doll's head to the back, pulling the thread tight again before knotting it. Slightly redden the cheeks with lipstick, if desired.

2. The Hair. Wind rug yarn four times around two fingers, and cut the end; slip the loops of yarn off your fingers, holding them together at one end. With matching thread, secure the loops together in one spot, and sew the bunch of hair to the head with the same thread. Repeat to make a total of fifty bunches for each doll. Sew them to the heads, leaving about ½" (13 mm) of space between bunches, until the tops and backs of the heads, including the neck tabs, are covered. Use the hairline on the original cutting pattern as a guide. Cut the loops of yarn open and trim the hair to an even length.

The dolls' clothes

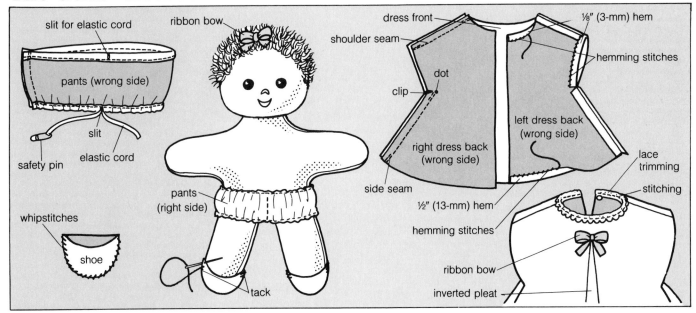

1. The Pants. For each doll cut a 3½" × 12" (8.9 × 30.5-cm) piece of print fabric, and seam the short edges right sides together. Make a ⅜" (9.5-mm) hem along both long edges to serve as casings for the elastic. Cut a tiny hole on the wrong side of each casing. Work a strip of oval elastic cord equal in length to the circumference of the doll's waist plus 1½" (3.9 cm) through each casing at the end of a safety pin. Turn the pants right side out, and slip them on the doll. Adjust the elastic to fit the doll, and stitch the ends together, overlapping them slightly. Stitch the front and back of the pants together between the doll's legs to form the crotch.

2. The Shoes. Using the shoe pattern (cut earlier), cut two shoe backs and two fronts from the black felt. Whipstitch a front and a back piece together along the outer curved edges for each shoe. Slip the shoes onto the doll, and tack them to the feet at the side seams.

3. The Dresses. Fold the dress fabric for each doll in half wrong side out, and using the patterns made earlier, cut the dress front, placing the fold line of the pattern along the fold of the fabric. Then cut two dress-back pieces. With right sides facing, seam the front and back pieces together at the shoulders and at the sides below the dots. Clip the seam allowances at each dot, and press open

the seam allowances at the shoulders and at the sides below the dots. Turn and stitch ⅛" (3-mm) hems at the neck and arm openings. Make ⅜" (9.5-mm) hems along the center-back edges and a ½" (13-mm) hem at the bottom of the skirt. Pin and then stitch the lace along the neck edge of the dress on the wrong side. Close the back of each dress with two snaps, one at the neck and one at the waist. Cut the satin ribbon in half, and tie two bows. Make a small vertical pleat at the center front of each dress 1⅜" (3.5 cm) below the neckline, and tack it in place. Stitch one bow over the top of the pleat to hide the tacks, then sew the other bow to the hair.

Waking-Sleeping Girl

Materials

½ yard (45.7 cm) of 36"-wide (.91-m) pale-pink cotton fabric

¼ yard (22.9 cm) of 36"-wide (.91-m) small-print cotton fabric

Scraps of felt to match one of the colors in the cotton print

Sewing thread: to match fabric, felt, yarn, and ribbons

Polyester fiber for stuffing

6-strand embroidery floss: brown, medium blue, and red

31 yards (28 m) light-yellow knitting worsted

Cellophane tape

1 yard (.91 m) of ½"-wide (13-mm) ribbon to match one of the colors in the cotton print

¾ yard (68.6 cm) of ½"-wide (13-mm) pregathered embroidered white edging

The doll's body

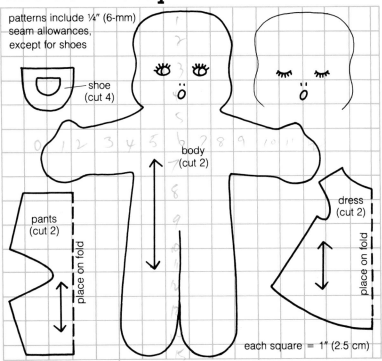

patterns include ¼" (6-mm) seam allowances, except for shoes

shoe (cut 4)

body (cut 2)

pants (cut 2)

place on fold

dress (cut 2)

place on fold

each square = 1" (2.5 cm)

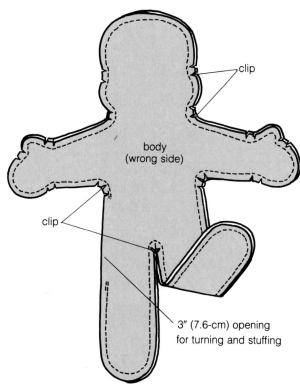

clip

body (wrong side)

clip

3" (7.6-cm) opening for turning and stuffing

1. Cutting the Fabric. Enlarge the patterns to the scale indicated and cut them out, following the instructions on page 155. Placing the patterns with the arrow along the lengthwise grain of the wrong side of the fabric, cut the following: two bodies from the pale-pink fabric; two dress pieces and one pant piece from the print fabric; four shoe pieces from

felt. Transfer all pattern markings to the fabric.

With a soft pencil, trace the features from the enlarged pattern on tissue or tracing paper. Turn the paper over, and retrace the features, transferring the "awake" features to the right side of one body piece, and the "asleep" features to the right side of the other.

2. The Doll's Body. Join the body sections, right sides together, around the edges, leaving a 3"-long (7.6-cm) opening along one side for turning and stuffing. Clip the seam allowances along the curves. Turn the body right side out, and stuff it softly with polyester fiber. Turn under the seam allowances along the opening; slipstitch them together.

The features and hair

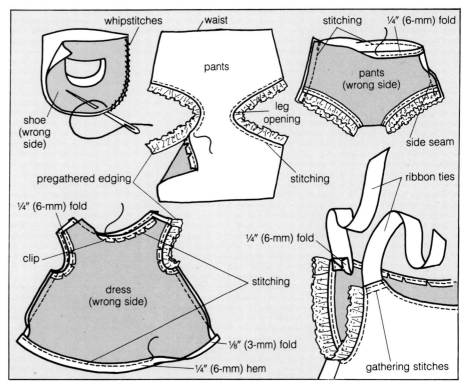

6" (15.2 cm)

2" (5 cm)

8" (20.3 cm)

yarn

paper

cellophane tape

stitching

running stitches

straight stitches

outline stitches

satin stitches

ribbon bow

braid

running stitches

outline stitches

1. The Features. To make the features, use two strands of embroidery floss. Work the outside lines of the eyes in brown outline stitches and the lashes with straight stitches. Fill in the irises with blue satin stitches. Using red floss, make two short straight stitches for the nose, and fill in the mouth with vertical satin stitches.

2. The hair. To make the **bangs,** loop yellow yarn in close parallel rows back and forth across the width of a 6" × 8" (15.2 × 20.3-cm) piece of paper until it measures 2" (5 cm) across. Place a strip of cellophane tape over the center of the yarn perpendicular to the loops. Machine stitch through the center of the tape; remove the paper and tape from the yarn. Center the stitching line of the bangs along

the top seam of the head, and sew the bangs to the head along the stitching line with small, hidden running stitches made with matching thread.

The braids. Cut eighteen 14" (35.6-cm) lengths of yarn, and place them side by side, aligning the ends. Wrap a 7" (17.8-cm) length of ribbon around the yarn 1" (2.5 cm) from one end, and tie a bow. Divide the yarn into three equal sections and braid them to within 1" (2.5 cm) of the opposite end. Wrap and tie a ribbon bow as before.

Center the braid over the bangs so it covers the head seam. Tack the braid down across the top of the head and along each side down to eye level with hidden running stitches made with matching thread.

The doll's clothes

1. The Pants. Stitch ¼" (6 mm) from the edges of the leg openings. Clip the edges along the curves, then turn the edges under along the stitching and press. Pin pregathered embroidered edging right side up to the underside of the leg-opening edges, so the ruffle extends out. Stitch the edging in place, easing it around the curves.

Fold the pants in half wrong side out, aligning the waist edges, and stitch the side seams. Press the seam allowances open. Turn under ¼" (6 mm) of fabric along the waist edge and stitch it down.

2. The Dress. To make the dress, first stitch ⅛" (3 mm) from the neck and armhole edges of the front and back. Clip the edges along the curves, outside the stitching line, then turn the edges under along the stitching line and press. Stitch down the fold along the neck.

Place the front and back right sides together, and stitch the side seams. Press the seam allowances open.

Turn under ⅛" (3 mm) along the hem edge and press. Turn up and stitch a ¼" (6-mm) hem.

Stitch pregathered edging right side up to the wrong side of the armhole.

Turn under ¼" (6 mm) of fabric along each shoulder edge. Stitch the folds with two parallel rows of gathering stitches, and gather the fabric to a width of ½" (13 mm). Knot the threads.

The shoulder ties. Cut four 5½" (14-cm) lengths of ribbon for the shoulder ties. Turn up one end of each tie ¼" (6 mm) to the side of the ribbon that will face out; sew a tie to the inside of each shoulder edge with the turned-up end facing the fabric. Slip the dress on the doll, and tie it in place with bows.

3. The Shoes. With matching thread, sew two shoe pieces together along the edges with ⅛" (3-mm) whipstitches to make each shoe.

Turn the shoes right side out, slip them on the doll's legs, and tack them to the legs at both side seams.

The Yarn Dolls *(from left to right, down the stairs):* (1) Needle-point Farm Family, (2) Kitchen Duet, (3) Yarn Couples, (4) Knitted Nelly, (5) Crocheted Jack and Jill, (6) Victorian Lady.

Yarn Dolls

Needlecrafters will be delighted by this collection of irresistible yarn dolls. Thankful too, perhaps, that at last the grab bag of yarn remnants at the back of the closet can be put to excellent use; indeed, much of what is needed may be found there. The projects range from very simple ones that even a small child can take part in to ones that require more complex stitchery.

Needlepointers will find the pliant, three-dimensional "Needlepoint Farm Family" (1) immensely creative and colorful. Convenient charts for stitching the canvas, as well as tracing and blocking instructions, simplify this highly original project. Worked in plain half-cross stitch, the ménage includes the farmer and his wife, gamboling horses, a pink-cheeked pig, an amusing scarecrow, a sunflower-bedecked silo, and a hinged-roofed barn that houses the separate pieces, when playtime is over. Needlepoint techniques are explained on page 157.

A knitted "Kitchen Duet" (2) features intriguingly embroidered features and other details: the salad chef holds a bowl of vegetables while the mustachioed pastry chef, hands in pockets, wears a blue-and-white striped apron. The accompanying charts indicate shaping, all the changes of yarn color, and embroidery placement for each doll.

A veritable UNICEF of interracial harmony is exemplified by the four "Yarn Couples" (3). Many of the techniques for making these ingenious dolls are transferable from one pair to another. A bit of stuffing and looped, tied, and braided yarn form their bodies; all you need to do is change the yarn color, the dolls' expressions, and their costumes to create an endless variety of entertaining new friends.

"Knitted Nelly" (4) requires a knowledge of basic knit stitches and procedures; you'll find these explained on page 158. Fashioned in one piece, except for her attached skirt, this lovely, old-fashioned looking doll has curled hair, imaginatively achieved by unraveling knitted yarn that has been immersed in water, dried, and steam-pressed.

Loose-limbed and jointed, "Crocheted Jack and Jill" (5) are all crocheted, except for their yarn features. Children love this rosy-cheeked pair that move, bend, and sit much like "real" people. You can change the color of the crocheted clothes and vary the expressions as your imagination suggests.

Ready for tea in the parlor, the coquettish "Victorian Lady" (6) is also crocheted (page 159). Her body sections, raffish chapeau, stylish ruffled dress with leg-o'-mutton sleeves, and accessories are all made separately, then sewed together.

Yarn Couples

The dolls' bodies

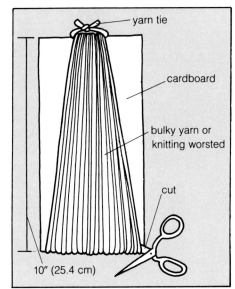

1. Cutting the Yarn. For each body, wind the yarn around a 10"-long (25.4-cm) piece of cardboard: fifty times for bulky yarn, 120 times for knitting worsted. Tie a 10" (25.4-cm) length of yarn around the yarn loops at one end of the cardboard, and knot it securely. Cut across the yarn strands at the other end of the cardboard.

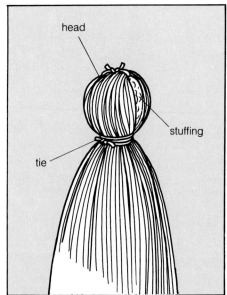

2. Making the Body. To form the head, place a small amount of polyester stuffing under the tie at the center of the yarn, and cover it smoothly on all sides with the loose strands of yarn. Cut another 10" (25.4-cm) length of the remaining yarn, and wrap it tightly around the strands 3½" (8.9 cm) below the tie at the top to form the head; knot the yarn.

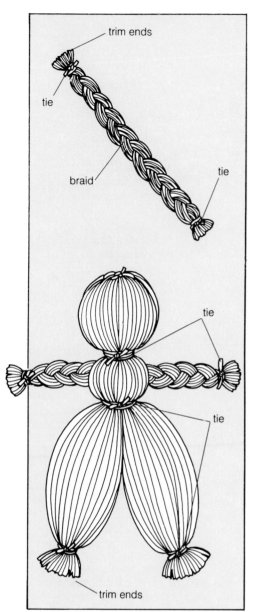

Materials

70 yards (64.1 m) bulky yarn or 4
ounces (103.4 grams) knitting worsted
for the bodies of each couple:
Indians, light gold; Orientals, ivory;
whites, pale peach; blacks, brown
A 10″-long (25.4-cm) piece of
cardboard
Polyester fiber for stuffing
Scraps of red and black knitting
worsted
Sewing thread: to match all fabrics and
trimmings, plus black
11 snaps

The Indian couple

1¾ ounces (50 grams) brown sport-
weight yarn
A 6″-long (15.2-cm) piece of cardboard
An 8″ × 11″ (20.3 × 27.9-cm) piece of
rose-coral cotton fabric
An 8″ × 9″ (20.3 × 22.9-cm) piece of
light-brown cotton fabric
An 8″ (20.3-cm) length of blue bias-fold
tape
An 8″ (20.3-cm) length of burnt-orange
bias-fold tape
A 4″ (10.2-cm) length of green rickrack
½ yard (45.7 cm) white rickrack
½ yard (45.7 cm) blue rickrack
A 7″ (17.8-cm) length of olive-green
rickrack
1 yard (.91 m) yellow rickrack
½ yard (45.7 cm) gold rickrack
An 8″ (20.3-cm) length of white bias-
fold tape
A 9″ × 10″ (22.9 × 25.4-cm) piece of
white cotton fabric
A scrap of brick-red suede or
felt

The Oriental couple

4 ounces (103.4 grams) black knitting
worsted
A 4″-long (10.2-cm) and a 3″-long (7.6-
cm) piece of cardboard
A 10″ × 15″ (25.4 × 38.1-cm) piece of
dark-blue floral-print fabric for the
kimono
A 20″ (50.8-cm) length of 1″-wide (2.5-
cm) red ribbon

2 small artificial flowers
A 9″ × 8″ (22.9 × 20.3-cm) piece of
light-blue floral-print fabric
A 30″ (76.2-cm) length of light-blue
bias-fold tape
An 8″ (20.3-cm) length of bright-rose
rickrack
A 9″ × 10″ (22.9 × 25.4 cm) piece of
blue fabric

The white couple

Tiny scraps of blue felt
4 ounces (103.4 grams) brown knitting
worsted
A 10″ (25.4-cm) length of pink ribbon
4 ounces (103.4 grams) yellow knitting
worsted
A 10″ square (25.4-cm) of floral print
fabric
1 yard (.91 m) bias-fold tape to match
one color in the floral-print fabric
½ yard (45.7 cm) of ⅛″-wide (3-mm)
elastic
An 8″ × 9″ (20.3 × 22.9-cm) piece of
striped shirting fabric
½ yard (45.7 cm) blue bias-fold tape
8″ (20.3 cm) of white bias-fold tape
A 9″ × 10″ (22.9 × 25.4-cm) piece of
light-blue fabric
A 7″ × 7″ × 10″ (17.8 × 17.8 × 25.4-
cm) triangle of red cotton fabric

The black couple

Scraps of white and black felt
4 ounces (103.4 grams) black knitting
worsted
A 20″ × 7″ (50.8 × 17.8-cm) piece of
pastel checked fabric
½ yard (45.7 cm) of ¾″-wide (19-mm)
embroidered ribbon
A 5″ (12.7-cm) length of ¼″-wide (6-
mm) red ribbon
Elastic cord
A 9″ × 8″ (22.9 × 20.3-cm) piece of
blue-and-white checked gingham
fabric
½ yard (45.7 cm) red bias-fold tape
A 9″ × 10″ (22.9 × 25.4-cm) piece of
red fabric
1⅛ yard (1 m) blue bias-fold tape

The arms and torso. Cut twenty-one
10″ (25.4-cm) lengths of bulky yarn, or
forty-two 10″ (25.4-cm) lengths of knitting
worsted. Lay the strands parallel to
each other with the ends even, and tie
them together ¾″ (19 mm) from one end
with a 6″ (15.2-cm) length of yarn. Divide
the yarn into three groups of seven (or
fourteen) strands each, braid them for
7½″ (19.1 cm) and tie the end of the braid
with another 6″ (15.2-cm) length of yarn.
Trim the free ends of the yarn ¾″ (19
mm) from the last tie.

Divide the yarn in half below the neck
and insert the arms from side to side
between the halves. Wrap a 10″ (25.4-
cm) length of yarn around the doll 1½″
(3.8 cm) below the neck to form the waist
and secure the arms.

The legs. Divide the yarn below the
waist into two equal side sections for
legs. Wrap an 8″ (20.3-cm) length of yarn
tightly around each section 3½″ (8.9 cm)
below the waist, and knot it to form
ankles. Trim the yarn ends even ¾″ (19
mm) below the ankle ties.

The features and hair

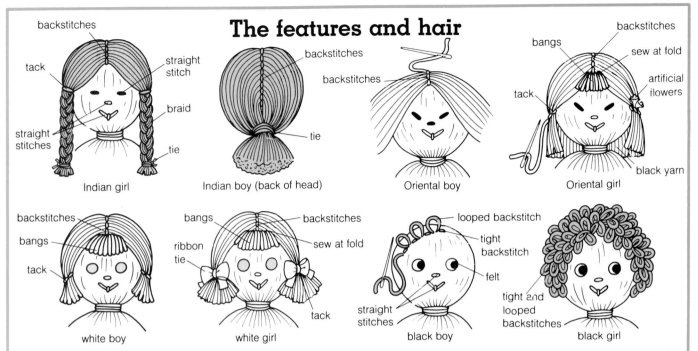

Indian girl — backstitches, tack, straight stitch, braid, straight stitches, tie

Indian boy (back of head) — backstitches, tie

Oriental boy — backstitches

Oriental girl — backstitches, bangs, sew at fold, artificial flowers, tack, black yarn

white boy — backstitches, bangs, tack

white girl — bangs, backstitches, ribbon tie, sew at fold, tack

black boy — looped backstitch, tight backstitch, felt, straight stitches

black girl — tight and looped backstitches

Note: For all of the dolls, knot the yarn specified for the features at one end. To begin, run an embroidery needle from the back of the doll's head to the front, and to end, bring the needle out the back and tie the yarn before cutting it.

1. The Indian Couple. With doubled red yarn, make each mouth with a straight stitch—1" (2.5 cm) long—on the face ¾" (19 mm) above the neck. Make a tiny vertical stitch just below and over the center of the first stitch to pull the mouth into a smile. Make a tiny straight horizontal stitch in red 1¼" (3.2 cm) above the neck for the nose. Using doubled black yarn, make one straight horizontal stitch for each eye 1½" (3.8 cm) above the neck and 1¼" (3.2 cm) from the other eye.

The hair. Wrap brown sport-weight yarn around a 6"-long (15.2-cm) piece of cardboard about 150 times, and cut the yarn at one end. For each doll, center a few parallel strands of yarn across the head from side to side, beginning 1¼" (3.2 cm) above the eyes. Using brown yarn, backstitch them in place at the center, moving from front to back.

For the girl, attach the hair in parallel rows until it reaches ½" (13 mm) above the back of the neck. Smooth the yarn to the sides of the face, bringing it forward over the brow and pulling it back at eye level; tack it to the sides of the head. Make two 1¾"-long (4.4-cm) braids, and tie each with a piece of brown yarn. Trim the ends even.

For the boy, attach the hair until it reaches 1½" (3.8 cm) above the back of the neck. Smooth the hair around the head to the center back of the neck. Tie the hair in a ponytail at the back of the neck with brown yarn, tack it to the head around the edges, and trim the ends even.

2. The Oriental Couple. Make the mouth and noses just as for the Indian dolls, except make the horizontal stitch for the mouth ¾" (19 mm) long for both, and make a black nose for the boy. For each doll's eyes, make a tiny slanting straight stitch with doubled black yarn 1½" (3.8 cm) above the neck and 1¼" (3.2 cm) from the other eye.

The hair. Wrap black knitting worsted 150 times around a 4"-long (10.2-cm) piece of cardboard for the girl's hair and a 3"-long (7-cm) piece for the boy's hair. Cut the yarn along one edge of each piece of cardboard.

Attach the hair for both dolls with matching yarn as for the Indian couple, ending at the same level in back, but

beginning 1½" (3.8 cm) above the eyes in front. Using black thread, tack the girl's hair to the sides of the head at eye level and continue with tiny running stitches that curve downward to the neck in back. Trim the ends even at the back. For bangs, cut ten 2" (5-cm) lengths of black yarn, fold them in half, and, one by one, stitch them through the fold along the front of the hairline. Tack one or two small fake flowers to the sides of the hair.

Tack the boy's hair to the side of the head at eye level and continue stitching around the head, securing the hair 1¼" (3.2 cm) above the neck edge at the center back.

3. The White Couple. Using red yarn, make each mouth and nose as for the Indian dolls, except make the horizontal stitch for the mouth ¾" (19 mm) long for the girl and 1¼" (3.2 cm) long for the boy. To make the eyes for each, cut two ¼" (6-mm) circles from blue felt. Glue or slipstitch them to the face 1¼" (3.2 cm) above the neck and 1¼" (3.2 cm) apart.

The hair. For the **girl,** wrap brown knitting worsted around a 4"-long (10.2-cm) piece of cardboard about fifty times. Cut the yarn along one edge of the cardboard. Attach the hair with matching yarn as for the other dolls, beginning 1¼" (3.2 cm) above the eyes and ending ½" (13 mm) above the neck. Smooth the hair, and tie each side with a pink ribbon bow at mouth level. Tack the underside to the head above the ribbon. For bangs, cut twelve 2" (5-cm) pieces of brown yarn, and, one by one, stitch them through the center to the center front of the hairline.

Make the **boy's hair** with yellow yarn as for the Oriental boy's hair, adding bangs as for the white girl.

4. The Black Couple. Make the mouths and noses for both dolls exactly like those for the white dolls. For each doll, cut two ⅜" (9.5-mm) circles from white felt and two 3/16" (5-mm) circles from black felt for the eyes. Glue or slipstitch the black circles on the white circles so the edges touch at one point. Glue or slipstitch the eyes to the face, with the pupils of each doll looking in the same direction, 1¼" (3.2 cm) from the neck and 1½" (3.8 cm) apart.

The hair. Thread a needle with a length of single black yarn, and make a tiny backstitch just above the hairline; then make another backstitch, leaving a loop about 1¼" (3.2 cm) high on the girl and ⅝" (16 mm) high on the boy. Continue working around each head from the outside to the center in spiraling rows of alternating tight and looped backstitches until the head is completely covered.

The dolls' clothes

1. Making the Patterns. Enlarge the patterns to the scale indicated and cut them out, following the instructions on page 155.

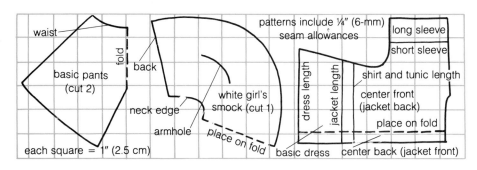

each square = 1″ (2.5 cm)

waist — basic pants (cut 2) — fold — back — neck edge — armhole — white girl's smock (cut 1) — place on fold — basic dress

patterns include ¼″ (6-mm) seam allowances — long sleeve — short sleeve — shirt and tunic length — center front (jacket back) — place on fold — dress length — jacket length — center back (jacket front)

2. The Indian Couple's Clothes. First make the girl's dress and the boy's tunic. These garments are made in the same manner with variations in color and trim. For the girl, cut one dress front and two dress backs from rose-coral fabric. For the boy, cut one shirt front and two shirt backs from light-brown fabric. Hem the center-back edges and seam the dress and tunic as for the black boy's shirt (page 72), and turn the garments right side out. Finish the neck of the dress with blue bias-fold tape and the tunic with burnt-orange bias-fold tape.

The trimmings. Cut a piece of rick-rack ½″ (13 mm) shorter than the length of the dress and tunic fronts: green for the dress, white for the tunic. Turn under ¼″ (6 mm) at one end of each strip of rickrack and attach it at the center front of the neck of the appropriate garment just below the seam binding. Similarly, turn under the opposite end of the rickrack, and stitch it down above the bottom edge of the garment. Measure a strip of blue rickrack to go around and ⅛″ (3 mm) away from the green strip, crossing it at the bottom as shown and adding ½″ (13 mm) for turning the ends under. Stitch the blue rickrack in place on the dress, as shown. Similarly, attach a strip of olive-green rickrack to the boy's tunic. Now stitch a band of yellow rickrack around the bottom of the neck binding on the dress, and a strip of gold on the tunic, making sure to turn the ends under. Sew a snap at the center back to close the necks of each garment and another 2½″ (6.4 cm) below the first. Fringe the bottom edge of both garments and the ends of the sleeves by making ⅜″-long (9.5-mm) cuts at ⅛″ (3-mm) intervals around the sleeves and lower edge of the tunic and ¾″-long (19-mm) fringe around the bottom of the dress. Tie a 16″ (40.6-cm) length of yellow rickrack around the girl's waist, and make a bow in the back.

The boy's pants. Cut two pants pieces from white fabric. Stitch them together and finish the waist edge, as for the black boy's pants (page 72), with bias-fold tape. Make a ½″-long (13-mm) fringe on the bottom of the legs.

The headbands and feather. Weave a 9″ (22.9-cm) length of yellow rickrack and a 9″ (22.9-cm) length of blue together to make a flat **headband** for the girl. Wrap it around her head, sew the

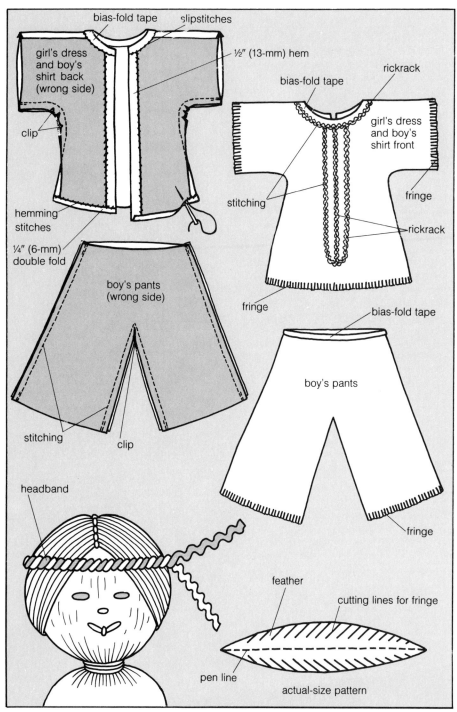

bias-fold tape — slipstitches — girl's dress and boy's shirt back (wrong side) — ½″ (13-mm) hem — clip — hemming stitches — ¼″ (6-mm) double fold

rickrack — bias-fold tape — girl's dress and boy's shirt front — stitching — fringe — rickrack — fringe

boy's pants (wrong side) — stitching — clip

bias-fold tape — boy's pants — fringe

headband

feather — cutting lines for fringe — pen line — actual-size pattern

ends together at the back, and tack it down at intervals. Repeat for the boy using gold and white rickrack.

Trace the actual-size pattern for the **feather** on tracing or tissue paper, and use the tracing to cut a feather from brick-red suede or felt. Draw a black line with a fine-point black felt-tip pen down the center, then fringe the edges as shown. Tack the broad end of the feather under the boy's headband at center back.

3. The Oriental Couple's Clothes. Begin with **the girl's kimono.** From dark-blue floral print, cut one 7¼″ (18.4-cm) square for the back and two 4¾″ × 7¼″ (12.1 × 18.4-cm) pieces for the front pieces. Mark the fabric 1½″ (3.8 cm) in from the center front on the neck edges and 1½″ (3.8 cm) down from the neck. Cut the corners off, in an outward curving line from one mark to the other. Align the unfinished edges of the front pieces with the back edges, right sides together. Stitch along the side edges beginning 2¾″ (7 cm) from the top. Join the top edge with a 2¾″-long (7-cm) line of stitching on each side, starting from the outside corner. Bind the center front and neck edges with one length of blue bias-fold tape. Turn up the bottom edge ¼″ (6 mm), then turn it up another 1″ (2.5 cm) and hem it.

Turn the kimono right side out, and slip it on the doll, overlapping the front edges. To make an *obi,* or **sash,** wrap a 6″ (15.2-cm) length of red ribbon around the waist, overlapping the ends at the back. Turn the outer end under, and slipstitch the two ends together. Wrapping red ribbon around two fingers to make a wide loop, cut it and pin the ends. Flatten and tack the bow to the sash with the seam hidden underneath.

The boy's jacket. Cut one jacket back and two front pieces from light-blue floral print. Stitch the jacket pieces together exactly as for the black boy's jacket. Make a ¼″ (6-mm) hem at the ends of the sleeves and a ½″ (13-mm) hem along the bottom edge. Turn the jacket right side out, and bind the center front and neck edges with light-blue bias-fold tape. Sew a snap to the edges at the top of the center front. Tie a bow made from a 4″ (10.2-cm) length of bright-rose rickrack, and then stitch it to the top of the overlapping side at the center front.

The boy's pants. Make the pants from blue fabric, following the instructions for the black boy's pants (page 72), but make a ¼″ (6-mm) hem along the bottom edge of the pant legs.

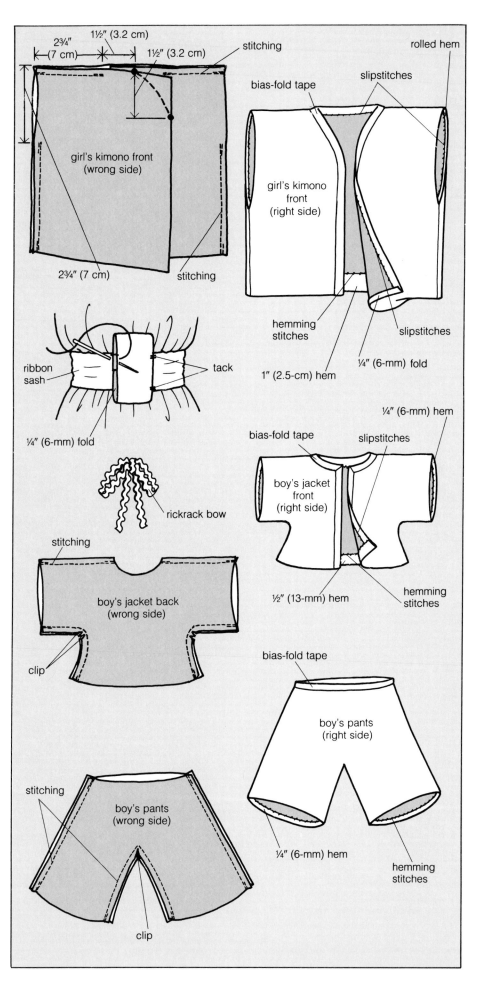

4. The White Girl's Clothes. Cut the circular dress, and a 12½″ × 3¼″ (31.8 × 8.3-cm) piece for the pants from the floral printed fabric. Make the **pants** following the instructions for the black girl's clothes (page 72).

The dress. Bind the entire edge of the dress with bias-fold tape, beginning at the lower edge of the center back, as for the black boy's shirt. Cut a 2″ (5-cm) length of bias-fold tape for each armhole. Press under ¼″ (6 mm) on each end. Fold it in half lengthwise, place it over the top edge of the armhole slit, and slipstitch around all the edges. Then stitch a narrow rolled hem along the lower edge of the armhole. Sew a snap to the center-back opening at the neck edge.

5. The White Boy's Clothes. Cut the **shirt** front and two backs from the striped fabric and two pant pieces from light-blue fabric. Make the boy's shirt following the instructions for the black boy's shirt (page 72), but omit the bow tie. Make the **pants** following the instructions for the black boy's pants, but stitch a ¼″ (6-mm) hem at the bottom edge of the legs.

The kerchief. Make a narrow ⅛″ (3-mm) hem along the edges of the red triangle of fabric and tie it around the boy's neck for a kerchief.

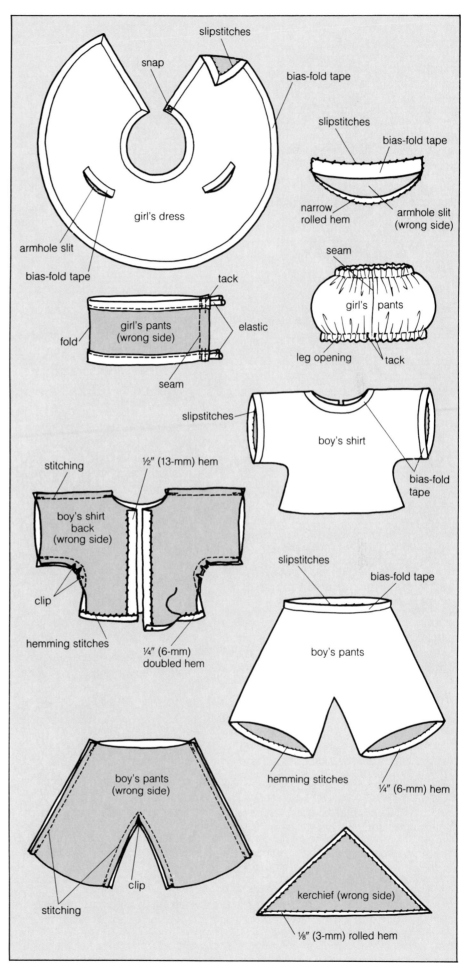

71

6. The Black Girl's Clothes. To make the girl's **pants,** cut a 12½" × 3¼" (31.8 × 8.3-cm) rectangle from pastel checked fabric. Turn under ¼" (6 mm) of fabric twice on each long edge, press, and stitch along the inside edge to make a casing for the elastic. Cut a 4" (10.2-cm) length and an 8" (20.3-cm) length of ⅛" (3-mm) elastic cord. Insert the shorter piece of elastic in the top casing and the longer piece in the bottom casing, tacking the ends securely at each end of the casing. Fold the pants in half, short ends and right sides together, and seam the ends. Turn the pants right side out, lay them flat with the seam down the middle of one side, and tack the lower, wider edges together at the center to make two leg openings.

The dress. From the pastel checked fabric, cut a 20" × 3¾" (50.8 × 9.5-cm) rectangle for the skirt. Align the short edges of the fabric wrong side out, and seam them together beginning 1¾" (4.4 cm) from the top end. Roll and stitch a narrow hem along each edge above the seam. Turn up ¼" (6 mm) of fabric along the lower edge of the skirt, then turn up another ¾" (19 mm) and press. Stitch the hem in place with hemming stitches.

Make a row of gathering stitches ¼" (6 mm) from the top edge of the skirt, and gather the fabric along the thread to a length of 6" (15.2 cm). Turn the skirt right side out. Cut a 7" (17.8-cm) length of ¾"-wide (19-mm) embroidered ribbon, center the ribbon, wrong side down, along the top of the skirt so that the bottom of the ribbon covers the gathering stitches, and sew the ribbon bodice to the skirt. Turn under the ends of the ribbon, and slipstitch them in place. Cut two 4" (10.2-cm) lengths of the embroidered ribbon for shoulder straps. Turn up ¼" (6 mm) at both ends of each strap, then slipstitch the straps to the ribbon bodice right side up, placing the front end of each strap ½" (13 mm) from the center and the back end ½" (13 mm) from the back opening. Slip the dress on the girl and stitch a snap on the bodice to close the back of the dress. Make a tiny bow from the red ribbon and tack it to the girl's hair just above the center-front hairline.

7. The Black Boy's Clothes. Cut one **shirt** front and two backs from the blue-and-white checked gingham. Make a ½" (13-mm) hem along the center edge of each back. Stitch both shirt backs to the front along the shoulders and side seams. Clip the seam allowances at the curve under the arms, and press them open. Hem a doubled ¼" (6-mm) fold along the bottom edge.

Turn the shirt right side out, and bind the neck and sleeve edges with red bias-fold tape as shown in the drawing. Align one edge of the bias-fold tape with the edge of the fabric right sides together, and stitch along the edges. Fold

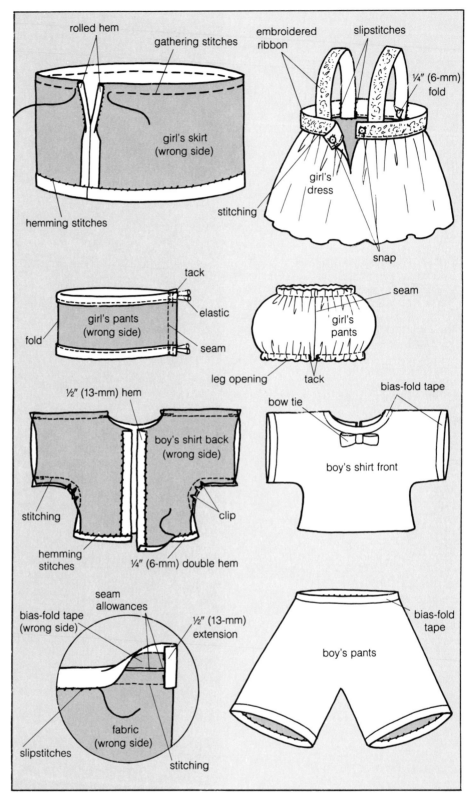

the tape over the seam allowances to the wrong side of the fabric and slipstitch it in place, turning the ends under.

Cut a 2¼" (5.7-cm) length of blue bias-fold tape, fold both ends ⅝" (16 mm) to the wrong side, and tack them down. Fold a 1"-long (2.5-cm) strip of bias-fold tape in half lengthwise, wrap it around the center of the first piece to make a bow tie, stitch it in place, and tack the bow to the center-front neck edge. Put the shirt on the doll, and overlap the

edges of the back opening to fit. Sew a snap in place at the neck and one 1¼" (3.2 cm) below it.

The pants. Cut the two pants pieces from the red fabric. Align the pants pieces right sides together, and join them along the side and inside leg edges. Clip the seam allowances at the top of the inside leg seam. Turn the pants right side out, and bind the top and lower edges with blue bias-fold tape, as explained for the shirt.

The doll's body

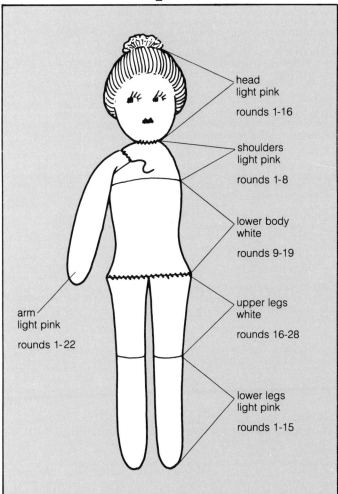

head
light pink

rounds 1-16

shoulders
light pink

rounds 1-8

lower body
white

rounds 9-19

upper legs
white

rounds 16-28

arm
light pink

rounds 1-22

lower legs
light pink

rounds 1-15

Victorian Lady

1. The Head. Using light-pink Speed-cro-sheen ch 2. *Round 1:* Work 6 sc in the second ch from hook. Do not join this or the following rounds. Place a marker at the beginning of the round. *Round 2:* Work 2 sc in each sc (12 sc). *Round 3:* * Sc in next sc, 2 sc in next sc (increase made). Repeat from * around — 6 sc increase (18 sc). *Round 4:* * Sc in next 2 sc, 2 sc in next sc. Repeat from * around (24 sc). *Rounds 5-13:* 1 sc in each sc. *Round 14:* * Draw up a loop in each of the next 2 sc, yo and draw through all three loops on the hook (decrease made). Sc in next 2 sc. Repeat from * around (18 sc). Turn the work wrong side out — this will be the right side of the head. Stuff the head firmly with polyester fiber. *Round 15:* Continue working on the right side. * Dec 1 sc, sc in next sc. Repeat from * around (12 sc). *Round 16:* Decrease every sc (6 sc); fasten thread. The head should measure 4¼" (10.8 cm) around at the widest part and 3" (7.6 cm) from top to bottom.

2. The Body. Using light-pink Speed cro-sheen, follow the instructions for the head for *Rounds 1 - 8* (24 sc). *Rounds 9-11:* Using white, work 3 rounds on 24 sc. *Round 12:* * Decrease 1 sc, sc in next 10 sc. Repeat from * (22 sc). *Round 13:* * Decrease 1 sc, sc in next 9 sc. Repeat from * (20 sc). *Round 14:* * Decrease 1 sc, sc in next 8 sc. Repeat from * (18 sc). *Round 15:* * Decrease 1 sc, sc in next 7 sc. Repeat from * (16 sc). *Round 16:* Sc in each sc (16 sc). *Round 17:* * 2 sc in next sc, 1 sc in next 3 sc. Repeat from * 3 times (20 sc). *Round 18:* * 2 sc in next sc, 1 sc in next 4 sc. Repeat from * 3 times (24 sc). *Round 19:* * 2 sc in next sc, 1 sc in next 5 sc. Repeat from * 3 times (28 sc). Turn the work wrong side out, using a pencil with a rubber eraser to push the top end of the body through the bottom opening. Stuff the body firmly, stretching it lengthwise until it measures 4" (10.2 cm) around the chest and 3¾" (9.5 cm) in length. Sew the lower edges of the body together.

Materials

- Speed-cro-sheen: 1 ball each of white and light pink
- Knit-cro-sheen: 1 ball each of cream-colored and black
- 6-strand embroidery floss: red, medium blue, white, and brown
- Scraps of 4-ply knitting worsted: red and bright green
- 15 yards of gold 2-ply sport-weight knitting yarn
- Polyester fiber for stuffing
- Scraps of cardboard
- A 5" × 12" (12.7 × 30.5-cm) piece of cream-colored organdy (optional)
- A 12" (30.5-cm) length of ¼" (6-mm) pregathered cream-colored lace edging (optional)
- A 4½" (11.4-cm) length of bias-fold tape (optional)
- Sewing thread: to match all yarn and fabric
- A No. 3 steel crochet hook
- Six ¼"-diameter (6-mm) pearl buttons
- **Crochet abbreviations:** ch (chain); sc (single crochet); dc (double crochet); sl st (slip stitch); yo (yarn over)
- **Gauge:** Speed-cro-sheen — 6 sc = 1" (2.5 cm); 5 rounds = 1" (2.5 cm); Knit-cro-sheen — 8 dc = 1" (2.5 cm); 3 rows = 1" (2.5 cm)

The features and hair

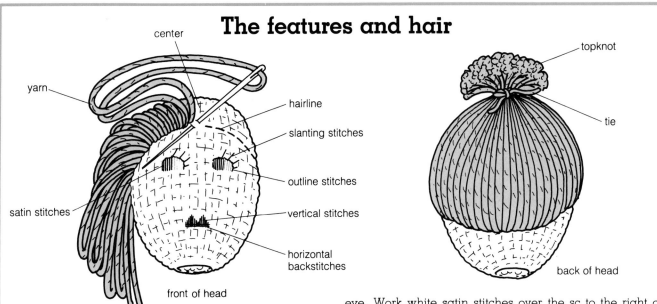

center

yarn

hairline

slanting stitches

outline stitches

satin stitches

vertical stitches

horizontal backstitches

front of head

topknot

tie

back of head

1. The Features. Use three strands of six-strand embroidery floss to make the features. For each one, knot the end of the thread, and draw the knot to the inside of the stuffing to hide it, then bring the needle out at the position instructed. On the fifth round from the bottom, using red embroidery floss, work the **mouth** in vertical straight stitches over 2 sc (one on each side of the center), forming two inverted Vs; make horizontal backstitches below the straight stitches.

The eyes. On the fourth round above the mouth, make blue satin stitches over the fourth sc from the center for the right eye; repeat over the third sc from the center for the left

eye. Work white satin stitches over the sc to the right of each blue section; leave 4 sc free between the eyes. Using brown, work outline stitches around the side and upper edges of each eye. Work four slanting stitches over each eye for lashes, as shown.

2. The Hair. Mark the hairline 2 rounds above the eyes in front to 4 sc beyond the eyes, tapering to 4 rounds above the lower edge in the back. Make stitches through the sc along the hairline, leaving 2½" (6.4-cm) ends and loops. Use 1 yard (.91 m) of gold yarn at a time, doubled in the needle. Draw the ends and loops upward into a ponytail, wrap them tightly with gold yarn, and tie them securely. Trim to ⅜" (9.5 mm) to simulate a topknot.

3. Joining the Head to the Body. Keeping the decrease rows above the waistline at the sides of the body, pin, then slipstitch the head securely to Round 2 of the body.

4. The Legs. With light-pink Speed-cro-sheen, starting at the toe, ch 2. *Round 1:* 5 sc in the second ch from the hook. *Rounds 2-15:* 1 sc in the next sc. 2 sc in each of the next 4 sc (9 sc). *(Note:* After Round 4, keep the work wrong side out, but insert the hook into the right side.

The work is too narrow to be turned after the leg is finished.) *Round 16:* Using white Speed-cro-sheen, work 1 sc in the next 4 sc, 2 sc in the next sc, 1 sc in each of the next 4 sc (10 sc). *Rounds 17-24:* Continue, making 1 increase in each round—do not increase over an increase in the previous round—(17 sc). *Rounds 25-28:* Work 17 sc in each row; fasten off. Stuff the leg firmly with polyester fiber, using the blunt end of the crochet hook to push the stuffing in. Sew

the upper edges of the leg together. Repeat to make the other leg. Sew the legs securely to the body so the edges of the legs meet at the center of the body.

5. The Arms. Using light-pink Speed-cro-sheen for the entire arm, follow the instructions for the legs, working 9 sc in each round through Round 22. Stuff the arm firmly, and sew the upper edges together. Repeat for the other arm. Sew an arm securely to each side of the body two rounds below the neck seam.

The doll's clothes

1. The Pants. *Row 1:* Using cream-colored Knit-cro-sheen, ch 38; 1 dc in the third ch from needle and in each remaining ch (36 dc—count ch 2 at the beginning of each row as 1 dc). Ch 2, turn. *Row 2:* 2 dc in the next dc, * dc in the next 5 dc, 2 dc in the next dc. Repeat from * 4 times (6 increases; 42 dc), ch 2, turn. *Row 3:* Dc in each dc, join with sl st at the top of ch 2. Do not turn. *Rows 4 - 5:* Ch 2, repeat Row 3. With the opening at the left side, mark the center front and center back of Row 5. To finish the leg edges, start at the center front, work sc in each dc, with 3 ch between; join with sl st at center back; fasten off. Repeat for the other leg edge.

To finish the upper and opening

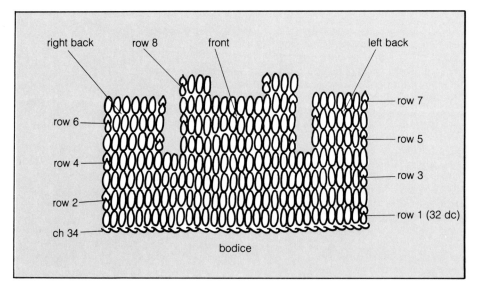

right back

row 8

front

left back

row 7

row 6

row 5

row 4

row 3

row 2

row 1 (32 dc)

ch 34

bodice

edges, start at the top of the opening, and work sc around the upper and opening edges; fasten off. For the drawstring, work ch 4" (10.2 cm) longer than the waistline; knot the ends and trim them. Insert the drawstring through the casing (Row 1), weaving in and out of each dc.

2. The Petticoat (optional). Turn and sew a ¼" (6-mm) hem on one long edge of the organdy. Stitch lace edging to the right side of the hem. Join the short edges, right sides together, to make the center-back seam, leaving a 1½" (3.8-cm) opening at the top. Turn under the opening edges, and stitch them. Make a row of gathering stitches ¼" (6 mm) from the upper edge of the petticoat; draw the fabric along the thread until it measures 4" (10.2 cm); fasten the thread. Bind the upper edge with bias-fold tape, adjusting the gathers evenly. Put the petticoat on the doll, overlap the opening edges, and sew on a snap or tack the petticoat in place.

3. The Bodice. With cream-colored Knit-cro-sheen, ch 34. *Row 1:* Dc in third ch from the hook, dc in each remaining ch (32 dc). *Row 2:* Ch 2, 1 dc in the next dc and in each remaining dc. *Rows 3-4:* Repeat Row 2. *Row 5* (left back): Ch 2, 1 dc in second dc and in the next 5 dc (7 dc). *Rows 6-7:* Repeat Row 5; fasten off. *Row 5* (front): Skip 2 dc of Row 4, join Speed-cro-sheen cotton in third dc; ch 2, dc in the next dc and in the next 12 dc (14 dc). *Rows 6 - 7:* Repeat Row 5. *Row 8:* Ch 2, dc in second dc and in the next 2 dc; fasten off. Skip 6 dc, join cotton in the next dc, ch 2, dc in the next dc and in the 2 remaining dc; fasten off. *Row 5* (right back): Skip 2 dc of Row 4, join Speed-cro-sheen cotton in the third dc; * ch 2, dc in the next dc and in the next 5 dc (7 dc). *Rows 6-7:* Repeat from *; fasten off.

With matching sewing thread, start at the armhole edge and join 4 dc of the front to the first 4 dc of the back on each side to make the shoulder seams. To finish the neck and back opening edges, start on the inside of the right back, and work 18 sc around the neck edge, ch 1. On the outside, work sc in each sc and 2 sc around dc at the right back edge. Ch 4 (loop) sc in bottom of second dc from top, * ch 4, dc in bottom of next dc. Repeat from * 4 more times (6 loops made). Fasten off.

4. The Sleeves. Starting at the bottom with cream-colored Knit-cro-sheen, ch 16. *Row 1:* Dc in third ch from hook and in each remaining ch (14 dc). Turn at the end of each row. *Rows 2-3:* Ch 2, dc in each dc. *Row 4:* Ch 2, dc in first dc (1 increase) and in each remaining dc (15 dc). *Row 5:* Repeat Row 4 (16 dc). *Row 6:* Ch 2 dc in the next 2 dc * 2 dc in the next dc, dc in the next dc. Repeat from * to end of row (6 increases), ending 1 dc in ch 2 (22 dc). *Row 7:* Ch 2, * dc in the next 2 dc, 2 dc in the next dc. Repeat from * to end of row (6 increases; 28 dc). *Rows

8-11:* Ch 2, dc in each dc across. *Row 12:* Ch 2, * yo hook, insert hook in dc, draw yarn through, yo hook and draw it through 2 loops. Repeat from * 5 more times, yo hook and draw through 7 loops, ch 1. Repeat procedure with 7 dc 3 more times; fasten off.

Using matching sewing thread, sew each sleeve to the bodice, placing the sleeve seam at the center of the underarm opening and the top center of the sleeve at the shoulder seam.

5. The Skirt. With black Knit-cro-sheen, ch 34. *Row 1:* Dc in third ch from hook, dc in each remaining dc (32 dc). *Row 2:* Ch 2, dc in the next 2 dc, 2 dc in the fourth dc, * dc in the next 3 dc, 2 dc in the next dc. Repeat from * to the last dc, ending in 2 dc (40 dc). *Row 3:* Ch 2, 1 dc in each dc across (40 dc). *Row 4:* Ch 2, dc in the next 3 dc, 2 dc in fifth dc, * dc in the next 4 dc, 2 dc in the next dc. Repeat from * to last dc, ending in 2 dc (48 dc). *Row 5:* Repeat Row 3 (48 dc). Continue, increasing 8 dc every other row through *Row 14* (88 dc).

The ruffle. Ch 88. *Row 1:* 2 sc in each ch (176 sc). *Row 2:* Ch 2, 1 dc in the next sc and in each remaining sc. *Rows 3-4:* Repeat Row 2. For heading, turn the work with sc edge at top. Join Speed-cro-sheen cotton in first sc, * ch 3, sc in next sc. Repeat from * to the end of the ruffle. Pin Row 1 of the ruffle to the lower edge of the skirt. With matching sewing thread, join the ruffle to the skirt, keeping the heading free.

6. Finishing the Dress. With matching sewing thread, join the back edges of the skirt and the ruffle, matching rows of dc and leaving 1" (2.5 cm) open at the upper end. Sew the bodice to the skirt, keeping the edges even. Close the back opening with six pearl buttons sewed on the left edge opposite the loops. Slip the dress on the doll.

The corsage. Wrap red yarn around a pencil three times, and cut the end; slip the loops off, and tie them tightly around the center with a 3" (7.6-cm) length of green yarn. Make a double knot to secure the loops. Similarly, make three more "flowers." Wind green yarn around the stems ¼" (6 mm) below the flowers. Trim the ends evenly; tack the corsage to the left-front waistline seam.

The jabot. Using black Knit-cro-sheen, ch 10; 3 dc in third ch from needle and in each of the remaining 9 ch (30 dc). Repeat on the opposite side of the ch; fasten off. For the neckband, work ch 4" (10.2 cm) long. Sc in second ch from hook and in each remaining ch; fasten off. Tack the jabot to the inside center of the neckband, turning the upper end of the jabot ½" (13 mm) to the outside. Adjust the band to fit the neck; sew on a tiny black snap fastener.

7. The Hat. Make the **crown** in the following fashion. *Round 1:* Using black Knit-cro-sheen, ch 2, 7 sc in second ch from needle. Do not join rounds; mark the

end of each round with contrasting thread. *Round 2:* 2 sc in each sc (14 sc). *Round 3:* * Sc in the next sc, 2 sc in the next sc (increase made). Repeat from * around (7 sc increase). *Round 4:* * Sc in each of the next 2 sc, 2 sc in the next sc. Repeat from * around (28 sc). *Rounds 5-7:* Increasing 7 sc evenly spaced around, sc in each sc (49 sc). *Round 8:* Sc in each sc (no increase). Repeat for 2 more rows.

The brim. Sc in each of the next 6 sc, 2 sc in the next sc (7 sc increase). Continue working 4 more rows, increasing 7 sc evenly spaced around each row.

Finishing the hat. Turn the hat wrong side out. Cut a 1½"-diameter (3.8-cm) circle of lightweight cardboard. Insert it into the crown to reinforce the shape. For a hatband, make a ch of cream-colored Knit-cro-sheen, to fit loosely around the crown. Work sc in second ch from hook and in each ch to end; fasten off. With the wrong side out, place the band around the crown, and tack the ends at the center front. Make three flowers, following the instructions for the corsage; wrap the stems close to the flowers and trim the stems to ½" (13 mm). Tack the flowers to the front of the hat over the ends of the hatband. Fasten the hat to the doll's head with glass-headed straight pins for hat pins at the front and back.

8. The Shoes. To start the **sole,** ch 10 using black Knit-cro-sheen. *Row 1:* 1 sc in second ch from needle and in each remaining 7 sc (9 sc). Ch 1, turn. *Row 2:* Sc in second sc and in each remaining 7 sc. *Rows 3-6:* Repeat Row 2.

The sides. *Row 7:* Sc around the sole, 9 sc on long edges, 5 sc at each end. Do not join rounds. *Rows 8-10:* Continue sc for 3 more rows. *Row 11:* At front end, work 3 sc across Row 10, ch 1, turn. *Rows 12-13:* Sc in 2 remaining sc, fasten off. With black sewing thread, join the edges of the tab to the top of Row 10.

Finishing the shoes. For each shoe, cut a ⅝" × 1" (16-mm × 2.5-cm) piece of lightweight cardboard, and round off the corners. Insert the cardboard into the shoe next to the sole. Stuff the toe and heel with polyester fiber. Place the shoe on the doll's foot, and sew the upper edge of the shoe to the top of Round 2 of the leg.

Knitted Nelly

Materials

Knitting worsted: 4 ounces (103.4 grams) each of off-white, dusty rose, and pale green, plus 25 yards (22.8 meters) of dark brown
Embroidery floss: pale blue, pale pink, dark brown, and navy
1 pair size 4 knitting needles, or whatever size gives correct gauge
A stitch holder
An embroidery needle

Polyester fiber for stuffing
1 yard of ⅛"-wide (3-mm) pale-green ribbon
21" (53.3-cm) length of pale-green ½"-wide (13-mm) ribbon or yarn
A 6" (15.2-cm) square of cardboard
Lipstick (optional)
Gauge: 6 stitches = 1" (2.5 cm); 7 rows = 1" (2.5 cm)

Knitting the doll

1. The Head. Cast on 10 stitches in off-white yarn; purl 1 row. Working in the stockinette stitch (knit 1 row, purl 1 row), increase 1 stitch at each end of every knit row four times, to give you a total of 18 stitches. Then begin to increase each knit row in the following manner: knit the first stitch; knit a stitch on the front, then one on the back of the second stitch; knit to within 3 stitches of the end of the row; knit the front and back of the next stitch; knit 2. Then work 12 rows, ending with a purl row. Still working in the stockinette stitch, decrease 1 stitch at each end of the next row (so that you have 16 stitches on the needle) as follows: knit 1 stitch; knit 2 together; knit to within 3 stitches of the end of the row; slip 1; knit 1; pass the slipped stitch over the knit stitch; knit 1. Purl 1 row, then knit 2 together across the next row; you should now have 8 stitches on the needle. Cut the yarn, leaving a 2"-long (5-cm) end.

2. The Body. Tie on dusty-rose yarn. Then cast on 6 stitches at the beginning of the next row, then work the 8 stitches remaining on the needle: knit 1, purl 1 four times to form a ribbing. Cast on 6 stitches at the end of the row to give you a total of 20 stitches. Make 16 more rows of ribbing, starting the next row with a purl stitch, and alternating knit and purl stitches for the first stitch of each row.

3. The Armholes and Waist. Continuing to make ribbing, cast on 4 stitches at the beginning of the next 2 rows, which will give you 28 stitches. Work even for 10 rows, ending with the right side facing you.

Working the garter stitch (knit each row), knit 1 row, then knit 2 together across the next row to give you 14 stitches; knit 1 row. Now work 2 rows in the stockinette stitch, starting with a knit row. Continuing with the stockinette stitch for 7 rows, increase 1 stitch at each end of every knit row four times, until you have 22 stitches. Work 11 more rows in the stockinette stitch.

4. The Legs. On the next row, knit 11 stitches and slip them onto a stitch holder until you are ready to work on the right leg; then knit the remaining 11 stitches.

The left leg. Make 1 row of elongated stitches in the following manner: insert the right needle in the first stitch, wrap the yarn around the right needle twice, and draw the two wraps through onto the right needle; repeat across the row. On the next row, knit across, dropping the second wrap on each stitch. Knit 2 rows in the usual manner, and cut the yarn, leaving a 2"-long (5-cm) end. Tie on the off-white yarn, and work 8 rows in the stockinette stitch. Continuing to work in the stockinette stitch, decrease 1 stitch on the next row by knitting to within 3 stitches of the end, then slip 1, knit 1, pass the slipped stitch over the knit stitch, and knit 1. Decrease in the same manner on the next fourth, eighth, and tenth rows, until there are 7 stitches on the needle. Purl 1 row, and cut the yarn, leaving a 2"-long (5-cm) end.

The left foot. Tie on the dusty-rose yarn, and working in the garter stitch, knit 4 rows. Continuing with the garter stitch, increase 1 stitch on the outer edge of each of the next 3 rows, as explained in the instructions for the head, until you have 10 stitches, then knit 6 rows. On the next row, knit 2 together five times. Bind off the remaining 5 stitches.

The right leg and foot. Transfer the stitches from the stitch holder onto a knitting needle. Work the right leg exactly as you did the left, except that increases and decreases are made on the opposite edge; use the appropriate instructions for decreasing from the section on the head (increasing is accomplished in the same way for both).

5. The Back. Knit the back of the doll exactly as you did the front. Then, with the right sides of the front and back together, join the head and shoulders, using yarn of a matching color and an embroidery needle.

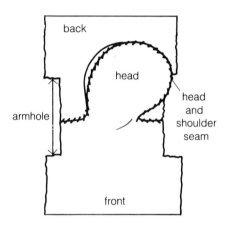

6. The Sleeves and Arms. Pick up 28 stitches across the entire left armhole including the cast-on stitches. Using dusty-rose yarn, purl 2 together across the row, decreasing to 14 stitches. Knit 1 row. Knit the next row, increasing each stitch and ending up with 28 stitches. For the next 6 rows, alternate a row of elongated stitches and a row of plain knit stitches in which you drop the second wrap of each elongated stitch from the previous row (as for the leg). Next row: Knit 1, knit 2 together across the row until the last stitch, then knit 1; there will be 15 stitches on the needle. Purl 1 row. Cut the dusty-rose yarn and tie on the off-white yarn. Work the stockinette stitch for 6 rows. Decrease 1 stitch at each end of the next knit row, then purl 1 row; knit 1 row, again decreasing 1 stitch at each end so that there are 11 stitches. Purl 1 row.

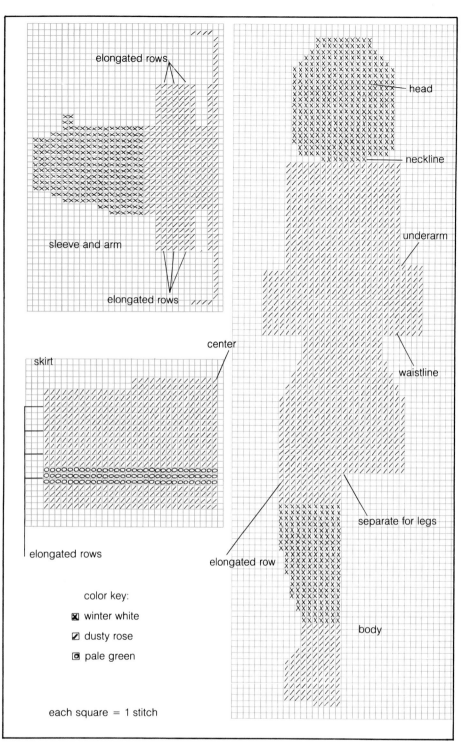

color key:

☒ winter white

☑ dusty rose

◙ pale green

each square = 1 stitch

The hand. Row 1: Knit 1, increase 1 stitch in the second stitch, knit 2, increase 1 stitch in the next stitch, knit 6; there should be 13 stitches. Row 2: Purl across. Row 3: Knit 5, increase 1 stitch in each of the next 2 stitches, knit 6; there will be 15 stitches. Row 4: Purl across. Row 5: Knit 1, knit 2 together, knit 2, knit 2 together, slip 1 stitch, knit 1 stitch, pass the slipped stitch over the knit stitch, knit 3, knit 2 together, knit 1; there will be 11 stitches. Row 6: Purl across. Row 7: Knit 3, knit 2 together, slip 1 stitch, knit 1 stitch, pass the slipped stitch over the knit stitch, knit 4. Row 8: Purl across. Bind off.

The right sleeve and arm. Make exactly as you did the left arm, reversing the order of stitches in each row.

7. The Skirt. Using dusty-rose yarn, cast on 30 stitches. Row 1 (wrong side): Knit across. Row 2: Knit, increasing each stitch so that you end up with 60 stitches. Row 3: Knit across. Row 4: Make a row of elongated stitches, as for the leg. Row 5: Knit across, dropping the second wrap of each elongated stitch. Rows 6-7: Knit across. Row 8: Make a row of elongated stitches. Row 9: Knit across, dropping the second wrap of each elongated stitch. Rows 10-11: Knit across. Row 12: Make an elongated row. Row

The features and hair

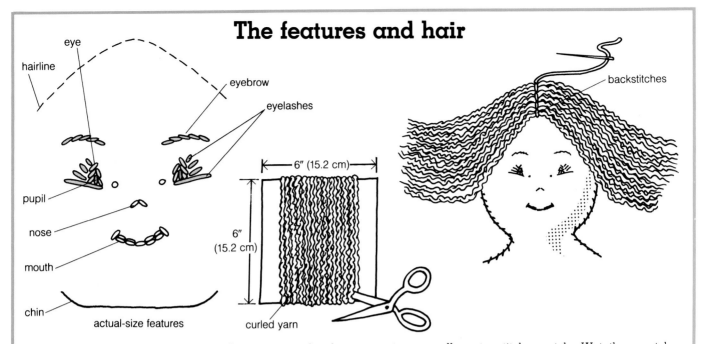

eye

hairline

eyebrow

eyelashes

pupil

nose

mouth

chin

actual-size features

curled yarn

6″ (15.2 cm)

6″ (15.2 cm)

backstitches

1. The Features. Trace the actual-size pattern for the eyes, eyebrows, and mouth on tracing paper with a soft pencil and use the chin line for positioning. Turn the paper over and retrace the features, transferring them onto the face. Using embroidery floss and satin stitches, embroider the features: pale blue for the eyes, navy for the pupils, pale pink for the nose and mouth, and dark brown for the eyelashes and eyebrows. Color the cheeks lightly with lipstick if desired, and tie the green ribbon or yarn around the waist.

2. The Hair. To curl the hair, knit all of the dark-brown yarn in a small garter-stitch swatch. Wet the swatch thoroughly in cold water, and let it dry. Steam-press and let dry. Unravel the swatch and wind the yarn around a 6″ (15.2-cm) square of cardboard. Cut across the strands at one end of the cardboard. Lay the strands close together side by side across the top of the head; sew along the center from front to back, securing the strands with backstitches of dark-brown yarn. Cut two 10″ (25.4-cm) lengths of ⅛″-wide (3-mm) pale-green ribbon, and tie the ends in two pigtails. Tack the hair where necessary to hold it in place, and trim the ends.

13: Knit across, dropping each second wrap, as before. Row 14: Knit across. Row 15: Knit across; cut the yarn and tie on the pale-green yarn. Row 16: Make an elongated row. Row 17: Knit across, dropping each second wrap. Cut the yarn and tie on the dusty-rose yarn. Rows 18-21: Knit across. Bind off loosely. Weave a 13″ (33.1-cm) length of ⅛″ (3-mm) pale-green ribbon in and out through the row of pale-green elongated stitches, overlapping the ends of the ribbon by 1″ (2.5 cm).

8. Finishing the Doll. Using an embroidery needle and the appropriate yarn, sew the sides and legs of the back and front together, leaving a 1½″ (3.8-cm) opening at one side for stuffing. Stuff firmly with polyester fiber, separating the body stuffing from that of the arms. Using dusty-rose yarn and an embroidery needle, sew the skirt to the doll's waist with the skirt seam at the center back, then seam the skirt shut.

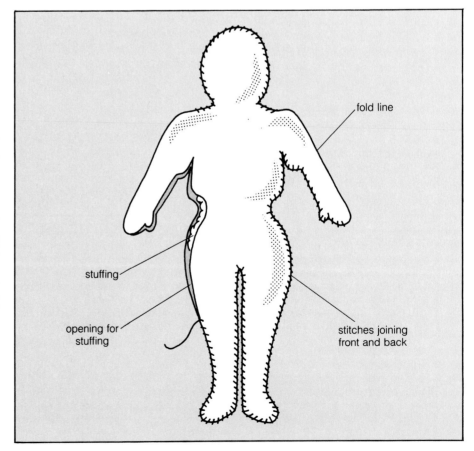

fold line

stuffing

opening for stuffing

stitches joining front and back

Kitchen Duet

Materials

Knitting worsted: 2 ounces (56.7 grams) white; 1 ounce (28.4 grams) black; 1½ ounces (42.5 grams) blue; ½ ounce (14.2 grams) each of beige, gold, and brown

6-strand embroidery floss: red, green, black, and brown

1 pair size 7 knitting needles, or whatever size gives correct gauge

Yarn bobbins

Stitch holders

An embroidery needle

2 buttons ¼" (3 mm) in diameter

Polyester fiber for stuffing

Gauge: 5 stitches = 1" (2.5 cm); 6 rows = 1" (2.5 cm)

Note: See knitting basics for changing colors and other knitting information. On the charts read knit rows from right to left, purl rows from left to right. Add yarn bobbins as needed.

The pastry chef

1. The Front. To make the **shoes,** use black yarn and cast on 5 stitches. *Rows 1-4:* Work in the stockinette stitch (knit 1 row, purl 1 row). Cut the yarn, and slip the stitches onto a stitch holder. Repeat for the second shoe.

The body. *Row 5:* With white knit across one shoe (5 stitches) picking it up from the holder and increasing 1 stitch in the first stitch, cast on 3 stitches, knit across the second shoe from the holder (5 stitches), increasing 1 stitch in the last stitch (15 stitches). *Row 6:* Purl across. *Row 7:* With white knit 1, with blue knit 1, with white knit 2, with blue knit 1, with white knit 2. with blue knit 1, with white knit 2, with blue knit 1, with white knit 2, with blue knit 1, with white knit 1. *Row 8:* Purl across, using each stitch's own color. *Rows 9-13:* Work in the stockinette stitch (knit 1 row, purl 1 row), using each stitch's own color. *Row 14:* With blue purl, increasing 1 stitch in the first stitch, purl 2, purl, using each stitch's own color, to within 3 stitches of the end, with blue purl 2, purl, increasing 1 stitch in the last stitch (17 stitches). *Row 15:* With blue knit, increasing 1 stitch in the first stitch, knit across, using each stitch's own color and increasing 1 stitch in the last stitch (19 stitches). *Row 16:* Purl across, using each stitch's own color. *Row 17:* With blue knit, increasing 1 stitch in the first stitch knit 3, with white knit 2, with blue knit 1, with white knit 2, with blue knit 1, with white knit 1, with blue knit 1, with white knit 2, with blue knit 3, knit, increasing 1 stitch in the last stitch (21 stitches). *Row 18:* Purl across, using each stitch's own color. *Row 19:* With white knit 4, knit, using each stitch's own color, to within 4 stitches of the end, with white knit 4. *Row 20:* Purl across, using each stitch's own color. *Row 21:* Knit across, using each stitch's own color. *Row 22:* With white purl 4, with blue purl 2, with white purl 1, with blue purl 1, with white purl 2, with blue purl 1, with white purl 2, with blue purl 1, with white purl 1, with blue purl 2, with white purl 4. *Row 23:* With white knit 5, with blue knit 1, with white knit 1, with blue knit 1, with white knit 2, with blue knit 1, with white knit 2, with blue knit 1, with white knit 1, with blue knit 1, with white knit 5. *Row 24:* With white purl 5, with blue purl 3, with white purl 2, with blue purl 1, with white purl 2, with blue purl 3, with white purl 5. *Row 25:* With white knit 4, with blue knit 1, with white knit 1, with blue knit 2, with white knit 2, with blue knit 1, with white knit 2, with blue knit 2, with white knit 1, with blue knit 1, with white knit 4. *Row 26:* With white purl 4, with blue purl 1, with white purl 1, with blue purl 1, with white purl 1, with blue purl 5, with white purl 1, with blue purl 1, with white purl 1, with blue purl 1, with white purl 4. *Row 27:* With white knit 2 together, knit 2, knit 15 in each stitch's own color, knit 2 together (19 stitches). *Row 28:* With white purl 3, with blue purl 1, with white purl 1, with blue purl 1, with white purl 7, with blue purl 1, with white purl 1, with blue purl 1, with white purl 3. *Row 29:* With white knit and bind off 3 stitches, with blue knit 1, with white knit 1, with blue knit 1, with white knit 7, with blue

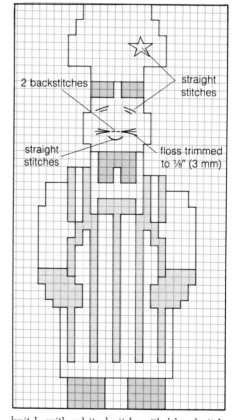

knit 1, with white knit 1, with blue knit 1, with white knit 3 (16 stitches). *Row 30:* With white purl and bind off 3 stitches, with blue purl 1, with white purl 1, with blue purl 1, with white purl 1, with black purl 2, with white purl 1, with black purl 2, with white purl 1, with blue purl 1, with white purl 1, with blue purl 1 (13 stitches). *Row 31:* With white knit and bind off 3 stitches, knit 1, with black knit 2, with white knit 1, with black knit 2, with white knit 1, with blue knit 1, with white knit 1, with blue knit 1 (10 stitches). *Row 32:* With white purl and bind off 3 stitches, purl 1, with black purl 5, with white purl 1 (7 stitches). *Row 33:* Knit across, using each stitch's own color. *Row 34:* With pale beige purl across. *Row 35:* With pale beige knit across, increasing 1 in the first and last stitches (9 stitches). *Rows 36-38:* Work in the stockinette stitch. *Row 39:* With black knit 2 together, knit 2, with pale beige knit 1, with black knit 2, knit 2 together (7

The salad chef

1. The Front. Rows 1-4: With brown only, work the **shoes** in the same manner as for the pastry chef.

The body. Wind one bobbin with blue yarn. *Row 5:* Cast on 6 stitches in blue. With the right side of the shoes facing you, knit 5 across one shoe, picking it up from the holder, cast on 1, knit 5 across the second shoe, and cast on 6 stitches (you will have 23 stitches). *Row 6:* Purl across. *Rows 7-10:* Work even in the stockinette stitch (knit 1 row, purl 1 row). *Row 11:* Knit 2 together, knit 5, with white knit 9, with blue knit 5, knit 2 together (21 stitches). *Row 12:* Purl across, using each stitch's own color. *Row 13:* With blue knit 5, with white knit 11, with blue knit 5. *Row 14:* Purl across, using each stitch's own color. *Row 15:* With blue knit 2 together, knit 2, with white knit 13, with blue knit 2, knit 2 together (19 stitches). *Row 16:* Purl across, using each stitch's own color. *Row 17:* With blue knit 2, with white knit 15, with blue knit 2. *Row 18:* Purl across, using each stitch's own color. *Row 19:* With white knit across, knitting the first and last 2 stitches together (17 stitches). *Row 20:* Purl across. *Row 21:* With white knit across, knitting the first and last 2 stitches together (15 stitches). *Row 22:* Purl across. *Row 23:* With pale beige knit 2 together, knit 4, with white knit 3, with pale beige knit 4, knit 2 together (13 stitches). *Row 24:* Purl across, using each stitch's own color. *Row 25:* With pale beige knit 4, with white knit 5, with pale beige knit 4. *Row 26:* Purl across, using each stitch's own color. *Row 27:* With white knit, increasing 1 stitch in the first stitch, knit 1, with blue knit 9, with white knit 1, increase 1 stitch in the last stitch (15 stitches). *Row 28:* Purl across, using each stitch's own color. *Row 29:* Knit across, using each stitch's own color and increasing 1 stitch in the first and last stitches (17 stitches). *Row 30:* Purl across, using each stitch's own color. *Row 31:* With white knit, increasing 1 stitch in the first stitch, knit 2, with blue knit 11, with white knit 2, increase 1 stitch in the last stitch (19 stitches). *Row*

stitches). *Row 40:* Purl across, using each stitch's own color. *Rows 41-44:* With white work in the stockinette stitch. *Row 45:* Cast on 3 stitches, knit 7, cast on 3 stitches (13 stitches). *Rows 46-48:* Work in the stockinette stitch. *Row 49:* Knit 2 together, knit 9, knit 2 together (11 stitches). *Row 50:* Purl across. *Row 51:* Knit 2 together, knit 7, knit 2 together (9 stitches). *Row 52:* Purl across, binding off.

2. The Back. Work the two **shoes** as for the front with black.

The body. Follow the instructions for the front, using white only.

3. Finishing the Doll. With an embroidery needle and matching yarns, sew the front to the back, wrong sides to-

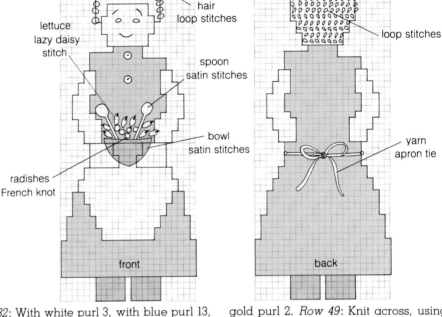

lettuce lazy daisy stitch

hair loop stitches

spoon satin stitches

bowl satin stitches

radishes French knot

front

loop stitches

yarn apron tie

back

32: With white purl 3, with blue purl 13, with white purl 3. *Row 33:* Knit across, using each stitch's own color. *Row 34:* Purl across, using each stitch's own color. *Row 35:* With white knit 2 together, knit 2, with blue knit 11, with white knit 2, knit 2 together (17 stitches). *Row 36:* Purl across, using each stitch's own color. *Row 37:* With white knit 2 together, knit 1, with blue knit 11, with white knit 1, knit 2 together (15 stitches). *Row 38:* Purl across, using each stitch's own color. *Row 39:* With blue knit across, knitting the first and last 2 stitches together (13 stitches). *Row 40:* Purl across. *Row 41:* Knit, binding off the first 4 stitches, knit 9 (9 stitches). *Row 42:* With blue purl, binding off the first 4 stitches, with pale beige purl 5 (5 stitches). *Row 43:* With pale beige knit across, increasing 1 stitch in the first and last stiches (7 stitches). *Row 44:* Purl across. *Row 45:* With pale beige knit across, increasing 1 stitch in the first and last stiches (9 stitches). *Row 46:* Purl across. *Row 47:* With gold, knit 1, with pale beige increase 1 in the next stitch, knit 5, increase 1 in the next stitch, with gold knit 1 (11 stitches). *Row 48:* With gold purl 2, with pale beige purl 7, with

gether, leaving a small opening. Stuff the doll firmly with polyester fiber, and close the opening. With white yarn make a few running stitches along the line between the white apron and the green arms, working the stitches through from front to back and back to front and pulling tightly on them to indent the outline of the arms. Following the embroidery chart, work the mouth and the star on the hat with straight stitches of red embroidery floss. Use black floss and a couple of straight stitches for each eye; make the black mustache with two or three back-stitches, cutting the ends of the floss ⅛" (3 mm) long.

gold purl 2. *Row 49:* Knit across, using each stitch's own color. *Row 50:* With gold purl across. *Row 51:* Knit 2 together, knit 7, knit 2 together (9 stitches).

2. The Back. Follow the directions for the front (shoes and body), except work rows 11-26 with blue only, and rows 42-52 with gold only.

3. Finishing the Doll. Following the instructions for the pastry chef, sew the front and back together, and stuff with polyester fiber, indenting the arm outline in white. With gold yarn work loop stitches for the hair, using the chart, as follows: bring the yarn through from the wrong side; leaving a small loop on the surface, make a small stitch where the yarn came out, to hold the loop in place. Using the embroidery chart as a guide, work the eyes and eyebrows in straight stitches with brown embroidery floss, and the mouth with red. Embroider the bowl and spoons with satin stitches using brown floss, the lettuce with lazy daisy stitches using green floss, and the radishes in French knots with red floss. Sew buttons to the front as shown. Knot strands of white yarn for the apron ties at the side seams, and tie them in a bow at the center back.

Crocheted Jack and Jill

The dolls' bodies

1. The Head and Torso. Using winter-white yarn and an F hook, make two head-and-torso sections, one at a time, for each doll, working in rounds, as follows: Ch 2. *Round 1:* Make 6 sc in the second ch. *Rounds 2-12:* Without joining and marking the ends of the rounds, work around, increasing 6 sc in each round, making a total of 72 sc stitches at the end of the twelfth round. *Round 13:* Ch 1, turn, sc in the next 16 sc, ch 1, turn. *Round 14:* Sc in 16 sc, ch 7. *Round 15:* Sc in the second ch and the next 5 chains, sc across, ch 7. *Round 16:* Sc in the second ch and the next 5 chains, sc across (28 stitches). *Rounds 17-46:* Work even, and fasten off.

For each doll, sew the head-and-torso sections wrong sides together, leaving a small opening for stuffing. Stuff them

firmly with polyester fiber, keeping them somewhat flat.

2. The Arms. Using winter-white yarn and an F hook, make two arms for each doll as follows: Ch 2. *Round 1:* Work 5 sc in the second ch. *Round 2:* Make 2 sc in each sc. Mark the ends of the rounds. *Round 3:* Increase 5 sc on the round (making a total of 15 sc). *Rounds 4-5:* Work even. *Round 6:* Increase 3 sc on the round (18 sc). *Round 7:* Increase 3 sc on the round (21 sc). *Round 8:* Increase 1 sc in each of the first 3 sc, ch 1, and turn. *Round 9:* Sc in 6 sc, ch 1, and turn. *Round 10:* Decrease 3 sc in the next 6 sc, decrease 1 sc down the sides of the increased rows, sc around. *Round 11:* Decrease 1 sc up increasing rows, sc around (23 sc). *Round 12:* Decrease 3 sc around (20 sc). *Round 13:* Decrease 3 sc around (17 sc). *Rounds 14-35:* Work even on 17 sc. *Round 36:* Decrease 5 sc around. Fasten off.

Materials

Knitting worsted: 12 ounces (340.2 g) winter white; 8 ounces (226.8 g) white; 8 ounces (226.8 g) red; 4 ounces (113.4 g) blue; 4 ounces (113.4 g) yellow; 2 ounces (56.7 g) black; scrap of brown
Polyester fiber for stuffing
1 yard (.91 m) elastic cord
Scraps of felt: blue, off-white, and red
3 sew-through white buttons, ¾" (19 mm) in diameter
Pink chalk or blusher (optional)
F and J crochet hooks
Crochet abbreviations: ch (chain), dc (double crochet), join (join last row with a slipstitch), sc (single crochet), sl st (slipstitch), st (stitch), sts (stitches), tc (triple crochet).
Gauge: with F hook, 4 sc = 1" (2.5 cm); with J hook, 3 sc = 1" (2.5 cm)

Stuffing the arms. Count from the beginning to the twenty-first round, and mark the round with thread. Stuff the hand-and-arm section firmly to the twenty-first round with polyester fiber. Form the bend in the elbow by sewing through the arm from front to back with a doubled strand of winter-white yarn between the twenty-first and twenty-second rounds, as shown, so the bulge of the thumb is up when the arm is seen from the side.

Stuff the upper arm firmly, and sew the open end closed, keeping it flat, and making the seam parallel to the elbow joint. Sew the arm to the upper body at the shoulder line, thumb side in. Repeat for the other arm.

3. The Legs. Using winter-white yarn, make two legs, one at a time, for each doll, as follows: Ch 25, join to begin rounds. *Rounds 1-20:* Make 1 sc in each ch around, marking the end of each round and working even. For **Jill:** *Round 21:* Change to red yarn, and sc around. *Rounds 22-41:* With red, sc around (making 20 rows of red). For **Jack:** *Round 21:* With winter white, sc around. *Rounds 22-41:* Change to blue yarn and alternate 2 rounds of blue sc with 2 rounds of winter white sc. For **both dolls:** *Round 42:* Attach black yarn to front of leg, sc around, join with slip stitch to first black stitch. *Round 43:* Ch 6, sc in second ch and next 4 ch, sc around, sc 5 on opposite side of starting chain. *Rounds 44-49:* Work even. *Round 50:* Decrease 3 sc on heel and toe. *Round 51:* Decrease 2 sc on heel and toe. Fasten off. Sew the bottoms of the feet closed.

Stuffing the legs. Stuff the foot and sock section of each leg firmly. At the top of the sock form the knee joint as for the elbow, using a doubled strand of winter-white yarn, and flattening the leg from one side to the other across the front, as shown. Stuff the upper leg firmly, sew the open end of the leg closed, keeping it flat and making the seam parallel to the knee joint. Sew the leg to one side of the bottom of each body; sew the other leg to the other side.

The features and hair

1. The Features. Trace the actual-size patterns for the features on tissue or tracing paper, and use them to cut the following: four circles from blue felt for the eyes, two noses from off-white felt, and two mouths from red felt. Following the chart, lightly mark the face with a soft pencil to show the position of the features. Slipstitch the eyes, nose and mouth into place. Thread a needle with brown yarn, and make the eyelashes with straight stitches. Use red yarn to make the smile with outline stitches and a straight stitch at each corner of the smile. Using pink chalk or blusher, lightly color the cheeks in the areas indicated, if desired.

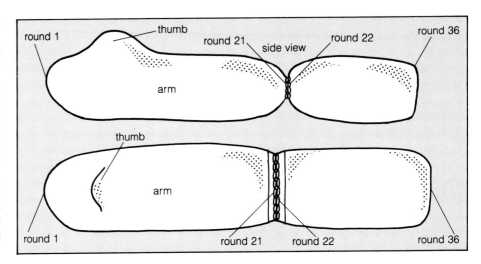

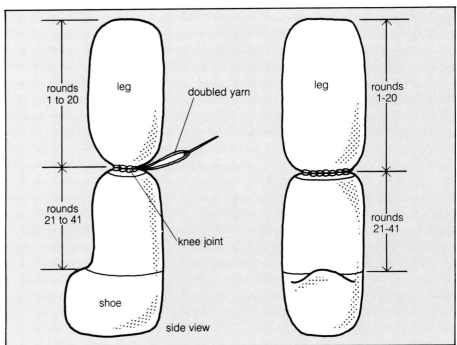

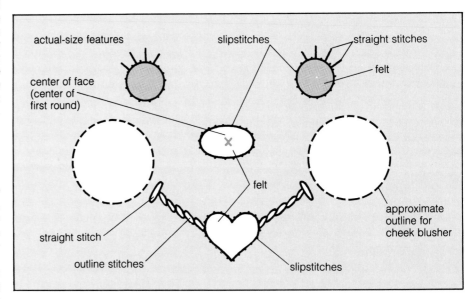

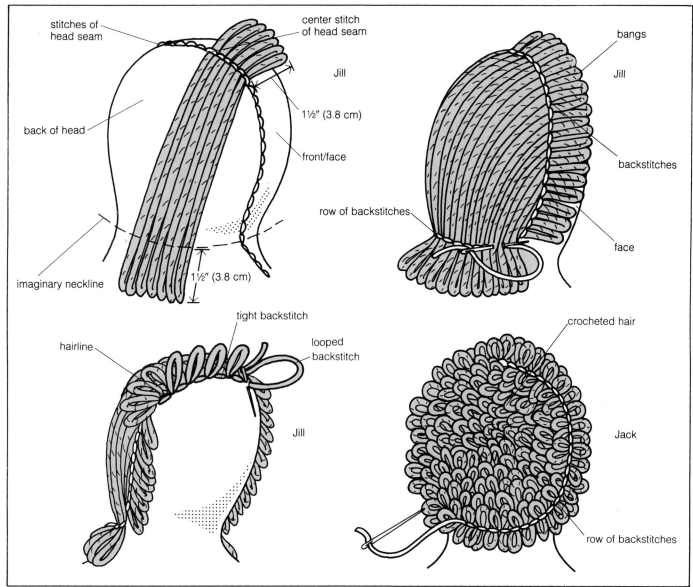

2. Jill's Hair. Use yellow yarn and an F hook to make the girl's hair: Begin at the center back of the head, holding the end of the yarn against the doll's neck so that approximately 1½" (3.8 cm) of yarn falls below her neckline. Using the crochet hook, pull a loop of yellow yarn through the center-top stitch of the head seam. Extend the loop approximately 1½" (3.8 cm) beyond the seam toward the face. Holding the loop in place on the forehead, bring the yarn back down the head and make a loop that extends approximately 1½" (3.8 cm) below the neckline. Repeat, bringing the yarn back up the head again and making a second loop through the same stitch at the head seam. Continue making the hair in this manner, working from the top down one side of the head to the neckline and holding the yarn flat against the back of the head while making the loops at the back of the neck and at the head seam. Work two loops through each head seam stitch. Repeat to cover the side of the head.

With a knotted doubled strand of yellow yarn, begin a row of backstitches where the hair ends at one side of the head. Backstitch over the seam line of the head, covering the seam and securing the hair. In the same fashion, secure the hair with a row of backstitches around the back neckline, taking care to keep the hair neat and flat against the back of the head, as shown.

Use a needle threaded with a single strand of yellow yarn to make bangs. Starting 2" (5 cm) to the right of the center front, make a backstitch just in front of the loops of hair along the hairline. Make another backstitch along the hairline, working toward the center, but do not pull it tight; leave a loop about 1½" (3.8 cm) long. Continue working across the hairline, alternating tight and looped backstitches, and ending 2" (5 cm) to the left of center.

The hair ribbon. Using red yarn and a J hook, ch 12. Work 2 rows in sc, and fasten off. Wrap red yarn tightly around the center of the crocheted strip six times to make it look like a bow, and knot the yarn, leaving the ends long enough for tacking the bow to the hair. Place the bow 1" (2.5 cm) to the left of the center front between the bangs and other hair loops, and tack it in place.

3. Jack's Hair. Using red yarn and an F hook, ch 2. *Round 1:* Work 6 sc in the second ch from the hook. Join with a sl st to the first sc and ch 1, turn. *Round 2:* Work 2 loop sts in each sc. Join, ch 1, turn. (To make a loop st, loop the yarn over your forefinger. Insert the hook in an sc, and draw the yarn through from under your finger, complete the sc, and drop the loop from your finger.) *Round 3:* Sc around, increasing 6 sc on the round. *Round 4:* Loop st around, increasing 6 sc on the round. *Rounds 5-12:* Alternate rounds of sc with rounds of loop st, increasing 6 sc on each round (making 72 sc at the end of Round 12).

After Round 12, continue on with 36 loop sts without increasing, ch 1, turn. Work 36 sc, ch 1, turn. Work 36 loop sts, fasten off. Sew the hair to the back of the head, with the last 36 loop sts at the front and top of the head. Make bangs exactly as you did for Jill.

Jill's clothes

1. The Pants. With white yarn and a J hook, ch 64. *Round 1:* Join to begin rounds, work 64 sc in a circle, working over elastic cord. *Round 2:* Ch 3, dc around (64 dc). Join in the top of the chain. *Rounds 3-7:* Dc around. *Round 8:* Ch 3, dc in the next 31 dc. Join in the top of the chain. *Rounds 9-15:* Dc around on 32 stitches. *Round 16:* Sc around on 32 stitches, working over elastic cord. *Round 17:* 2 dc in each sc around, join, and fasten off. Work the other leg in the same fashion. Slip the pants on the doll, and tie the elastic to fit the doll's waist.

2. The Dress. Make two identical pieces for the dress, one for the front and another for the back, as follows: With red yarn and a J hook, start the neck edge by chaining 19. *Round 1:* Sc in the second ch and across making 18 sc, ch 5. *Round 2:* Sc in the second ch and the next 3 ch, sc across, ch 5. *Round 3:* Sc in the second chain and the next 3 ch, sc across (26 stitches). *Rounds 4-10:* Work even on 26 sc. *Round 11:* Decrease 2 sc on each side (22 stitches). *Rounds 12-18:* Work even on 22 sc. *Round 19:* Ch 3, dc across, including the first stitch so as to increase each row. *Rounds 20-28:* Work the same as Round 19. Fasten off. Stitch the front and back of the dress together, right sides out, along the shoulders. From the right side, pick up 18 sc across the armhole. *Round 29:* Ch 1, turn, and sc across (18 stitches). *Round 30:* Ch 1, turn, and sc across (18 stitches). *Round 31:* Ch 1, turn, increase 1 sc at the beginning and end of the row (20 stitches). *Round 32:* Work even. *Round 33:* Increase 1 sc on each side (22 stitches). *Round 34:* Work even on 22 sc. *Rounds 35-36:* Ch 3, dc across, working all stitches to increase. *Round 37:* Drop red and pick up white. Sc across. *Rounds 38-39:* Working over elastic cord, make a picot edge across, as follows: Sc in the first st, ch 2, sc in the same st, ch 1, skip 1 sc. Repeat Rounds 29-39 for the other sleeve. Work a picot edge over elastic around the edge of the neck by repeating the sequences used in Round 10 and 11. Sew the sides of the dress together, and slip it on the doll.

3. The Apron. To make the belt use white yarn and a J hook. *Row 1:* Ch 65, turn. *Row 2:* Work 64 sc across the ch. *Rows 3-5:* Work even. Fasten off.

The skirt. *Round 1:* Attach yarn in the eleventh stitch in from the end of the belt, on the edge. Sc in 45 sc across. *Round 2:* Ch 4, work 2 tc in each of 40 sc, ch 1, turn. *Round 3:* Sc across, ch 4, turn. *Round 4:* Tc across, ch 1. *Round 5:* Repeat Round 3. *Round 6:* Repeat Round 4. *Round 7:* Repeat Round 3. *Round 8:* Repeat Round 4. *Round 9:* Repeat Round 3. Fasten off.

The bib. Attach yarn in the twenty-first stitch from one end on the top side of the belt. *Round 1:* Sc in 23 sc, ch 3, turn. *Round 2:* Work 2 tc in each sc across, ch 1, turn. *Round 3:* Sc across. Fasten off.

The straps. Work 14 rows of 4 sc and fasten off. Sew one end of each strap to a top corner of the bib. Wrap the apron around the doll, stitch a button on the back of the belt to hold it closed; slip the button into a space in the crochet on the other end of the belt. Wrap the straps over the doll's shoulders, cross them in back, and secure them inside the belt, about 2″ (5 cm) apart.

Jack's clothes

1. The Shirt. Using white yarn and a J hook, make identical front and back sections for the shirt, as follows: Ch 19. *Row 1:* Sc across the ch (making 18 stitches), ch 5. *Row 2:* Sc in the second ch and across, ch 5 (22 stitches). *Row 3:* Sc in the second ch and across (26 stitches). *Rows 4-12:* Work even on 26 sc. *Row 13:* Decrease 2 sc on each side (22 stitches). *Rows 14-20:* Work even on 22 stitches. Fasten off.

Align the front and back of the shirt, wrong sides together, and join them across the top of the shoulders. Pick up 20 sc across the armhole, work even on 20 sc for 10 rows. Fasten off. Sew the sides and lower arm edges together.

The collar. Attach white yarn in the center front st of the neck edge. Sc around, making 3 sc in the stitch at the shoulder seam. At the end of the row turn, but do not ch 1. Skip the first sc, and sc around, working 3 sc at the center sc at each shoulder increase. Repeat the round once more, decreasing at the front edge and increasing at the shoulders. Fasten off.

2. The Hat. With blue yarn and a J hook, ch 2. *Round 1:* Work 4 sc in the second ch until you have 32 sc. *Rounds 2-8:* Marking the ends of each round with contrasting thread, work around in sc, increasing 4 sc in each row. *Rounds 9-10:* Work even. *Round 11:* Change to white yarn. Work 2 sc in each sc around. *Round 12:* Work 1 sc in every other sc. *Rounds 13-14:* Work even. Fasten off.

Turn up the brim of the hat, and sew it to the head.

3. The Pants. With blue yarn and a J hook, ch 48, and join the ch to start rounds.

The pants top. *Round 1:* Work 48 sc in a circle, working over elastic cord. *Round 2:* Sc increasing 4 stitches (52 stitches). *Round 3:* Work even in sc. *Round 4:* Increase 4 sc (56 stitches).

The legs. *Rounds 5-21:* Work even. *Round 22:* Sc in 28 sc for the first leg, and join to start rounds. *Rounds 23-35:* Work even (making 31 rows from the start of the leg). Fasten off. Repeat for the other leg.

Slip the pants on the doll, and tie the elastic to fit the waist.

The straps. Work 32 rows of 4 sc for each strap. Fasten off. Sew one end of each strap to the front of the waist, spacing them about 3½″ (8.9 cm) apart at the center. Cross the straps in the back and sew to the back waist. Sew a white button over the end of each strap on the front waistband.

Needlepoint Farm Family

Materials

1 yard (.91 m) of 36"-wide (.91-m) plain mono canvas, 10 meshes to the inch

Fine-point waterproof felt-tip marking pen in a light color

A size 18 tapestry needle

A darning needle

Persian yarn: three 40-yard (36.4-m) skeins of bright red; four 8-yard (7.3-m) skeins each of medium gray and dark gray. Small amounts of the following: orange; pale, medium, fuchsia, and coral pink; gray-blue and deep blue; beige, tan, buff, cream, cocoa, brown, and rust; pale yellow, yellow, deep yellow and gold; red; spring green; white; and black

White glue

Polyester fiber for stuffing

A 1½" × 3" (3.8 × 7.6-cm) piece of beige suede or felt

A 2" × 2" (5 × 5-cm) piece of black felt

Cardboard: two 8½" × 9" (21.6 × 22.9-cm) pieces for the front and back, two 6½" × 9" (16.5 × 22.9-cm) pieces for the sides, and one 9½" × 11½" (24 × 29-cm) piece for the roof

½ yard (45.7 cm) blue cotton fabric

A 6"-high × 3"-diameter (15.2 × 7.6-cm) metal-rimmed cardboard container (an 8-ounce—227-gram—bread-crumb container is ideal)

A 2"-long (5-cm) wooden stick, ¼" (6 mm) in diameter

A small lump of modeling clay

Note: One yard of yarn will cover 1 square inch (2.5 cm) of canvas. Leftover knitting worsted may be substituted in small areas, if 1 strand is separated from regular 4-ply yarn.

Needlepoint lends itself to shapes that follow the lines of the canvas. This group makes the most of that with colorful shapes that have moving parts. The limbs of the farmer, his wife, and the animals can be adjusted, the barn doors open, and the roof of the barn lifts up for storage of the whole set, including the silo.

General information

1. Stitching. Every piece in this project is made with the half-cross stitch, which can be worked horizontally or vertically, as shown on page 157. This economical stitch leaves little yarn on the back of the canvas, where it forms a straight stitch.

2. Reversing a Stitching Chart. The easiest way to make the reverse of a stitching chart is to trace it on tracing paper and then flop the tracing sideways. Mark the second side.

3. Blocking. If needlepoint gets pulled out of shape while you are working, it can be straightened by correct blocking. If the piece is fairly straight, simply press it on the wrong side, covered by a damp terry-cloth towel and let it dry thoroughly before moving it. If the needlepoint is really out of shape, roll it in a very damp terry-cloth towel and leave it overnight until it is thoroughly damp. Lay the needlepoint face down on heavy cardboard or pressboard, and straighten it by pulling opposite corners; anchor it every ¾" (19 mm) around the edges with rustproof thumbtacks or pushpins. Allow the needlepoint to dry thoroughly. Remove it from the board, cover it with a damp cloth, and steam it with a hot iron to fluff the yarn, but do not let the iron touch the needlepoint or it will become flat.

4. Trimming the Needlepoint. After each needlepoint section is completely finished and blocked, trim the canvas ⅜" (9.5 mm) away from the stitches. Except for the barn, turn under the excess canvas, clipping it outside the stitching along the curves and inner corners as necessary to turn it easily. Glue the edges down on the wrong side.

5. Joining the Canvas. Using a darning needle and doubled matching yarn, join the designated edges with overcast stitches.

Preparing the canvas

1. Marking and cutting the canvas. Make sure that the selvage edges are parallel to the sides of every piece of canvas cut; the lengthwise grain of the canvas should run from the top to the bottom of every figure in this project.

Using a soft pencil and the following measurements, mark off the outer dimensions of each piece on the canvas and label it. It is easiest to arrange all pieces of the same size in columns on the canvas wherever possible.

Measure 1" (2.5 cm) in from the edge of every section marked on the cutting diagram before penciling the outline of each figure on the canvas. Make each barn door 23 stitches across and 27 stitches deep. There should be 1" (2.5 cm) of free canvas around the outside of all stitched areas on the finished work for ease in working and blocking.

Cut the rectangles of canvas apart. *Do not cut* the shape shown by the outer line on the stitch charts; it is only there as a visual aid. And remember, the canvas is trimmed only after all the stitching has been completed and the needlepoint has been blocked.

Each square on a chart represents one mesh of canvas or one stitch of needlepoint. The area for the roof has been doubled to allow for both sides.

		inches	centimeters
Wife:	head (cut 2)	3½ × 3½	(8.9 × 8.9)
	body (cut 2)	4 × 4½	(10.2 × 11.4)
	arm (cut 2)	3½ × 3½	(8.9 × 8.9)
	leg (cut 2)	3½ × 3½	(8.9 × 8.9)
	foot (cut 2)	3 × 3½	(7.6 × 8.9)
Farmer:	head (cut 2)	3½ × 3½	(8.9 × 8.9)
	body (cut 2)	4 × 4½	(10.2 × 11.4)
	arm (cut 2)	3½ × 3½	(8.9 × 8.9)
	leg (cut 2)	3½ × 3½	(8.9 × 8.9)
	foot (cut 2)	3 × 3½	(7.6 × 8.9)
Scarecrow:	head (cut 2)	3 × 3½	(7.6 × 8.9)
	body (cut 2)	4 × 4½	(10.2 × 11.4)
Large Horse:	head (cut 2)	3½ × 3½	(8.9 × 8.9)
	body (cut 2)	3½ × 4½	(8.9 × 11.4)
	leg (cut 4)	3½ × 4	(8.9 × 10.2)
Small Horse:	head (cut 2)	3½ × 3½	(8.9 × 8.9)
	body (cut 2)	3½ × 4	(8.9 × 10.2)
	leg (cut 4)	3½ × 4	(8.9 × 10.2)
Pig:	head (cut 2)	3½ × 3½	(8.9 × 8.9)
	body (cut 2)	3½ × 3½	(8.9 × 8.9)
	leg (cut 4)	3 × 3½	(7.6 × 8.9)
Barn:	front (cut 1)	8½ × 9	(21.6 × 22.9)
	back (cut 1)	8½ × 9	(21.6 × 22.9)
	side (cut 2)	6½ × 9	(16.5 × 22.9)
	door (cut 2)	4½ × 6	(11.4 × 15.2)
	roof (cut 1)	9½ × 11½	(24 × 29)
	horse's head (cut 2)	3½ × 3½	(8.9 × 8.9)
Silo:	roof (cut 1)	7½ × 7½	(19 × 19)
	sides (cut 1)	8 × 12	(20.3 × 30.5)

The farmer's wife

Work the front and back of the head and the body sections, two arms, and two legs, following the stitching charts. Also work two shoes in black yarn, following the chart for the farmer's shoes. Block the canvas. When the canvas has dried, trim the edges and glue them under as explained in the general information.

1. The Head. Join the head sections, right sides out, along the edges as explained in "General Information."

2. The Body. Join the body sections in a similar fashion, except stuff the body compactly with polyester fiber before closing the edges completely. Stitch the head to the body, aligning them at the center front and center back. Wrap pale-pink yarn around the neck to cover the joining stitches, and secure it.

3. The Hair. Roll orange yarn tightly into a ¼"-thick (6-mm) ball; then roll the yarn crosswise around the ball to flatten it and make a bun of hair that is ¼" (6 mm) thick and ½" (13 mm) wide. Attach the hair to the back of the head at the position indicated by the dotted line on the chart, and tack any loose loops on the bun securely.

4. The Bows. Make a stitch with a 3" (7.6-cm) length of yellow yarn at the center front of the neck; tie the ends in a bow and trim them. With a 5″ (12.7 cm) length of white 4-ply yarn, take a stitch at the center back of the apron tie section; tie the yarn into a 1″-long (2.5-cm) bow, with 1″-long (2.5-cm) ends.

5. The Arms and Legs. Join the long edges and both ends of each arm and leg, right side out. Keeping the top end of the arm aligned with the end of the shoulder and the seam toward the back, stitch an arm to each side of the body. Make a loose loop of pale pink yarn for the thumb at the front of each arm, in the position indicated on the chart, and secure it.

With the seams to the inside, secure the legs side by side at the center of the lower edge of the body.

6. The Feet. Join the long edges and ends of each foot. With the side seam along the outside edge, secure each foot on the top back edge to the bottom of one of the legs.

The farmer

Work the front and back head and body sections, two arms, two feet, and two legs, omitting the red patch on the front of one leg. Block, trim, glue, and join the parts as for the farmer's wife, but do not stuff the body sections.

1. The Ears and Thumbs. Make a loop of pale-pink yarn at either side of the head and at the front of each arm (see the stitching chart) for the ears and thumbs.

2. The Hat Brim. Fold a 1½″ × 3″ (3.8 × 7.6-cm) piece of beige suede or felt in half lengthwise, and from it cut an oval 2¾″ (7 cm) long and 1¼″ (3.2 cm) wide. Cut a 1⅜″ (3.5-cm) slit down the center of the oval, to fit over the farmer's head. Slip the brim on the farmer's head and pull it down to the hairline.

The scarecrow

Work the front of the scarecrow's head following the chart; repeat to work the back of the head, but omit the features. Work the body front following the chart; work the body back in reverse following the general information on page 86 for obtaining a reverse stitching chart. Block, trim, glue, join, and attach the head sections and body sections as was done previously, but leave a ¼″ (6 mm) opening at the center of the lower body edge.

1. The Straw. To simulate straw, stitch through the neck with yellow yarn, leaving a ½″- to 1″-long (13-mm to 2.5-cm) loose end of yarn protruding on one side. Clip the yarn, leaving an equally long end free on the other side of the neck. Repeat stitching through the neck and clipping the yarn in a radiating

fashion so that the scarecrow appears to have a straw ruff around its neck.

Using the same technique, but making ½″-long (13-mm) yarn loops on either side, stitch back and forth about five or six times through the lower edge of the arms in the position indicated on the chart. Clip the ends of the yarn so that it looks as if the scarecrow's hands are made of straw.

2. The Clay Base. Mold the lump of clay to resemble the shape of a half walnut shell. Insert the 2″-long (5-cm) stick into the center; let the clay dry thoroughly. Insert the other end of the stick through the hole in the scarecrow's body; glue it securely in place.

3. The Hat Brim. Cut a 1¾″ (4.4-cm) circle from black felt. Cut a straight slit in the center to fit over the black crown section of the head. Fold the circle of felt in half and cut an oval at the center that measures 1⅛″ (2.8 cm) long and ⅜″ (9.5 mm) across.

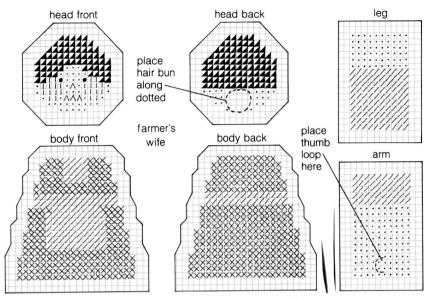

head front   head back   leg

place hair bun along dotted

farmer's wife

body front   body back   place thumb loop here

arm

color key: ◪ orange · black ⊡ pale pink ⊞ medium pink △ coral pink
⊠ fuschia pink ⊘ white

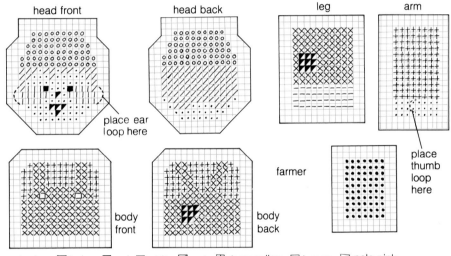

head front   head back   leg   arm

place ear loop here

farmer   place thumb loop here

body front   body back

color key: ⊙ beige ◪ red ☐ white ⊘ rust ⊞ deep yellow · brown ⊡ pale pink
■ black ⊡ medium pink ⊟ pale blue ⊠ deep blue △ coral pink

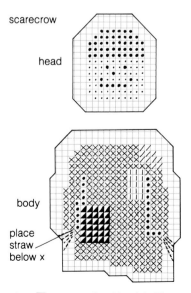

scarecrow

head

body

place straw below x

color key: · black ⊡ fuschia pink ⊠ deep blue
⊘ spring green ⊡ yellow ◪ red

The barn

Work the front following the chart. Work two identical doors in plain red. Work the back the same as the front, but omit the opening and add the window in the lower left section as shown on the inset. Work the right side of the barn following the chart; work the left side in the same manner, but see the left-side chart for details of the windows. Start the roof at the center edge of the design (marked on the chart), by a row of black stitches representing the peak of the roof. Work one half completely, following the chart; then repeat the pattern in reverse for the other half, omitting a second row of black stitches at the center of the canvas. (See "General Information" for reversing a pattern.)

1. The Hay. To simulate hay in the loft at the front of the barn, make small stitches around the edges and middle of the gold section of the hayloft, mixing gold and yellow yarn and clipping the ends to random lengths ranging from ½" (13 mm) to 1" (2.5 cm).

2. The Horse's Tail. Using black yarn, make the horse's tail in the left-hand window on the right side of the barn, following the directions for the large horse's tail.

3. Reinforcing the Barn Sections. To reinforce the barn sections, mark and cut cardboard pieces to the size of each worked area, except for the doors. With a ruler and a sharp knife, lightly score (do not cut through) the top center of the cardboard for the roof from end to end. Then score a line 2" (5 cm) to each side of the center for ease in shaping the roof.

Cut blue cotton fabric to line each section, making each piece ½" (13 mm) larger all around than the corresponding piece of cardboard or the doors.

Trim the canvas of each section to within ⅜" (9.5 mm) of the worked area. Center a matching piece of cardboard under each worked area (except for the doors), turn the excess canvas over the edges of the cardboard, clipping at the inner corners, and glue the canvas securely to the cardboard.

4. Lining the Barn Sections. Turn under ½" (13 mm) of fabric on all the edges of the lining pieces, and press. Place each piece of lining on the inside of its corresponding barn section and glue it into place. Bend the roof into shape first, and then glue the lining into position. Readjust the fabric to fit smoothly, wherever necessary.

5. Joining the Barn Sections. Using red yarn, join the four barn sections together at the corners, then overcast all upper edges of the barn, covering the exposed canvas and catching the top edge of the lining. From the inside, join one long edge of each door to one side of the barn opening at the front. For the

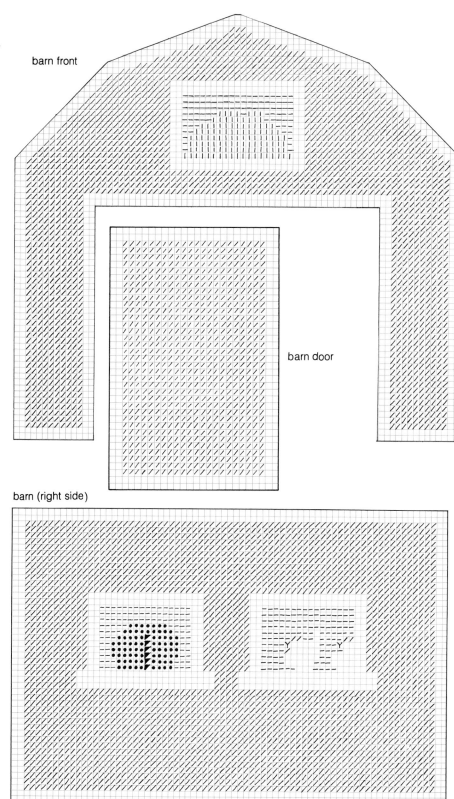

barn front

barn door

barn (right side)

color key:
▨	red	⊡	tan
Ⴤ	yellow	◨	brown
☐	white	⊙	cocoa
⊠	black	⊙	dark gray
⊞	gold	⊟	gray-blue

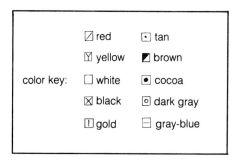

horse head for barn window

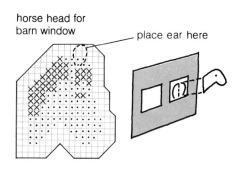

place ear here

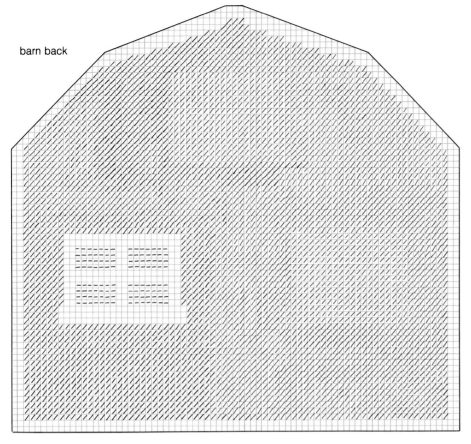

barn back

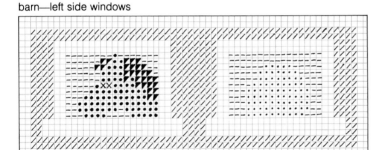

barn—left side windows

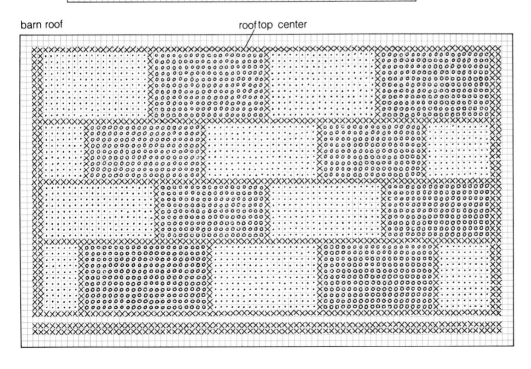

barn roof   rooftop center

door handles, make nine or ten ¾"-long (19-mm) black loosely looped stitches in the same place, ½" (13 mm) in from the front edge of each door, and starting 1½" (3.8 cm) from the lower edge of the door. Then wind the end of the yarn around the loops to make a solid handle before securing it.

6. The Barn Floor. Cut two pieces of heavy cardboard, one 7¼" × 7½" (18.4 × 19.1 cm) and the other 6¾" × 7" (17.1 × 17.8 cm), rounding the corners very slightly. For each piece of cardboard, cut a piece of lining fabric that is ⅝" (16 mm) larger all around than the cardboard. Place each piece of cardboard on the wrong side of its corresponding lining. Turn the edges of the lining over the cardboard and glue them securely in place. Center the smaller piece of cardboard over the larger one, lining sides out, so that the larger piece extends ¼" (6 mm) beyond the smaller one on all sides. Glue them together.

7. Assembling the Barn. Set the lower edges of the barn on the barn floor so they rest on the extensions of the larger piece of cardboard. Glue the barn securely in place.

From the inside, join one side of the roof to the top of one side of the barn with red yarn, making slightly loose stitches through the lining only, to form a sort of hinge.

8. The Horse's Head. Work one side following the chart, and make a loop of tan yarn for the ear at the position indicated by the dotted line on the chart. Repeat, in reverse, for the other side of the head. Block, trim, glue, and join the sections together. Make a ¼" (6-mm) fringe for the forelock with black yarn. Secure the head to the center of the buff stitches in the window on the left side of the barn.

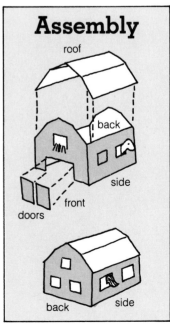

Assembly

roof

back

side

front

doors

back   side

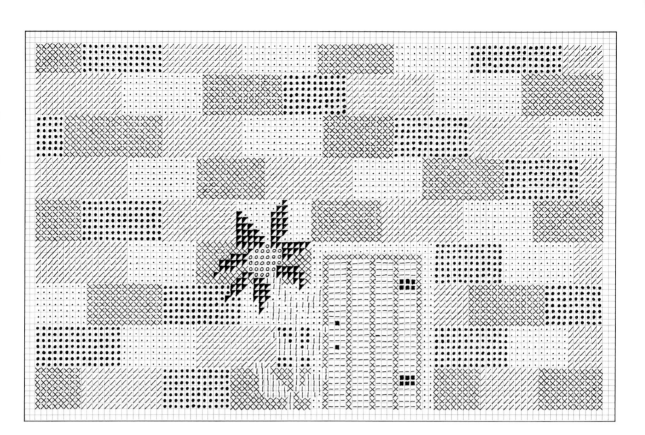

silo
color key:
- ⊡ buff
- ⊠ medium gray
- ⊿ beige
- ⊡ cream
- ⊞ spring green
- ◪ deep yellow
- ⊟ pale yellow
- ⊙ brown
- ■ black

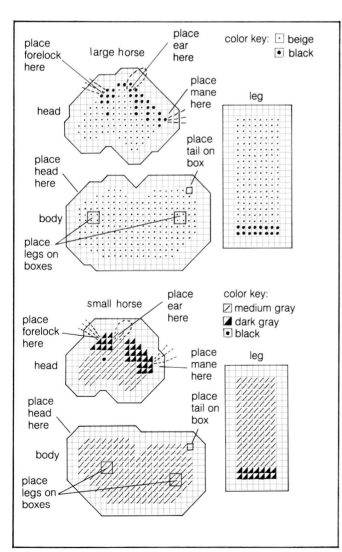

place forelock here
large horse
place ear here

color key: ⊡ beige ⊡ black

place mane here

head

place head here

place tail on box

body

place legs on boxes

leg

place forelock here
small horse
place ear here

color key:
- ⊿ medium gray
- ◣ dark gray
- ⊡ black

place mane here

head

place head here

place tail on box

leg

body

place legs on boxes

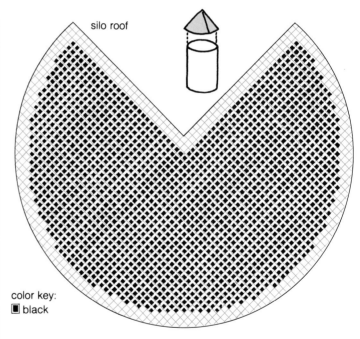

silo roof

color key:
- ■ black

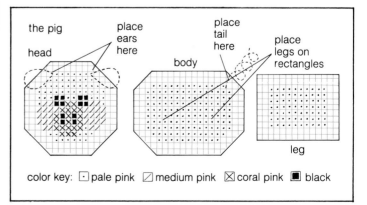

the pig

place ears here

place tail here

place legs on rectangles

head

body

leg

color key: ⊡ pale pink ⊿ medium pink ⊠ coral pink ■ black

90

The silo

Work the silo following the chart. Block and trim the canvas, and glue the edges as you did for the other pieces. Using black yarn and following the directions for the barn door, work a ⅝"-long (16-mm) door handle at the side of the door opposite the hinges. Join the short ends of the canvas together, with matching yarns to form a tube. Insert the cardboard container inside the needlepoint, and glue it in place.

1. The Roof. Work the silo roof following the chart and finish it as you did the other sections. Cut a piece of black felt the same shape as the roof and ⅛" (3 mm) smaller all around. Join the straight edges of the needlepoint roof, then glue the felt to the insides of the needlepoint. Stuff the roof firmly with polyester fiber, then glue the roof to the top of the silo so that the edges extend evenly beyond the silo on all sides.

The animals

1. The Large Horse. Work the front and back sections for the head and body of the large horse following the charts, but reverse the charts for the back sections of the head and body as described in "General Information." Work four leg sections. Block, trim, and glue the canvas as before. Join the neck edge of the head section to the body section. Make a beige yarn loop on each side of the head for ears, in the position indicated by the dotted lines on the chart.

Join the head-and-body sections together around the edges, stuffing the head and body areas firmly as you stitch.

The mane and tail. Using black yarn, stitch back and forth three or four times from the top to the bottom of the mane at the position marked by dotted lines on the chart, leaving ⅛"-long (3-mm) loops of yarn at either end. Clip the ends of the loops for the forelock.

Again using black yarn, make the tail in the position indicated by the small square on the chart. Stitch through the top of the horse's rump, with the needle pointing from top to bottom along the center seam, and leaving a 1"-long (2.5-cm) end of yarn protruding at the top of the horse's hindquarters. Bring the needle back to where it first went in, leaving a 1" (2.5-cm) loop of yarn below the loose end. Clip the yarn 1" (2.5 cm) from the body. Repeat to anchor seven more loops of yarn together at the rump. Pull the loose ends of yarn through the loops and draw them tight to form a knot. Clip the loose ends of yarn even, and unravel the yarn to make the tail full.

The legs. Join the long edges and each end of the four legs. With matching yarn, secure the upper inside edges of the legs to the body, making stitches through the body at the centers of each larger square and keeping the leg seams toward the back. The legs should remain movable. Fasten the yarn.

2. The Small Horse. Work the sections for the small horse following the charts, and assemble them as you did for the large horse. Use medium-gray yarn for the ears and dark-gray yarn for the mane and tail.

3. The Pig. Work the front of the pig's head following the chart. Work the back in the same shape as the front, but entirely in pale pink, omitting the face. Work the front and back body sections following the chart. Work four legs following the leg chart. Block, trim, and glue the sections as directed in "General Information." Join the front and back of the head.

The ears. Braid three strands of pale-pink yarn into a 3" (7.6-cm) length, cut it in half, and stitch the ends to keep them from raveling. Loop each braid and anchor the ends of the loop on the pig's head at one of the positions indicated by the dotted lines on the chart.

Join the body sections, but stuff the body firmly before closing the seam completely.

Join the short edges and each end of the four legs and attach them to the body as for the large horse. Secure the center back of the head to one side of the front end of the body so that the pig's head is facing sideways but slightly angled toward the front.

The tail. Wind two 2"-long (5-cm) strands of Persian yarn around a uniformly narrow heat-resistant object no more than ⅛" (3 mm) in diameter, and steam the loops with an iron. Let the yarn dry thoroughly. Anchor one end of the curly yarn to the back of the pig at the position indicated on the chart.

The Novelty Dolls (clockwise from left): (1) Little Red Ridinghood Story Doll,
(2) Dolley Doorstop, (3) Shaker Woman, (4) Abigail and Ebenezer, (5) Maude and
Cecil, (6) Grandmother Pillow Doll, (7) Kitchen Witch, (8) Cuddly Kitten, (9) Pillow Girl.

Novelty Dolls

Human ingenuity and skill have created a vast category that can best be classified as "novelty" dolls. Often the term signifies playthings made from materials and objects not originally intended for dollmaking, such as dried fruits, nuts, seashells, clothespins, soap, twigs. You'll find examples of this kind of novelty doll here, as well as witty and appealing creatures intended for unusual or humorous purposes.

The "Little Red Ridinghood Story Doll" (1) follows a time-honored tradition in American dollmaking: the turn-about doll. Flip Little Red's skirt over, and there's her grandmother. Pull off the old lady's cap, and there lurks the big, bad wolf.

Toting a tiny flower basket, "Dolley Doorstop" (2) rests on a sandbag, cleverly concealed in her calico dress. Her miniature spectacles are simply the eye of a hook and eye.

A pair of bent pipe cleaners for arms, neck, and parasol, plus a few small scraps of fabric, are virtually the only materials required for the beautifully simple "Shaker Woman" (3), a descendant of an authentic American colonial design.

American folk artisans often recycled corncobs to make dolls. "Abigail and Ebenezer" (4), a gingham-and-denim clad couple, continue the tradition. Their heads are simply slices of cobs glued to longer pieces; their arms are pipe cleaners and their noses are beans.

Snooty, fur-bedecked dowager "Maude," and her stuffy husband "Cecil" (5), are hand puppets that fairly beg to be manipulated. Their expressive faces are stuffed felt, molded with hand stitches. Their heads and garments—into which their hands are sewed—are glued to cardboard-tube necks.

Cream-colored and quietly serene, the "Grandmother Pillow Doll" (6) makes a cozy bedtime companion. This lacy, limbless creation uses machine zigzag stitching to join the sections and to outline the features.

Swooping in on her broomstick, the "Kitchen Witch" (7) isn't a wicked witch at all. On the contrary, this enchanting little sorceress of Norwegian descent is believed to guard against scorching pots, fallen cakes, and other culinary disasters. This droll adaption of an authentic Scandinavian design is unusual in that she is crocheted and has pipe cleaners for limbs.

No mother would put a real cat in a baby's crib, but this "Cuddly Kitten" (8) would be a welcome companion. Extremely simple to make, this snoozing kitty has a soutache-braid tail, embroidered features, and a cheerful bow around her neck.

Blonde braids, embroidered features, and floppy limbs that extend beyond the body characterize the "Pillow Girl" (9). This sweetly sleeping child is lightly stuffed to cradle a dozing head.

Dolley Doorstop

Materials

A 22″ × 10½″ (55.8 × 26.7-cm) piece of calico printed fabric

A 22½″ × 8½″ (57.2 × 21.6-cm) piece of muslin

A 6″ × 4¾″ (15.2 × 12.1-cm) piece of pale-pink broadcloth

A 12″ × 8″ (30.5 × 20.3-cm) piece of red wool, homespun, or challis

Polyester fiber for stuffing

Thread: to match all fabrics, plus red and gray

1 straight black metal eye (from a hook and eye),

approximately ½″ (13 mm) long

A soft gray pencil

A 6″ (15.2-cm) length of white or natural lace, approximately 1″ (2.5 cm) wide

A small amount of lamb's wool (available in a drugstore)

A 2″ (5-cm) length of natural eyelet or lace, approximately 1″ (2.5 cm) wide, finished on both edges

3 pounds, approximately, of very fine sand

A 1″ (2.5-cm) basket of flowers

The doll's body and clothes

1. Cutting the Fabric. Enlarge the patterns to the scale indicated and cut them out, following the directions on page 155. Using the patterns, cut two dress pieces and one bonnet from calico, the apron and two pieces for the sandbag from muslin, two head pieces from pale-pink broadcloth, and the shawl from red wool, homespun, or challis. Transfer any pattern markings to the fabric.

2. The Sandbag and Dress. Sew the muslin **sandbag** pieces right sides together along all four sides, leaving a 2″ (5-cm) opening at the center of the shortest (top) edge. Turn the sandbag right side out.

The dress. Similarly, join the two pieces of dress fabric, but leave the entire top edge of the dress open. Fold down the top edge ¾″ (19 mm) to the wrong side, and press. Turn the dress right side out.

3. The Apron. Turn under and press a double ¼″ (6-mm) hem along the side and bottom edges of the apron. Stitch the hem in place. Make six or seven small, even tucks along the top edge of the apron so that it measures 3″ (7.6 cm) wide, and baste them in place. Center the top edge of the apron wrong side down, along the top edge of the right side of the dress. Pin the apron in place. Make a row of gathering stitches with doubled thread ¼″ (6 mm) from the top edge of the dress. Start and stop at the same point. Make sure to stitch through all thicknesses of both dress and apron across the front. Leave 4″-long (10.2-cm) thread ends at both ends.

Pattern diagram

apron (cut 1)

bonnet (cut 1)

sandbag (cut 2)

dress (cut 2)

fold line

shawl (cut 1)

head (cut 2)

each square = 1″ (2.5 cm)

patterns include ¼″ (6-mm) seam allowances for the head and ½″ (13-mm) seam allowances for the other sections

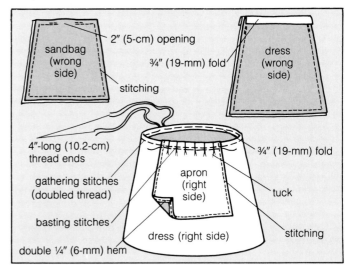

sandbag (wrong side)

2″ (5-cm) opening

stitching

dress (wrong side)

¾″ (19-mm) fold

4″-long (10.2-cm) thread ends

gathering stitches (doubled thread)

basting stitches

double ¼″ (6-mm) hem

apron (right side)

dress (right side)

¾″ (19-mm) fold

tuck

stitching

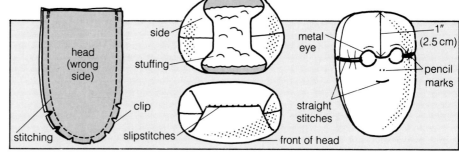

4. The Head. Stitch the head pieces, right sides together, around the curved edges, leaving the straight edge open. Clip the seam allowances around the curves and turn the head right side out. Stuff the head firmly to within ¾" (19 mm) of the top edge with polyester fiber. Then fold down the fabric around the top of the head as though you were wrapping a package. First, fold the sides toward the center, flattening the top of the head. Then fold the fabric at the back forward, over the side folds, then fold the front fabric back, and slipstitch it in place.

The features. Flatten the top of the head into a rectangular shape. Measure 1" (2.5 cm) down the center front of the face from the top, and make a light mark for placement of the eyes. Center the metal eye over the mark, and fasten each side of it in place, to resemble eyeglasses, with two or three long stitches starting and ending at the nearest side seam to resemble earpieces. Pull the thread taut to the face as you work, and knot it securely at the side.

Make a ¼"-long (6-mm) stitch of red thread for the mouth ½" (13 mm) below the glasses at the center of the face. Using a soft gray pencil, draw eyebrows above the glasses and make two dots for the nose halfway between the glasses and the mouth.

5. The Bonnet and Hair. Place the **bonnet** fabric wrong side up and fold back one long edge 1" (2.5 cm). Press. Place a strip of lace approximately ¼" (6 mm) in from the folded edge, so that the lace extends beyond the edge, and stitch it in place.

The hair. Shape the lamb's wool into a rectangle that measures approximately 3½" × 1⅜" (8.9 × 3.5 cm). Wrap the lamb's wool hair around the top of the head from ear to ear so that it extends approximately ½" (13 mm) out from around the forehead. Center the bonnet, wrong side down and lace edge forward, across the top of the head and along the sides of the face, about ¼" (6 mm) in front of the side seams. Tack the bonnet in place at the center top and at the sides and lower front corners.

6. Assembling the Doll. Place the muslin sandbag inside the dress. With a small funnel, fill the muslin bag with sand, leaving enough room at the top for the fabric to close completely over it. Stitch the opening closed with tight, closely spaced stitches. Pull the gathering threads around the top of the dress until the opening of the dress measures approximately 2" (5 cm) across.

Place the head in the neck opening, aligning the center of the face with the center of the apron. The top edge of the dress should reach about ½" (13 mm) below the mouth. Pull the gathering threads tight around the head and knot them securely. Whipstitch the head to the dress and sandbag.

7. The Shawl, Bow, and Basket. Turn under the edge of the neck opening ½" (13 mm), and wrap the shawl around the doll's neck. Overlap the shawl under the doll's chin, and tack it in place.

Twist the 2" (5-cm) length of lace at the middle to form a bow-like shape. Press it, and then stitch to hold it. Place the bow on top of the shawl under the chin, and slipstitch it in place.

Stitch the tiny basket of flowers to the left front of the shawl, approximately 1" (2.5 cm) from the hem and front edge.

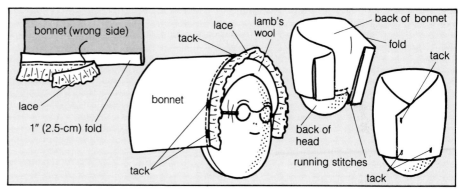

Folding the back of the bonnet. With the back of the head facing you, fold the center back of the bonnet straight down against the back of the head. Attach the bonnet to the back of the head with a row of running stitches that extends ½" (13 mm) to each side of the center. One at a time, fold each side vertically across the back, turning back the end of the first side and turning under the end of the second side to make it look smooth. Tack the corners in place, as shown.

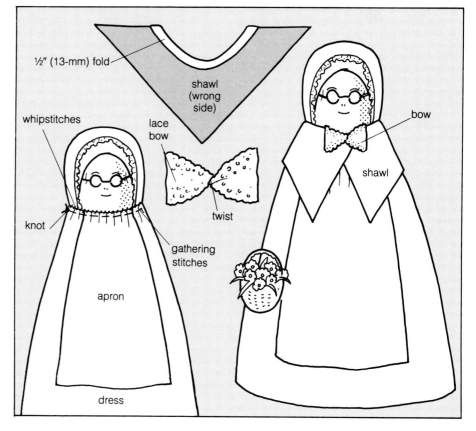

Maude
and Cecil

Materials

A 9″ × 18″ (22.9 × 45.7-cm)
   piece of flesh-colored felt
A 9″ × 12″ (22.9 × 30.5-cm)
   piece of bright-pink felt
A 9″ × 12″ (22.9 × 30.5-cm)
   piece of brown felt
A 9″ × 30″ (22.9 × 76.2-cm)
   piece of deep-pink
   corduroy
A 5″ × 6″ (12.7 × 15.2-cm)
   piece of blue-and-brown
   printed cotton fabric
A 1¼″ × 14″ (3.2 × 35.6-cm)
   piece of blue felt
A 9″ × 30″ (22.9 × 76.2-cm)
   piece of aqua crepe fabric
A 3″ × 13″ (7.6 × 33-cm)
   scrap of real or fake fur
Sewing thread: deep pink,
   brown, bright pink, and
   aqua
Polyester fiber for stuffing
A 4″ (10.2-cm) length of
   cardboard tubing, 1″ (2.5
   cm) in diameter
White glue
Masking tape
6-strand embroidery floss:
   white, black, brown, blue,
   and red
Flesh-colored nylon thread
2 star-shaped green sequins
3 pearl beads
An 8″ (20.3-cm) length of 18-
   gauge copper wire
A red pencil
Coarse sandpaper
Cardboard
A 58½″ (1.49-m) length of
   gray 4-ply knitting worsted
A 10½″ (26.7-cm) length of
   black 4-ply knitting worsted
1 ounce (28.35 grams) of
   brown mohair yarn
An 18″ (45.7-cm) length of 1″-
   wide (2.5-cm) off-white lace
   edging
A ½″ × 10″ (13-mm × 25.4-
   cm) strip of lightweight
   cardboard
1½ yards (1.4 m) of 1″-
   wide (2.5-cm) red satin
   ribbon
A small cluster of red
   maribou trim
2 pearl-headed corsage pins
A straight pin with a blue
   plastic head

The puppets' bodies

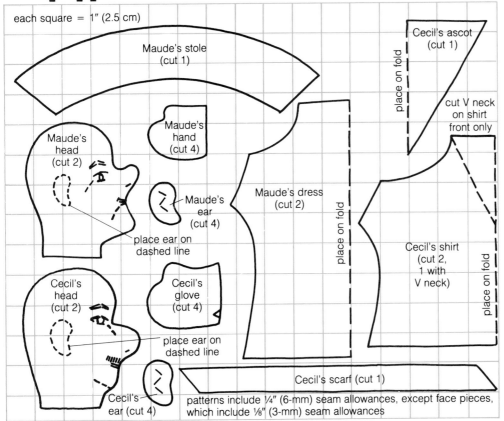

each square = 1″ (2.5 cm)

Maude's stole (cut 1)

Cecil's ascot (cut 1)

place on fold

cut V neck on shirt front only

Maude's hand (cut 4)

Maude's head (cut 2)

Maude's ear (cut 4)

place ear on dashed line

Maude's dress (cut 2)

place on fold

Cecil's head (cut 2)

Cecil's glove (cut 4)

place ear on dashed line

Cecil's shirt (cut 2, 1 with V neck)

place on fold

Cecil's ear (cut 4)

Cecil's scarf (cut 1)

patterns include ¼″ (6-mm) seam allowances, except face pieces, which include ⅛″ (3-mm) seam allowances

1. Cutting the Fabric. Enlarge the patterns to the scale indicated and cut them out, following the instructions given on page 155.

Using the patterns, cut the following pieces for the bodies: from folded flesh-colored felt, two pieces for each head; from folded bright-pink felt, eight ears (four pieces for each doll) and four pieces for Maude's hands.

For the clothes, cut the following: from folded brown felt, four pieces for Cecil's gloves; two pieces from folded deep-pink corduroy for Cecil's shirt; one piece from folded blue-and-brown print for his ascot; one piece of blue felt for his scarf.

For Maude, cut two pieces from folded aqua crepe for the dress and one piece of real or fake fur for her stole. Trace the pattern on the skin side of the fur and cut with scissors, or use a single-edged razor blade for real fur. Lightly transfer all the pattern markings indicated onto the felt.

2. The Heads. For each puppet, align and pin the two head pieces, right sides together, matching the pattern markings. Stitch 1/8" (3 mm) from the edges, leaving the neck edges open. Turn the heads right side out, and stuff them firmly with polyester fiber.

The necks. Cut the cardboard tubing into two 2"-long (5-cm) sections. Spread white glue on the fabric around the inside of the neck opening on each head and also spread it around one end of each tube in a band 3/4" (19 mm) wide. Insert the glued end of the tubing into the neck opening of each doll. Press the glued edge of the fabric and tube firmly together and tape the fabric tightly around the tube with masking tape. When the glue has thoroughly dried, remove the tape.

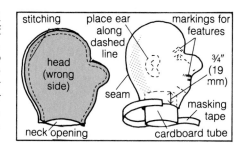

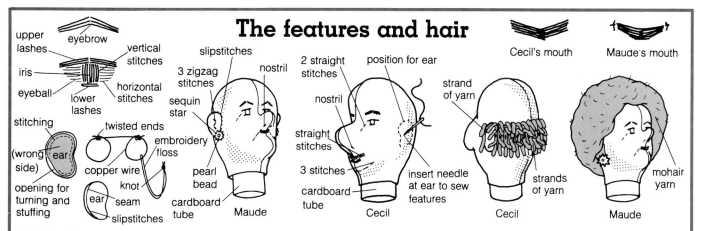

The features and hair

1. The Features.
Use three strands of 18"-long (45.7-cm) embroidery floss for making all the features. Insert an embroidery needle at the center of the pattern markings for the ear nearest the particular feature so the knots will be hidden under the ears. Stitch back and forth to the ear when stitches must be indented, pulling the thread taut.

The eyes. Using white embroidery floss, cover each eye area with about eight 1/2"-long (13-mm) horizontal stitches, pulling the stitches taut through the head to indent the eyes. Using black for Maude and brown for Cecil, sew straight stitches to make arched upper and straight lower lashes, indenting the stitches by pulling each one taut, as before. Using black for Cecil and blue for Maude, make irises with four or five small vertical stitches across the center of each eye; do not pull these stitches taut. Using black thread, sew long horizontal stitches to make arched eyebrows for both dolls, indenting Cecil's slightly.

The noses and mouths. Using red embroidery floss, make one tiny vertical, slightly indented stitch for each of Maude's nostrils and two for each of Cecil's, pulling Cecil's very tight. Cover each mouth area with 1/2"-long (13-mm) red stitches, as shown. Using brown floss, cover Cecil's mustache area with 1/2"-long (13-mm) vertical straight stitches, slanting them outward at the lower corners.

The cheeks and chin. Use flesh-colored nylon thread. For **Cecil,** sew three 1/2"-long (13-mm) stitches in a semicircle 3/4" (19 mm) below his mouth, pulling each stitch through either side of the head to make an indentation under the chin. Sew two 1/2"-long (13-mm) stitches under the inside corner of each eye beside the nose to indent the tops of his cheeks. For **Maude,** form the cheeks with two 1/2"-long (13-mm) indented stitches at either side of her mouth, slanting the stitches downward, and two 1/2" (13-mm) indented stitches at the outside corners of each eye, slanting down.

The ears. Stitch two matching ear pieces together around the edges for each ear, leaving the lower back edges open and keeping the ears for each doll separate. Turn each ear right side out, stuff it with polyester fiber, then turn the edges along the opening under and slipstitch them together. Attach the ears with slipstitches in the position marked on the fabric. Using flesh-colored nylon thread, indent each ear with three 1/2"-long (13-mm) stitches

drawn tightly in a zigzag pattern down the center. Sew one star sequin to each of Maude's earlobes, with a pearl bead to hold it in place. Backstitch on the underside of the lobe to secure the sequin.

Cecil's glasses. Shape the ends of the copper wire into two 3/4"-diameter (19-mm) circles with 1 1/4" (3.2 cm) of straight wire between. Turn the ends of the circles around the crosspiece to secure them. Loop a 6" (15.2-cm) length of black embroidery floss through one circle and knot the ends. Attach the knot behind Cecil's left ear with a few tiny stitches. Place the glasses on Cecil's nose and sew each end to the face with flesh-colored thread, taking stitches through the head, but without indenting the stitches.

The skin. Using a red pencil, give a glow to Maude's and Cecil's cheeks and chins. With sandpaper, roughen the seam of each head to cover the stitches with fuzz. Apply white glue to the heads and features with a brush, pushing the fuzz into the seams. Work back and forth with the end of the brush until the seam is covered. Allow the heads to dry.

2. The Hair.
For **Cecil,** cut a strip of cardboard 3/4" (19 mm) wide. Wind a 31 1/2" (80-cm) length of gray yarn and all of the black knitting yarn around the cardboard, and cut the yarn along one edge so that each strand is 1 1/2" (3.8 cm) long. Put glue on the strands for about 1/2" (13 mm) along the center. Beginning with gray yarn at each end and alternating three strands of gray with one of black, position them close together, vertically, in a row around the back of Cecil's head, starting just behind the ears. Using a 1/2"-wide (13-mm) strip of cardboard, cut the remaining gray yarn into 1" (2.5-cm) lengths. Glue 1/4" (6 mm) at the center of each strand and center the strands vertically over the first row of yarn. Also place one strand of yarn, in the same vertical direction, in front of each ear. Allow the glue to dry, then fluff the ends of yarn slightly.

Maude's hair. Roll the brown mohair yarn into a loose 4" (10.2-cm) ball and, working it with your fingers, mold it over Maude's head to form a caplike wig. When the top and back of her head are well covered, push a few waves into the yarn. Remove the wig carefully, apply glue to the underside, and replace it on her head. Allow the glue to dry. Then fluff the hair up slightly, and apply more glue to secure any loose loops.

The puppets' clothes

1. Maude's Clothes. Cut four 2½" (6.4-cm) lengths of off-white lace edging. Baste one piece to the right side of each sleeve edge on the dress front and back, aligning the straight edge of the lace ⅛" (3 mm) from the sleeve edges, with the lace facing in. Align one hand piece with the end of each sleeve, placing it over the lace, so it faces the center of the dress and the thumb points up. Pin and stitch the hand pieces to the front and back of the dress. Press the seam allowances toward the dress. Pin the dress front to the dress back, wrong sides out, aligning the edges, and stitch around the shoulder, hand, and side seams. Clip the seam allowances at the curves and the inner corner of the thumbs. Trim the seam allowances of the hands to ⅛" (3 mm) and turn up and pin a ⅜" (9.5-cm) hem. Stitch the hem ⅛" (3 mm) from the folded edge. Fold down ¼" (6 mm) of fabric around the neck edge, and sew it with gathering stitches. Turn the dress and hands right side out.

Finishing Maude's Clothes. To make a collar, run a row of gathering stitches around the straight edge of the remaining lace. Gather the lace to fit the dress neckline, and sew it to the dress along the edge, with the lace turned down.

Apply glue around the bottom of the felt on Maude's neck. Place the neck opening of the dress ½" (13 mm) above the felt edge. Pull the gathering threads at the top of the dress to fit the neck and knot them. Adjust the gathers evenly. Press the neckline of the dress firmly into the glue and let the glue dry.

The hat. Bend the 10"-long (25.4-cm) strip of lightweight cardboard into a circle, overlapping the ends by ½" (13 mm) and gluing them together. Fold the red ribbon in half lengthwise, and coil it around the cardboard, overlapping the open edges as you wind it and spacing the turns approximately ¼" (6 mm) apart. When the cardboard is covered, glue the ribbon end to the inside of the rim. Sew the maribou cluster on one side of the hat, and place the hat on Maude's head with the feather above one ear. Secure with a corsage pin.

The fur stole. Place the fur stole around Maude's neck, lapping the right end over the left, and secure it with the other corsage pin.

2. Cecil's Clothes. Join the glove pieces to the front and back of the shirt as the hands were joined to Maude's dress.

The ascot. Make a ¼"-deep (6-mm) clip at the center of the V neck on the shirt front. Align one edge of the ascot along one edge of the V neck opening, right sides together. Adjust the fullness, and pin. Stitch from the center of the V to the shoulder on each side. Press the seam allowances toward the shirt.

The shirt. Pin the shirt front to the shirt back, right sides together, aligning the edges. Stitch the shoulder, glove, and side seams. Stitch a row of gathering stitches around the edge of the neck. Clip the seam allowances at the curves. Trim the seam allowances of the gloves to ⅛" (3 mm). Turn up the hemline ⅜" (9.5 mm) and pin; then stitch ⅛" (3 mm) from the folded edge. Turn the shirt and gloves right side out.

Finishing Cecil's Clothes. Apply glue to the bottom of Cecil's neck about ½" (13 mm) above the felt edge. Place the neck edge of the shirt over the glue, then draw the gathering thread tight and knot it. Adjust the gathers evenly. Press the neckline of the shirt firmly into the glue and allow the glue to dry.

The scarf. Tie the blue-felt scarf around the neck to cover the unfinished edge of the shirt neckline. Slip the flower-shaped sequin and the remaining pearl bead onto the blue-beaded straight pin, then fasten the scarf in place with the pin.

Grandmother Pillow Doll

Materials

¼ yard (22.9 cm) white-and-brown lengthwise-striped fabric

¼ yard (22.9 cm) cream-colored medium-weight cotton fabric

¼ yard (22.9 cm) cream-colored chintz fabric

A 4″ (10.2-cm) square of dark-beige cotton fabric

1 yard (.91 m) unbleached muslin

A 7″ × 10″ (17.8 × 25.4-cm) piece of white satin damask-type fabric

A 5″ × 6″ (12.7 × 15.2-cm) piece of lightweight white or beige fabric

Sewing thread: to match all fabrics, plus black, rust, gray, and pink

Polyester batting for padding

1 yard (.91 m) of 1¼″-wide (3.2-cm) off-white pregathered eyelet

½ yard (45.7 cm) of 1¼″-wide (3.2-cm) white flat lace

¾ yard (68.6 cm) of ½″-wide (13-mm) white pregathered lace

18 yards (16.4 meters) of 4-ply cream-colored knitting yarn

Polyester fiber for stuffing

Note: If a zigzag machine is not available, two rows of short straight stitching ⅛″ (3 mm) apart may be used to join the pattern pieces, and parallel hand stitches may be used for the features.

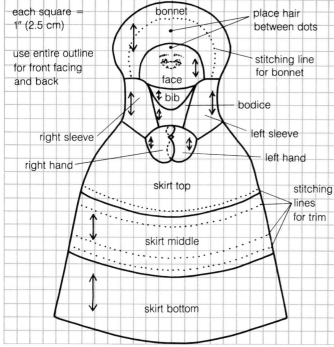

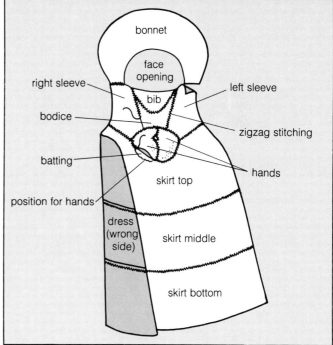

1. Cutting the Fabric. Enlarge the patterns, following the instructions on page 155. Cut one piece each for the front facing and back. Add ¼″ (6-mm) seam allowances along the upper edges of the three skirt pieces, the lower edges of the sleeves, and all edges of the bodice and face. Do not add any extra to the bib, bonnet, or hands. (**Note:** The upper edge of the hands is also the upper center line for the skirt top.) Transfer the markings to the patterns. Pin the patterns on the fabric with the arrows following the lengthwise grain. Cut one skirt bottom from striped fabric; one skirt middle, one bib, and two sleeves from medium-weight cream-colored cotton; one skirt top from chintz; one bodice from beige fabric; one back, one front facing, one face, and two hands from unbleached

muslin; and one bonnet from damask. Cut one face from white or beige lining fabric. Transfer the pattern markings to the fabric.

2. The Doll's Front. Align the skirt bottom along the bottom of the facing, and join the side edges with zigzag stitching. Continue joining the front pieces with zigzag stitching as follows: Lap the bottom of the skirt middle ¼″ (6 mm) over the top of the skirt bottom, right sides up. Pin and join the pieces on the muslin facing with closely spaced zigzag stitching. Similarly, join the skirt top to the skirt middle and the bib to the bodice, then join the bottoms of the sleeves to the skirt top. Pin the bib to the bodice, and slip them in place under the inner edges of the sleeves; join the bib and bodice, then attach them

99

to the inner edges of the sleeves. Lap the tops of the sleeves over the bottom of the bonnet, and join them. Lap the hands, and pin them. Cut a piece of batting ¼" (6 mm) smaller around than the hands, and cut a hole in it where the hands do not overlap. Center the batting on the hands position, and pin. Place the hands over the batting, and attach them with closely spaced zigzag stitching.

3. The Features and Face. Trace the actual-size **features** drawn here on tracing or tissue paper with a soft pencil. Turn the paper over and transfer the features to the right side of the face fabric.

Cut a piece of polyester batting ¼" (6 mm) smaller all around than the face, and center it, like a sandwich, between the face and the face lining with the features right side out. Baste the edges together. Using black thread, make the eyes, eyelashes, and the bridge of the nose with zigzag stitching, varying the closeness and width of the stitching as indicated in the drawing of the features. Use rust-colored thread for the zigzag stitching in the eyebrows. Make the mouth with pink thread, sewing a very narrow (¹⁄₃₂", or .8 mm) row of zigzag stitching, beginning and ending with a bar tack at the corners. If you wish, you can widen the stitching at the center of the mouth to make it look more bow-like.

Attaching the face. Lap and pin the opening edges of the bib, sleeves, and bonnet ¼" (6 mm) over the edges of the face. Join them with closely spaced zigzag stitching.

4. Trimming the Dress. Pin and stitch a row of 1¼" (3.2-cm) pregathered eyelet, ruffled edge down, ½" (13 mm) above the bottom edge of the skirt middle. Pin and stitch a row of 1¼" (3.2-cm) flat lace ¾" (19 mm) above the stitching for the eyelet. Pin and stitch a row of ½"-wide (13-mm) pregathered lace 1" (2.5 cm) below the top of the skirt middle. Pin and stitch a row of 1¼"-wide (3.2-cm) pregathered eyelet ¼" (6 mm) above the bottom edge of the skirt top. Add a 3½" (8.9-cm) collar of ½"-wide (13-mm) pregathered lace, ruffled edge down and ends turned under, across the bottom of the face from one end of the bib to the other; similarly, add 1¾" (4.4-cm) cuffs of pregathered lace across the sleeve bottoms.

5. The Hair. Cut eighteen 1-yard (.91-m) lengths of yarn, and lay them side by side with the ends even and the strands close enough together to measure 1½" (3.8 cm) across at the center. Secure the center with a strip of cellophane tape. Cut a 2½" × 1½" (6.4 × 3.8-cm) strip of tissue paper; fold the paper lengthwise into thirds. Carefully turn the strands of yarn over, and align the folded tissue paper with the cellophane tape, across the yarn; baste along the center of the tissue. Turn the strands over again, and stitch across the center of the yarn, through the tape and tissue paper. Remove the tape, tissue paper, and basting.

Position the yarn hair on the doll so that the line of stitching lies between the two dots marked on the face and bonnet patterns, and tack it securely in place. Divide the ends of the hair on each side into three sections; wind each section around your finger to form a curl, and tack it securely with matching thread so that each side of the face has three vertical, parallel ringlets.

6. Finishing the Doll. Pin the back to the front of the doll right sides together, keeping the yarn hair free of the ½" (13-mm) seam allowance. Seam the doll together all around the edge, leaving a 6" (15.2-cm) opening along the bottom for turning and stuffing. Clip the seam allowances along the curves, and press them open.

Turn the pillow right side out through the opening. Using beige thread, stitch the bonnet through all layers along the pattern markings. Stuff the doll firmly enough to give it body but softly enough to be comfortable as a pillow. Turn the seam allowance at the opening under, and slipstitch the opening closed.

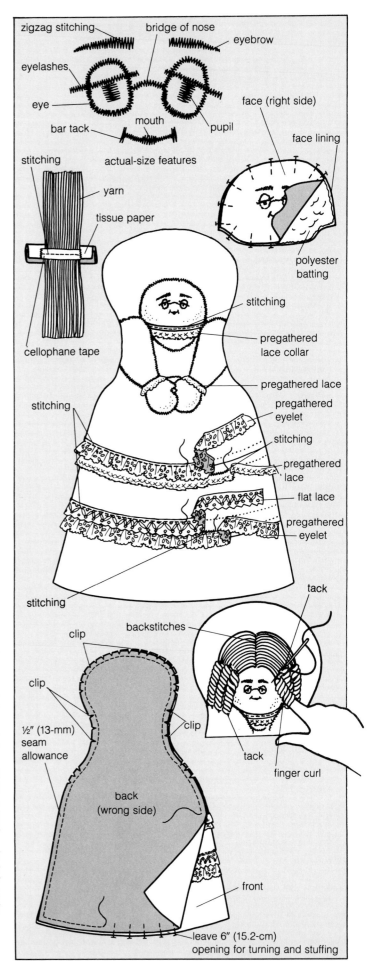

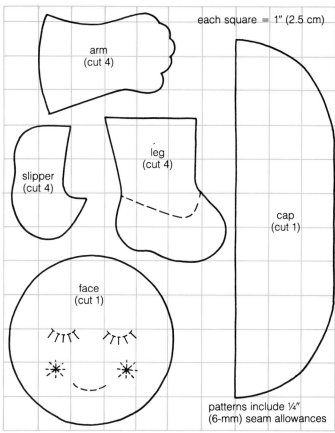

each square = 1" (2.5 cm)

arm
(cut 4)

slipper
(cut 4)

leg
(cut 4)

cap
(cut 1)

face
(cut 1)

patterns include ¼"
(6-mm) seam allowances

1. Cutting the Fabric. Enlarge the patterns to the scale indicated and cut them out, following the instructions on page 155. Using the patterns, cut one face, two arms, and two legs from off-white cotton and one cap from white cotton. Cut two slippers from the solid-blue fabric. Turn the arm, leg, and slipper patterns over sideways so that they face in the opposite direction, and cut two more of each.

For the dress, cut two 10½" × 16" (26.7 × 40.7-cm) pieces of printed fabric, then trim the pieces along the long edges so that they curve in from each end to a width of 9" (22.9 cm) at the center. Also cut two 3¼" × 7" (8.3 × 17.8-cm) sleeves and one 4" × 1¼" (10.2 × 3.2-cm) placket from the printed fabric. These measurements include ¼" (6-mm) seam allowances on the sleeves and placket and ½" (13-mm) on the dress pieces.

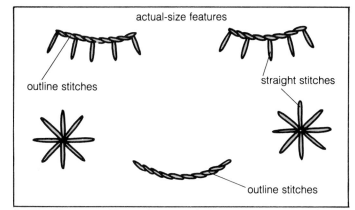

actual-size features

outline stitches

straight stitches

outline stitches

2. The Features. Trace the actual-size patterns on tracing or tissue paper. Turn the paper over and center it on the right side of the face, with the mouth 1¼" (3.2 cm) above the lower edge. Retrace, transferring the features onto the fabric.

Using four strands of black embroidery floss, make the eyes with outline stitches along the top line and straight stitches for the lashes. Sew the mouth with outline stitches, using six-strand dark-pink floss. Make rosy cheeks with six-strand light-pink floss by crossing straight stitches in a circular pattern.

Pillow Girl

Materials

¼ yard (22.9 cm) of 36"-wide (.91-m) off-white cotton
A 4" × 12" (10.2 × 30.5-cm) piece of white cotton
A 7" (17.8-cm) square of solid-blue fabric that coordinates with the floral printed fabric
½ yard (45.7 cm) of 36"-wide (.91-m) basically blue floral printed fabric
A soft pencil
Tissue paper
6-strand embroidery floss: light pink, dark pink, and black
Sewing thread: to match the fabrics and trimmings
A 5" (12.7-cm) square of

polyester batting for padding
½ yard (45.7 cm) baby rickrack to match the solid-blue fabric
1¼" (3.2 cm) of 1"-wide (2.5-cm) pregathered white eyelet
Cardboard
32 yards (29.1 m) yellow synthetic sportweight yarn
Polyester fiber for stuffing
1¼ yards (114.3 cm) of ¼"-wide (6-mm) ribbon to match the solid-blue fabric
2 white pom-poms, 1" (2.5 cm) across
3 white buttons, ½" (13 mm) in diameter

3. Attaching the Face, Placket, and Collar. Stitch around the **face** ¼" (6 mm) from the edge, clip the seam allowance to the stitching line at regular intervals, and turn it under; press. Cut a 4" (10.2-cm) circle from the polyester batting and place it on one dress piece, centered 2" (5 cm) from one wide end (top). Center the face over the polyester batting, and pin it to the dress.

The placket. Turn under ¼" (6 mm) of the fabric on the long edges and one short (lower) end of the placket. Fold the lower corners to the wrong side until they meet, forming a point, and press. Center the placket below the face, point down, and insert ¼" (6 mm) of the top end under the face. Stitch the placket ⅛" (3 mm) from the side and lower edges. Pin baby rickrack over the stitching line and stitch it in place.

The collar. Cut a 5½" (14-cm) length of pregathered eyelet. Turn under ½" (13 mm) on each end and make a rolled hem. Slip the flat edge of the eyelet under the lower edge of the face, centering it, and pin it in place. Stitch the lower half of the face in place ⅛" (3 mm) from the edge, catching the eyelet.

4. The Hair. Cut a 9" (22.9-cm) square of cardboard, and wrap yellow yarn around it, with the strands side by side and close together. Cut across the strands at one end of the cardboard so that you have sixty 18" (45.7-cm) lengths of yarn. Arrange the strands in a radiating fashion around the top of the head for 2" (5 cm) on either side of the center, with the bottom ends inserted ½" (13 mm) under the top edge of the face. Pin, then stitch the remaining free edge of the head to the body ⅛" (3 mm) from the edge, catching the hair.

Divide the hair in half at the center and smooth it to the sides of the face, about ¼" (6 mm) below the eyes. Wrap a short length of yarn around the hair at each side, tie it on the underside, and tack it to the face. Divide the loose hair at each side into three equal sections and braid them for 8½" (21.6 cm). Tie a short length of yarn around the lower end of each braid. Trim the ends of the braids even.

5. The Arms and Sleeves. For each **arm,** stitch two arm pieces together, wrong sides out, leaving the edge opposite the fingers open (use at least 12 to 15 stitches per inch around the fingers). Trim the seam allowances and clip them in the curved areas and between the fingers. Turn the arm right side out and stuff it, pushing the stuffing down into the finger area, but not stuffing it very firmly. Baste the open edges together. Using doubled thread and stitching completely through the hand from the front to the back, sew three ⅜"-long (9.5-mm) lines of tight, indented running stitches, spaced equally apart, from the end of the hand to form the fingers.

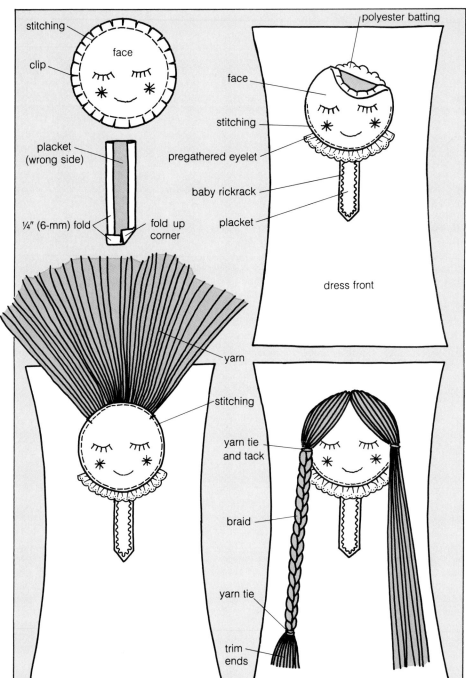

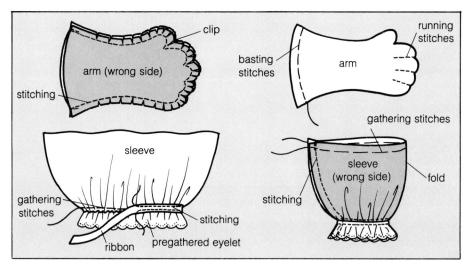

The sleeves. Press under ¼" (6 mm) of fabric on one long edge of each sleeve, and sew a row of gathering stitches ⅛" (3 mm) from the fold. For each sleeve, cut a 4½" (11.5-cm) length of pregathered eyelet. Gather the folded edge of each sleeve, pin it to fit over the flat edge of a piece of the eyelet, and stitch them together. Then pin a 4½" (11.5-cm) length of ribbon over the edge of the gathered fabric and stitch it in place along the edges of the ribbon. Fold the sleeve in half, short edges together and wrong side out, and seam the short edges. Make a row of gathering stitches ½" (13 mm) from the top edge of the sleeve.

6. Attaching the Arms. Place a sleeve over each arm, matching the underarm seams, and gather the sleeve to fit the top of the arm. Baste the sleeve to the arm ½" (13 mm) from the edge. Baste an arm to the right side of each side of the dress-front section 6¼" (11.6 cm) below the top edge, with the hand facing in.

7. The Legs. Make a row of stitching ¼" (6 mm) from the top edge of each slipper piece. Clip the seam allowance in the curved area and press it to the wrong side. Pin the wrong side of each slipper piece to the right side of the foot area of a leg piece, and stitch them together ⅟₁₆" (1.5 mm) from the top edge of the slipper. Baste along the remaining slipper edges. For each leg, pin two slippered leg pieces right sides together, and stitch around the edges, leaving the straight top edge open. Clip the seam allowances along the curves and turn the legs right side out. Stuff each leg semifirmly, and baste it closed ½" (13 mm) from the top edge.

8. The Body. Stitch the two dress sections, right sides together, along one long side. Clip the seam allowances along the curves, and press them open. Pin, then stitch the flat edge of a length of eyelet ½" (13 mm) above the lower edge of the dress sections. Place a length of ribbon over the binding on the eyelet, and stitch it in place along both edges of the ribbon. Stitch the top and unstitched side of the dress sections together to within 2" (5 cm) of the bottom edge. Turn the dress right side out, turn up the ½" (13-mm) seam allowance below the eyelet, and press. Align the straight edge of the legs, toes out, with the seam allowance along the top edge of the bottom of the back dress section, placing each leg ¾" (19 mm) away from the center. Baste the legs in place. Stuff the body and slipstitch the front to the back along the lower edge and the opening on the side edge, attaching the legs securely. Remove the basting. Sew a pom-pom to the toe of each slipper.

9. The Cap. Press under ¼" (6 mm) on the straight edge of the cap and make a row of gathering stitches along the fold. Then make a row of gathering stitches ¼" (6 mm) from the other edge of the

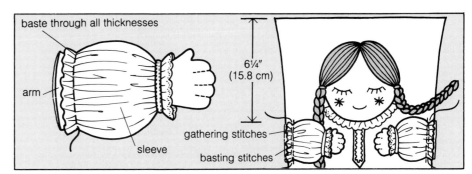

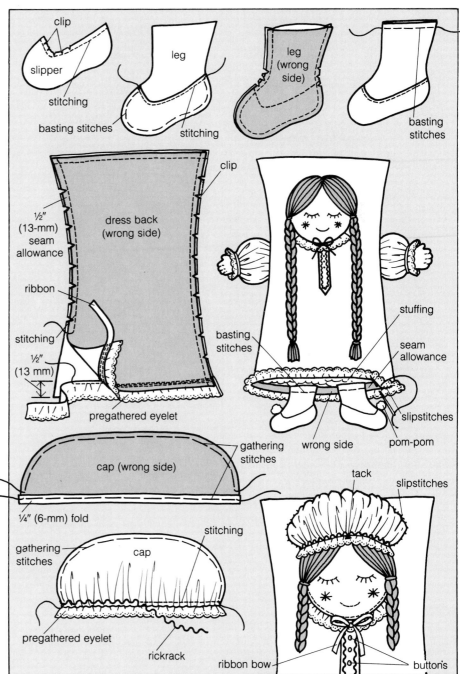

cap. Cut an 8" (20.3-cm) length of pregathered eyelet. Turn under ½" (13 mm) on each end and make a rolled hem. Gather the straight edge of the cap evenly along the thread to fit the flat edge of the eyelet. Pin it over the flat edge, and stitch in place. Then stitch baby rickrack over the edge of the fab-

ric. Pin the cap to the sides of the head, gather the top edge of the cap evenly, and slipstitch it to the dress section so that the center top is about ¼" (6 mm) below the top dress seam. Make a bow from the remaining ribbon and tack it to the center of the collar. Sew three buttons down the center of the placket.

Abigail and Ebenezer

Materials

2 dried, stripped corncobs, trimmed flat at top and bottom to a length of 7″ (17.8 cm)
2 white beans
White glue
Fine felt-tip markers: black and red
A small saw
A small pocketknife or penknife
10 white pipe cleaners
A 4″ × 5″ (10.2 × 12.7-cm) piece of navy fabric with tiny white polka dots
Sewing thread: to match all fabrics and trimming
A 6″ × 10″ (15.2 × 25.4-cm) piece of blue denim
A 4″-diameter (10.2-cm) circle of burlap
A 6½″ (16.5-cm) stick or twig
¼ yard (22.9 cm) of small-print red fabric
½ yard (45.7 cm) of ½″-wide (13-mm) white lace

The doll's bodies

1. The Head and Features. For each doll, cut a 1″ (2.5-cm) length off one end of each trimmed corncob to make the head. On the cut side, carve out a small ¼″-diameter (6-mm) hole to hold the bean for the nose, as shown in the drawings, and glue the bean in the hole. Use felt-tip markers to make the eyes and brows in black and the mouth in red. Cut a small slice off the bottom of the head to make it lie flat on the top end of the body.

2. The Torsos, Arms, and Legs. To make the man's legs, saw an opening ¼″ (6 mm) wide and 3″ (7.6 cm) long lengthwise along the corncob, starting at the center of one end of a 6″ (15.2-cm) piece of cob. Do not cut legs for the woman. For both dolls, carve a small armhole ¼″ (6 mm) in diameter and ¼″ (6 mm) deep with a small pocketknife or penknife on both sides of each cob ¼″ (6 mm) from the top end. Cut the pipe cleaners into 2½″ (6.4-cm) lengths. Twist five lengths together, and glue one end of them into each armhole. Glue the bottoms of the heads to the tops of the bodies.

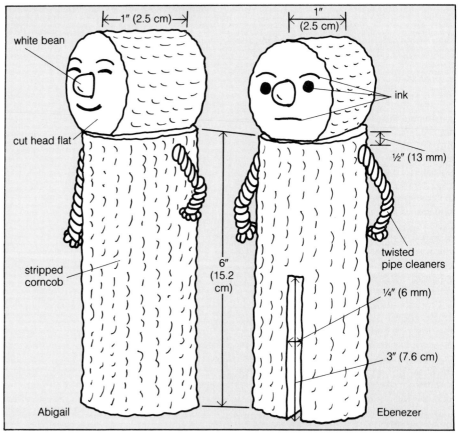

white bean

cut head flat

stripped corncob

Abigail

ink

½″ (13 mm)

twisted pipe cleaners

¼″ (6 mm)

3″ (7.6 cm)

Ebenezer

6″ (15.2 cm)

1″ (2.5 cm)

1″ (2.5 cm)

The doll's clothes

1. The Man's Clothes. To make the **shirt,** fold the piece of navy polka-dot fabric in half lengthwise, wrong side out. With the fold at the top, cut the fabric into a T shape through both thicknesses as shown in the drawing, so the body section excluding the sleeves is 2" (5 cm) wide and 2" (5 cm) long. Stitch the edges together under the sleeves and along the sides, leaving ¼" (6-mm) seam allowances. Clip the underarm corners. Slash one side of the shirt up the center from the bottom to the fold to make the front opening. Make a ½" (13-mm) cut along the fold on each side of the center slash for the neck opening. Turn the shirt right side out, and slip it on the doll. Glue or slipstitch the left side of the shirt in place over the right side.

The overalls. Cut two 3¾" × 4¼" (9.5 × 10.8-cm) denim pieces for the pants. Fold each piece in half lengthwise, wrong side out. Stitch the long side edges together, leaving a 1¼"-long (3.2-cm) opening at the top. Then turn the legs right side out, align the seams, and pin the open edges above them together to make the crotch seam. Sew the crotch seam by hand, clip the seam allowances at the curves, and put the trousers on the doll.

Cut a 1" (2.5-cm) square of denim for the bib. Trim the two top corners slightly to round them. Cut two ¼" × 3" (6-mm × 7.6-cm) denim straps. Stitch one end of each strap, right side out, to one of the top inside corners of the bib. Sew the bottom of the bib inside the center front of the trousers. Place the straps over the doll's shoulders, cross them at the back, and anchor the ends inside the back of the pants equidistant from the center.

The hat and stick. Glue the burlap circle on top of the corncob head. Cut a ¼" × 4" (6-mm × 10.2-cm) strip of denim for the hatband, and glue it around the hat ½" (13 mm) in from the edge so that it fits around the crown of the head. Twist the ends of one arm to form a hand, and shape the hand to fit snugly around the walking stick.

2. The Woman's Clothes. To make the **bodice,** cut a 6" × 6" (15.2 × 15.2-cm) piece of small-print red fabric. Cut and sew it exactly as for the man's shirt, but stitch a band of lace around the bottom edge of each sleeve and down the center front, on the right side. Also, sew a ½" (6-mm) hem along the bottom.

The skirt. Cut a 5" × 18" (12.7 × 45.7-cm) piece of small-print red fabric. Fold the fabric in half, short sides together and wrong side out. Seam the short edges, then stitch a rolled hem along the bottom edge. Sew a row of gathering stitches along the top edge of the skirt. Place the skirt on the doll and gather the skirt tightly along the thread before knotting it.

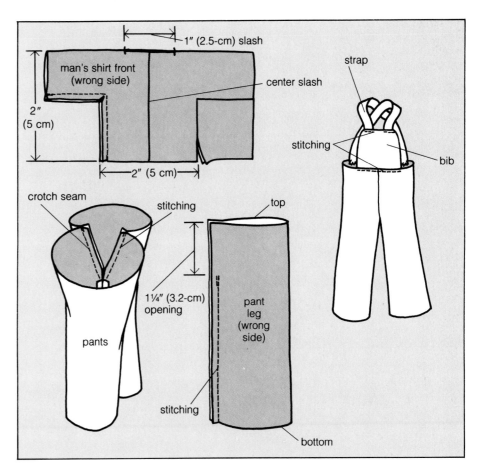

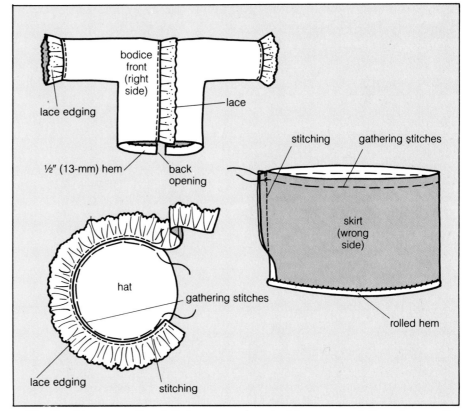

Slip the blouse on the doll, lap one side of the back opening over the other side, and glue or slipstitch it in place. Slipstitch the bottom edge of the blouse to the top edge of the skirt.

The hat. Cut a 4"-diameter (10.2-cm) circle of red printed fabric, and stitch a band of lace around the edge on the right side. Make a row of gathering stitches around the edge of the hat just inside the edge of the lace. Put the hat on the doll and pull the gathering thread tight before knotting it. Glue the hat in place on the head.

Shaker Woman

Materials

Sewing thread: white and purple
A 3" (7.6-cm) circle of white knit fabric
Polyester fiber for stuffing
1 small silver-colored eye from a metal hook and eye
6-strand embroidery floss: silver gray
Two 6"-long (15.2-cm) white pipe cleaners
A 4" × 9" (10.2 × 22.9-cm) and a 2" × 2" (5 × 5-cm) piece of nonwoven interfacing
A 5" × 9" (12.7 × 22.9-cm) and a 2" × 4" (5 × 10.2-cm) piece of light-purple-and-white printed cotton fabric
A 4" (10.2-cm) length of 2½"-wide (6.3-cm) white eyelet edging
3" (7.6 cm) white bias-fold tape
Two 4" (10.2-cm) squares of purple cotton fabric

The doll's body

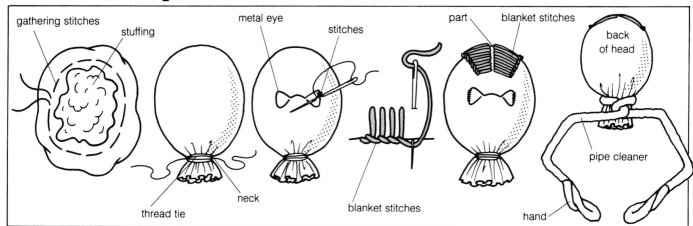

gathering stitches
stuffing
metal eye
stitches
part
blanket stitches
back of head
thread tie
neck
blanket stitches
hand
pipe cleaner

1. The Doll's Head. Using doubled thread, sew a row of gathering stitches about ⁵⁄₁₆" (8 mm) from the edge of the 3" (7.6-cm) circle of white knit fabric. Gather the fabric loosely to form a pouch with the thread ends on the outside, then stuff the pouch firmly inside the stitches with polyester fiber. Draw up the gathers tightly and fasten the thread. Wind the ends of the gathering thread around the gathers to form the neck. Pull the fabric smooth on one side of the head for the face. Stitch across the folds so that the face stays smooth and has an oval shape.

The eyes. Lay the silver-colored eye on the face where the eyes should go

and lightly mark the holes with a pencil. Using doubled white thread, knotted at the end, stitch through the head from back to front bringing the needle out next to one of the pencil marks for the eyes. Secure the eye to the face with a few stitches at each end, then end off the thread at the back of the head.

2. The Hair. Using two strands of six-strand silver-gray embroidery floss, make a row of blanket stitches close together on the left side of the center of the head. Start ⅛" (3 mm) above the eyes with ⅛"-long (3-mm) blanket stitches, and taper the length of the stitches to ½" (13 mm) at the top of the head. Repeat in reverse for the right

side, leaving a fine line of fabric uncovered at the center of the head, between the stitches, to make a part.

3. The Arms. Wrap a 6" (15.2-cm) white pipe cleaner around the neck from front to back so that the ends extend evenly on either side; then twist the pipe cleaner at the back of the head to secure the neck, and bring the ends straight out at each side. Sew the pipe cleaner securely to the fabric of the head. Bend the pipe cleaner down at both ends ½" (13 mm) from the neck to form the shoulders; bend it again ¾" (19 mm) below the shoulders to shape the elbows. Turn the ends back ¾" (19 mm) and twist them around the arms for hands.

The doll's clothes

1. The Dress. Center one long edge of the interfacing on the right side of one long edge of the 5″ × 9″ (12.7 cm × 22.9-cm) piece of dress fabric. Stitch them together, leaving a ½″ (13-mm) seam allowance. Turn the interfacing away from the fabric and press the seam allowances toward the fabric. Fold the fabric in half end to end, right sides together, and stitch the ends together. Press open the seam allowances.

Turn the fabric down over the interfacing until the edges are even, and sew a row of gathering stitches along the edges. Slip the dress up under the doll's arms, seam to the back and gathered side up. Gather the dress tightly and evenly, and secure the thread. Sew the dress through the gathers to the doll's neck.

2. The Apron. Gather the eyelet edging ¼″ (6 mm) from the upper edge to a length of 2″ (5 cm), and fasten the thread. Lay the edging over the dress front and sew it to the neck edge. Fold a 3″ (7.6-cm) length of bias-fold tape in half lengthwise, and stitch the long edges together. Wrap the binding around the top of the apron and dress, with the ends to the back. Turn the upper end of the binding under, and stitch the binding securely in place around the top of the skirt.

3. The Doll's Accessories. To make the **hat,** cut two 1¾″ (4.5-cm) circles from the print fabric and one 1¾″ (4.5-cm) circle from the interfacing. Baste the interfacing to the wrong side of one fabric circle. Join the fabric sections right sides together, stitching ⅛″ (3 mm) from the edges; leave a 1″ (2.5-cm) opening.

Turn the hat right side out through the opening and press it. Turn in the edges along the opening, and slipstitch them together. Make a ¼″ (6-mm) pleat from the center of the hat to one edge. Overcast the outer edges of the pleat together. Place the hat over the back of the doll's head, pleat to the back, and sew the hat securely to the neck.

The shawl. Draw out threads from all four sides of a 4″ (10.2-cm) square of purple fabric until the remaining fringe is ¼″ (6 mm) long. Fold the shawl in half diagonally, wrap it around the doll's shoulders, overlapping the ends across the front shoulders as shown in the photograph, and tack the folded edges to the bias tape at the center front and to each other toward the ends.

The umbrella. Cut a 4″ (10.2-cm) circle from the purple fabric, using pinking shears. With a sharp, pointed instrument, pierce a hole in the center of the fabric. Sew a line of gathering stitches a full ¼″ (6 mm) from the edge of the circle. Insert a 4″ (10.2-cm) length of pipe cleaner ½″ (13 mm) through the hole in the fabric. Wrap thread around the fab-

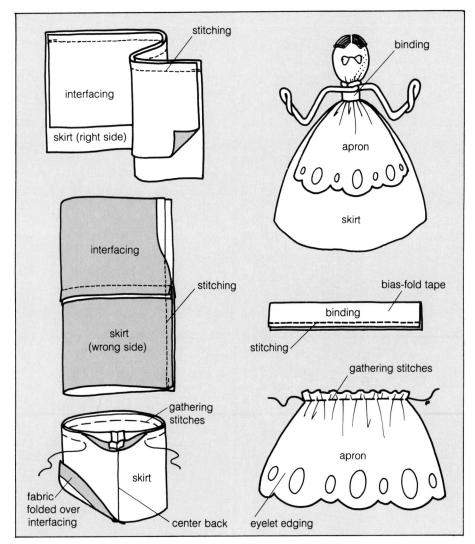

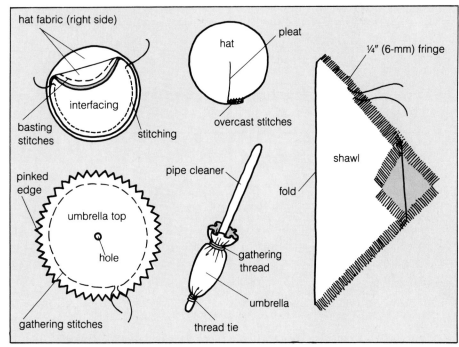

ric and the pipe cleaner at the hole and secure it. Draw the fabric tightly along the gathering thread, then secure the thread to the pipe cleaner, pushing the fabric along the pipe cleaner enough to make the umbrella a bit puffy. Insert the handle end of the umbrella through the doll's left hand, and bend the end so that it will not slip out.

To tell the story of Red Ridinghood, change the doll to whichever character is speaking. Turn Red Ridinghood upside down, pull her skirt over her head, and you will find Grandma. Turn Grandma backwards, flip her cap over her face, and there is the wolf.

Little Red Ridinghood Story Doll

Materials

¼ yard (30.5 cm) of 45″-wide (114.3-cm) flesh- or peach-colored cotton

¼ yard (30.5 cm) of 45″-wide (114.3-cm) gray fleece or fake fur

¼ yard (30.5 cm) of 45″-wide (114.3-cm) red chintz or plain cotton

½ yard (45.7 cm) of 45″-wide (114.3-cm) red-and-white polka-dot or printed cotton

½ yard (45.7 cm) of 45″-wide (114.3-cm) blue-and-white printed cotton

Sewing thread: light pink or peach, red, gray, blue, yellow, and white

Polyester fiber for stuffing

Embroidery floss: red and black

1 skein each of yellow and white needlepoint yarn

Scraps of black and white felt

White glue

A soft red pencil (optional)

1 yard (91.4 cm) of ⅞″-wide (22-mm) pregathered white eyelet

Four ¼″-diameter (6-mm) yellow buttons

A 9″ (22.9-cm) length of ⅜″-wide (9.5-mm) yellow grosgrain ribbon

Red single-fold bias tape

An 8¼″ (20.9-cm) length of ¼″-wide (6-mm) elastic

The doll's bodies

1. Cutting the Fabric. Enlarge the patterns to the scale indicated, and cut them out following the directions on page 155. Using the patterns with the arrow placed along the lengthwise grain of the fabric, cut the fabric pieces as follows, and transfer all the appropriate markings from the patterns to the fabric.

From folded flesh- or peach-colored fabric cut four body pieces, Red Ridinghood's face, and Grandma's face. From folded gray fleece or fake fur, cut the wolf's head, the ear front, and the ear back (making two pieces each). From folded solid-red fabric cut one cape, two hat brims, and one hat back. From red-and-white polka-dot fabric cut a 9¾″ × 34¾″ (23.1 × 88.3–cm) rectangle for Red Ridinghood's skirt. Then fold the fabric, and cut one bodice front, two bodice backs (left and right), and one cape lining. From blue-and-white printed fabric cut a 9¾″ × 34¾″ (23.1 × 88.3–cm) rectangle for Grandma's skirt. Then fold the fabric, and cut one bodice front, two bodice backs (left and right), and two 8¼″-diameter (20.9-cm) circles for Grandma's hat.

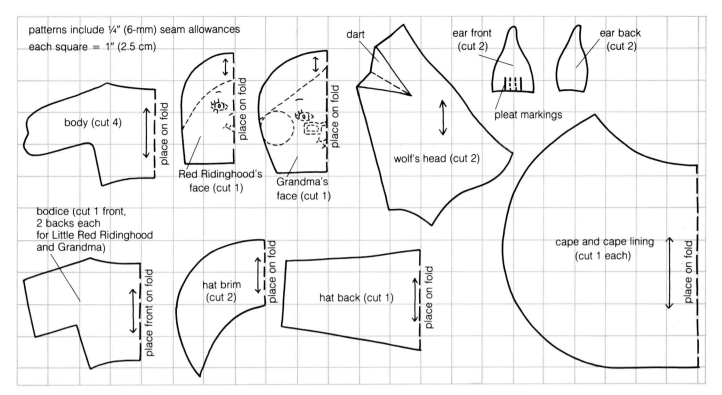

patterns include ¼″ (6-mm) seam allowances
each square = 1″ (2.5 cm)

dart

ear front (cut 2)

ear back (cut 2)

pleat markings

body (cut 4)

place on fold

Red Ridinghood's face (cut 1)

place on fold

Grandma's face (cut 1)

wolf's head (cut 2)

bodice (cut 1 front, 2 backs each for Little Red Ridinghood and Grandma)

place front on fold

hat brim (cut 2)

place on fold

hat back (cut 1)

place on fold

cape and cape lining (cut 1 each)

place on fold

2. Starting the Bodies. Join two body sections at the waist, right sides together. Then place Red Ridinghood's face on one body section, right sides together and neck edges aligned. Stitch the neck edges together. Pin Grandma's face to the other body section in the same fashion. Stitch a row of gathering stitches ¼″ (6 mm) from the edge around Grandma's face.

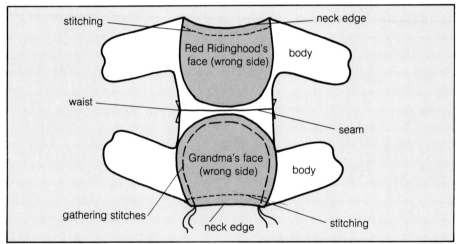

stitching

neck edge

Red Ridinghood's face (wrong side)

body

waist

seam

Grandma's face (wrong side)

body

gathering stitches

neck edge

stitching

3. Red Ridinghood's Hat. To make the back of the hat, fold the red hat-back piece in half, crosswise, wrong side out, and stitch the long straight edges together. Turn the hat right side out.

The brim. Place the two brim sections right sides together, and stitch around the outer curved edges. Trim the seam allowances and clip them along the curves. Turn the brim right side out, and press. Center the brim along the front edge of the hat, and baste them together along the edges. Join the remaining two body sections at the waist, right sides together. Align the neck edges of the hat and one body section right sides together and join them.

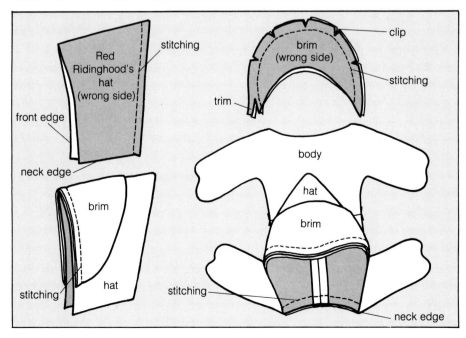

Red Ridinghood's hat (wrong side)

stitching

front edge

neck edge

brim (wrong side)

clip

trim

stitching

body

hat

brim

brim

hat

stitching

hat

stitching

neck edge

4. The Wolf's Head. To make the wolf's ears, make an inverted pleat in each ear front by lapping the inner pleat markings over the outer pleat markings as shown, and baste it. Join an ear front to each ear back, right sides together, around the edges. Trim the seam allowances, clip them at the curves, and turn the ears right side out. To make the wolf's head, slit each dart along the dashed line. Baste an ear to each dart, aligning the edges, with the pleated side of each ear facing down. Stitch the darts shut, right sides together.

Align the head sections right sides together, and stitch along the top, down the front of the nose, and around to the front edge of the neck. Trim the seam allowances, clip them at the curves, and turn the head right side out. Align the neck edges of the wolf's head and the remaining free body section, right sides together, and join them.

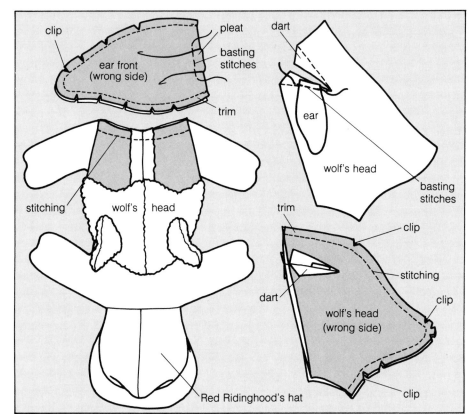

The features and hair

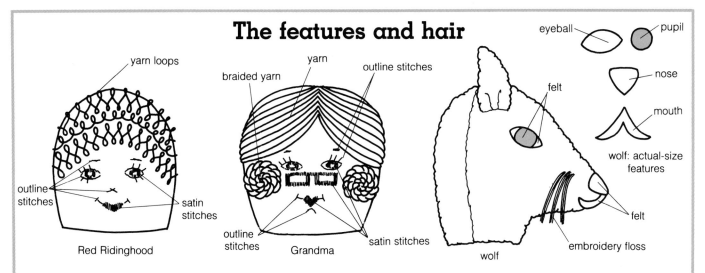

Red Ridinghood

Grandma

wolf

wolf: actual-size features

1. The Features. Stitch the faces on Little Red Ridinghood and Grandma using three strands of embroidery floss. Make satin stitches for the eyes, mouth, and glasses, and outline stitches for all other areas. Make the mouth, mouth corners, and chin red, and all the other areas black. If you wish, add a little color to Red Ridinghood's cheeks with a soft red pencil.

The wolf's face. Trace the actual-size features on tissue or tracing paper, and use them to cut two pupils, the nose, and the mouth from black felt, and two eyeballs from white felt. Glue the eyeballs to the head, about 2" (5 cm) from the end of the nose and 2½" (6.4 cm) apart at the inside corners. Center the pupils over them. Glue the nose, pointed end forward, to the end of the nose. Make the whiskers with black embroidery floss, as follows: Make a backstitch on one side of the nose about 1⅛" (2.8 cm) from the end, leaving a 1½"-long (3.8-cm) end of thread. Insert the needle through to the other side of the nose, make a backstitch, and clip the thread, leaving a 1½"-long (3.8-cm) end.

Repeat twice more close to the first stitches so that the wolf has three whiskers on each side.

2. The Hair. To make the hair for **Red Ridinghood,** cut approximately 70" (177.8 cm) of yellow yarn. Tack ¾"-long (19-mm) loops of yarn across the top of the head with yellow thread in two rows spaced about ¼" (6 mm) apart, alternating the direction of the loops from the forehead to the back of the head as shown. Make a third row of simple loops, all facing up, between the first two rows.

Grandma. To make the upper portion of Grandma's hair, cut individual strands of white yarn and glue them side by side, following the pattern marking so they curve down across each side of the forehead as shown. To make the braids, cut six 12"-long (30.5-cm) strands of yarn. Make two braids with three strands each and knot them at both ends. Tack the end of a braid to each side of the face ⅜" (9.5 mm) in from the side seam and even with the bottom of the glasses. Wrap and stitch the braid in concentric circles around the anchored end.

5. Assembling the Body. Turn both body sections wrong side out. Then, with right sides together, baste the edges, matching the back of the hat to Red Ridinghood's face and the wolf's head to Grandma's face, pulling up the gathering stitches around her face to fit the wolf's head. Stitch the edges, leaving one side open between the arms for turning and stuffing. Clip the seam allowances at the curves and turn. Stuff the entire body firmly with polyester fiber, and slipstitch the opening closed.

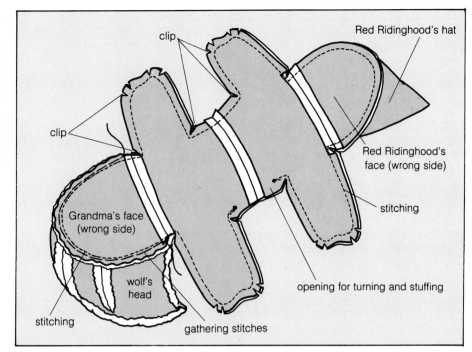

The doll's clothes

1. The Dresses. For each dress, join the **bodice** front to the left back and right back at the shoulder, right sides together. Press the seam allowances open. Turn under ¼" (6-mm) hems at the ends of the sleeves and stitch them ⅛" (3 mm) from the fold. Stitch the underarm seams, and clip the seam allowances at the corners.

Finish the neck edge of each dress with a 7" (17.8-cm) length of eyelet. Place the eyelet, wrong side down, on the right side of the dress, aligning the bound edge of the eyelet with the neck edge. Stitch them together. Clip the seam allowances along the curve and turn the bound edge of the eyelet under. Press. Repeat for the other dress.

The skirts. Sew a row of gathering stitches ¼" (6 mm) from the top long edge of each skirt. Then fold each skirt in half, end to end and wrong side out. Stitch the short edges together starting at the bottom and making a 7¼"-long (18.4-cm) seam. Press the seam allowances open. With the right sides together, join the bodice and skirt of each dress at the waist, pulling up the gathering stitches in the skirt to make it fit the waist of the bodice. Stitch.

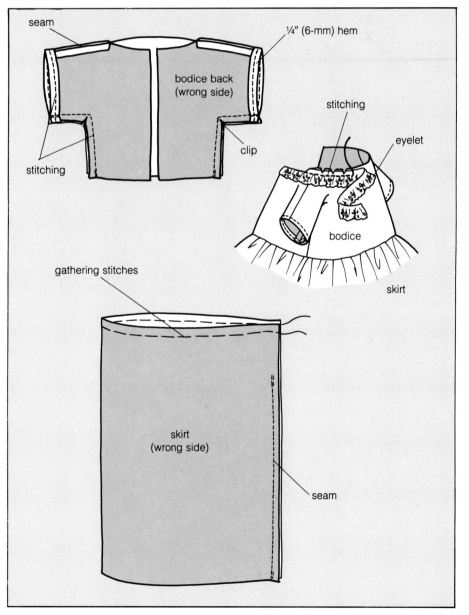

2. Joining and Finishing the Dresses.
Turn the dresses inside out, align the hems, right sides together, and stitch. Turn the dresses to the right side, press, and with the wrong sides together, stitch ½" (13 mm) from the edge of the hem with white thread. Slip Red Ridinghood into the red-and-white dress with the opening to her back. Then put Grandma and the wolf in the other dress with the opening on the wolf's side. Slipstitch both openings closed, turning under the edges. Then slipstitch the dress waist to the doll. Sew four buttons to the front of Red Ridinghood's dress. Cut the yellow ribbon in half and make a bow with each piece. Tack a bow to Grandma's neck and one to the wolf's neck.

3. The Cape. To make the cape, run a row of gathering stitches along the neck edge, between the dots, on both the cape and the lining. Gather the fabric between the dots to a width of 2" (5 cm). Align the cape and lining, right sides together, and stitch around the outer edges. Trim the seam allowances and clip them at the curves. Turn the cape right side out. Press. Topstitch ¼" (6 mm) from the outer edge. Stitch ¼" (6 mm) from the neck edge of the cape. Trim the fabric outside the stitching. Cut a 15" (38.1-cm) length of bias binding, fold it over the neck edge of the cape, and center it so that the ends extend 5" (12.7 cm) on each side. Tie the cape around Red Ridinghood's neck, with the solid-red side out.

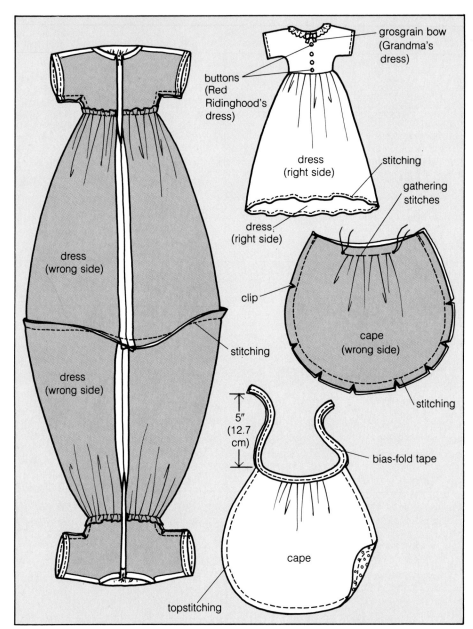

4. The Cap. To make a cap for Grandma and the wolf, remove the binding from the remaining eyelet and press the eyelet flat. Baste the eyelet to the right side of one circle of cap fabric, ¼" (6 mm) in from the edge with the finished side facing in. Place the two circles of fabric right sides together, and stitch ¼" (6 mm) from the edges all around, leaving a 1½" (3.8-cm) opening for turning. Clip the seam allowances at intervals, turn the cap right side out, and press. Then stitch around the cap ½" (13 mm) from the edge to make a casing for elastic.

Cut an 8¼" (20.9-cm) length of elastic. Fasten a safety pin to one end, and insert it through the opening at the edge of the cap. Work the elastic around the casing. Stitch the ends of the elastic together and slipstitch the opening closed. Slip the cap over the wolf's head and around Grandma's face. Turn Red Ridinghood right side up to ready her for the beginning of the story.

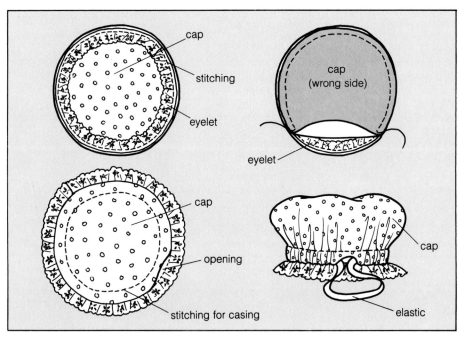

Kitchen Witch

Materials

Knitting worsted: approximately 1 ounce (28.35 grams) each of beige, black, blue, and paprika red; 25 yards (22.85 m) of olive green; 10 yards (9.14 m) of white; a scrap of red
Crochet hooks D and G
12″-long (30.5-cm) pipe cleaners: 3 white, 2 black
Polyester fiber for stuffing
A ¼″-thick (6-mm) wooden dowel, 12″ (30.5 cm) long
A scrap of lightweight nylon fishing line
Crochet abbreviations: ch (chain), sc (single crochet), dc (double crochet), tc (triple crochet)

The doll's head

1. The Head. Make two identical sections for the head as follows: With beige yarn and a D hook, ch 3. *Row 1*: Sc, increase in the second and third ch (making a total of 4 stitches). *Row 2*: Sc, increase in first and last sc (6 stitches). *Row 3*: Sc, increase in first sc only (7 stitches). *Row 4*: Sc, increase in last sc only (8 stitches). *Row 5*: Work even on 8 sc. *Row 6*: Sc across. Ch 6. *Row 7*: 2 sc in second ch, sc in next 4 ch, work across 8 sc (14 stitches). *Row 8*: Sc in 8 sc, ch 1, turn. *Row 9*: Sc in 8 sc, ch 1, turn. *Row 10*: Sc in 8 sc, ch 4. *Row 11*: Sc in 3 ch, sc in 6 sc across, decrease in last 2 sc (10 stitches). *Row 12*: Decrease in both of first 2 sc, work 4 sc, ch 1, turn (6 stitches). *Row 13*: Decrease in both of first 2 sc, work 2 sc, ch 1, turn (4 stitches). *Row 14*: Work even on 4 sc, fasten off. Repeat for the other head section.

Align the two head sections, and join the edges, inserting 1″ (2.5-cm) lengths of folded white pipe cleaner in the nose and chin, and stuffing the head completely with polyester fiber before closing the seam.

1. The Features. Using straight stitches and yarn in the needle, embroider the features. Make the eyes and eyebrows black, the mouth red, and the hair white. Place each eye ¼″ (6 mm) to the side of the top of the nose. Start the bottom of each eyebrow ⅜″ (9.5 mm) above the inner corner of its corresponding eye and end it 1″ (2.5 cm) back at the top of the head. For the hair, fill in the area between the eyebrows with about fourteen 1″-long (2.5-cm) parallel stitches of white yarn. Make the mouth just above the chin with one horizontal stitch the width of the chin and a ¼″-long (6-mm) stitch angled upward at each end of the first stitch.

2. The Body. Make two identical pieces for the body as follows: with black yarn and a D hook, ch 5. *Row 1*: Sc in 4 ch. *Row 2*: Sc, increasing in the first and last sc (6 stitches). *Rows 3-5*: Repeat Row 2 (making 12 sc at the end of the fifth row). *Rows 6-13*: Work even on 12 sc. *Row 14*: Decrease on both of first 2 sc, work across, increasing 1 sc in last sc (11 stitches). *Row 15*: Increase 1 sc in first sc, work across, decrease on both of last 2 sc (10 stitches). *Row 16*: Repeat Row 14 (9 stitches). *Row 17*: Repeat Row 15 (8 stitches). *Row 18*: Repeat Row 14 (7 stitches). *Row 19*: Repeat Row 15 (6 stitches). *Row 20*: Repeat Row 14 (5 stitches). Fasten off.

Sew the two body sections together around the edges, stuffing the body compactly before closing the edges. Sew the head to the top of the body, facing the concave side of the body.

The arms. Make the witch's arms as follows: Fold a 12″-long (30.5-cm) white pipe cleaner in half around a pencil. Wrap the pipe cleaner around the pencil to form a circle at the center (see the next page), and bend the ends parallel to each other, as shown. Attach beige yarn to the ring at the center of the pipe cleaner and, using a D hook, single-crochet around the outer part of the ring. Then single-crochet around the parallel ends of the pipe cleaner for 2½″ (6.4 cm). Fold the protuding ends of the pipe cleaner in and continue to single-crochet over the four thicknesses of the pipe cleaner until the top end is completely covered. Fasten off. Stitch the arm through the ring to one side of the body 1″ (2.5 cm) below the head. Repeat for the other arm.

The legs. Make the witch's legs in the following fashion: Bend a 12″-long (30.5-cm) pipe cleaner in half. Attach black yarn to the bend and single-crochet tightly over both thicknesses of the pipe cleaner to within 2″ (5 cm) of the free ends. Bend both ends under 1″ (2.5 cm) and continue to single-crochet over four thicknesses until they are completely covered. To make the foot, turn up the pipe cleaner 1″ (2.5 cm) from the narrower end. Form the knee by bending the pipe cleaner in the opposite direction from the foot 2″ (5 cm) above the end of the foot. Join the top (thick) end of the leg to one side of the bottom of the body so that the two overlap by 2″ (5 cm).

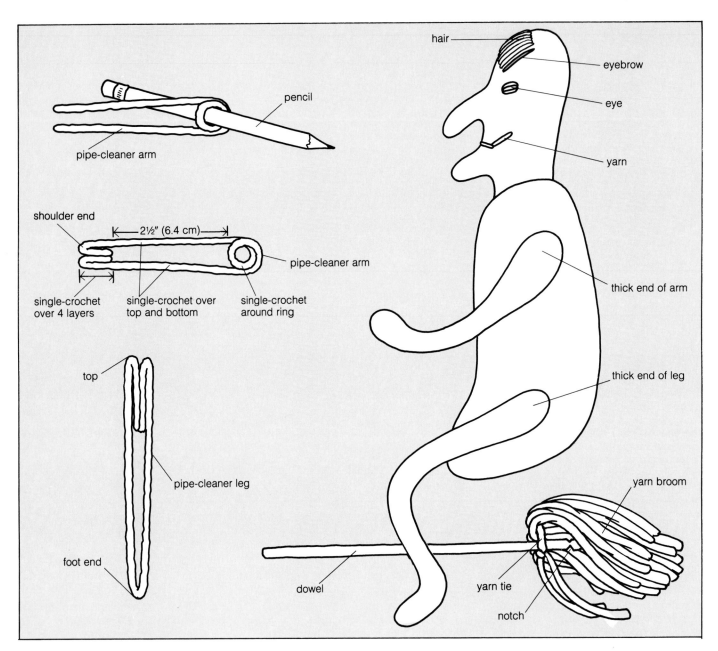

The doll's clothes and accessories

1. The Clothes. Using paprika-red yarn and a D crochet hook, make the **dress** as follows: ch 15. *Row 1*: 2 sc in each ch (28 stitches). *Rows 2-3*: Sc across. *Row 4*: Sc in 5 sc, ch 5, skip 5 sc, sc in 8 sc, ch 5, sc in last 5 sc. *Row 5*: Sc in 5 sc, sc in each of 5 ch, sc in 8 sc, sc in 5 ch, sc in last 5 sc, ch 3. *Row 6*: Dc in first sc, dc in next 9 sc, 2 dc in next 8 sc, dc in next 10 sc, ch 3. *Row 7-13*: Work even in dc. Fasten off.

The collar. Attach white yarn in the first ch at the neck, and work 2 dc across in each ch.

The sleeves and cuffs. Make two sleeves as follows: Attach paprika-red yarn at the end of one armhole on the dress, ch 1. *Row 1*: Sc around for a total 10 sc. *Row 2*: Ch 3, dc around. *Rows 3-5*: Dc around. Cut the paprika-red yarn and join white yarn to the cut end. Ch 2, 2 dc in each dc around. Join to the top of the chain and fasten off. Repeat to make the other sleeve and cuff. Slip the dress on the doll with the opening to the front. Then stitch the front edges together with matching yarn.

The hood. Using olive-green yarn and a D hook, ch 29. *Rows 1-3*: Sc across (28 stitches). *Row 4*: Skip first sc to 1 sc from the end, do not ch 1, turn. Continue with Row 4 until 2 sc remain. Decrease 2 sc and fasten off. Sew the hood around the doll's face with olive-green yarn.

The cape. Using blue yarn and a G hook, ch 23. *Row 1*: Work 22 sc across ch. Ch 4, turn. *Rows 2-8*: Work across in tc, working the first tc in the first stitch (or top of previous chain) to increase at the cape's outer edges, and increase 2 stitches at the center back by increasing 1 tc in each of the 2 center stitches. Fasten off. Wrap the cape around the witch's shoulders, sew the top ends together at the front, and tack the cape in place at the back of the neck.

2. The Broom. Cut a shallow notch around the dowel about ½" (13 mm) from one end. Cut thirty 5"-long (12.7-cm) strands of beige yarn. Lay them side by side, and tie them together across the center loosely with another strand of beige yarn; slip the notched end of the dowel through the yarn tie about ½" (13 mm) above the notch. Spread the yarn evenly around the dowel over the tie.

Tighten the tie, and knot it securely. Bring the ends of the yarn down over the end of the dowel, and tie another length of yarn tightly around the broom at the notch. Trim the ends of the tie, and trim the ends of the broom even. Insert the broomstick between the witch's hands and curl her legs around it. Attach a long loop of fishing line to the back of the witch's head, from which she can be suspended.

Cuddly Kitten

Materials

Two 6" × 9" (15.2 × 22.9-cm) scraps of cotton or cotton-blend fabric

A 3"-square (7.6-cm) scrap of white cotton or cotton-blend fabric

White glue

A 4" (10.2-cm) length of colored soutache braid

Embroidery floss: black, rose, and steel blue

Polyester fiber for stuffing

An 8" (20.3-cm) length of multicolor striped grosgrain ribbon ⅜" (9.5 mm) wide

Note: If a zigzag machine is not available, two rows of short, straight stitching ⅛" (3 mm) apart may be used where zigzag stitching is called for on the face

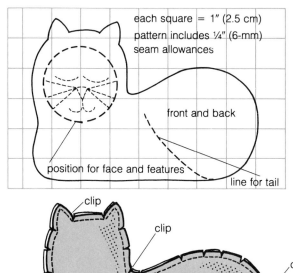

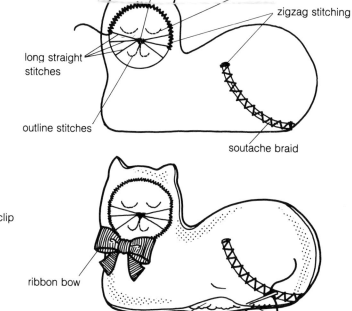

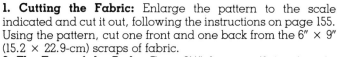

1. Cutting the Fabric: Enlarge the pattern to the scale indicated and cut it out, following the instructions on page 155. Using the pattern, cut one front and one back from the 6" × 9" (15.2 × 22.9-cm) scraps of fabric.

2. The Front of the Body. Cut a 2½"-diameter (6.4-cm) circle from a scrap of solid-white cotton or cotton-blend fabric for the **face.** Trace the features from the pattern onto tracing or tissue paper with a soft pencil. Turn the paper over on the face fabric and retrace the features, transferring them to the fabric.

Decide on which side you want the face, then glue it to the right side of the appropriate body section, aligning the face with the pattern markings.

With thread to match the body fabric, stitch around the edge of the face, using zigzag stitching.

The features. Working with two strands of embroidery floss, outline the kitten's eyes with black chain stitches and the

mouth with rose outline stitches. Fill in the nose with vertical satin stitches of rose floss, and make the whiskers with long, straight stitches in steel-blue floss.

The tail. Position the soutache braid along the pattern marking on the front of the body. Stitch the tail in place, using zigzag stitching the width of the braid. Anchor each end of the braid with a bar tack. (You can also attach the tail with zigzag hand stitches across the braid, or slipstitch both edges.)

3. Finishing the Body. Sew the front and back of the cat right sides together around the edges, leaving a 2" (5-cm) opening at the bottom. Clip the seam allowances along the curved edges. Turn the body right side out through the opening and stuff it compactly with polyester fiber. Turn under the edges along the opening and slipstitch them together.

The bow. Make a bow from the grosgrain ribbon and tack it securely below the face, as indicated in the photograph.

The International Dolls *(from left to right):* (1) Czech Couple, (2) Swiss Grandma, (3) East Indian Stick Dolls, (4) Greek Yarn Doll, (5) Chinese Man, (6) A Colleen from Kildare, (7) Sierra Leone Mother and Baby, (8) Peruvian Girl, (9) Gretel, (10) Navaho Woman.

International Dolls

Dolls exert their special magic all over the world. Although they vary in complexity and materials, most of the dolls in the international section of this book are authentic folk-art creations. Each has its own particular look and dress, but all share the same irresistible appeal.

In addition to dolls dressed in their colorful national costume, the Czechs also produce dolls made of linen and dressed in simple clothes, such as this charming "Czech Couple" (1). Soft, flat dolls, their realistic hair is creatively stitched linen thread.

Perched on an Alpine log, the wrinkled "Swiss Grandma" (2) knits away with miniature needles. Her sculpted face is formed by pinching and stitching a stuffed nylon stocking.

In East India, where a Sanskrit word for doll means "little daughter," Hindu children cherish simple dolls such as these authentic "East Indian Stick Dolls" (3). One turbaned and the other "shapely," the pair have embroidered faces. Their bodies are simply wooden dowels, padded and then wrapped and dressed with brightly colored cloth.

The "Greek Yarn Doll" (4) represents the Hellenic *evzone*, or elite guard. Made of bendable pipe cleaners, slightly padded and wrapped with yarn and floss, he wears the fez, the kilt, and the pom-pommed slippers of a soldier's dress uniform.

The "Chinese Man" (5) comes complete with braided hair in topknot style and Chinese ball buttons, made with soutache braid, to fasten his blue cotton jacket.

An Irish doll, the "Colleen from Kildare" (6), has a knitted rectangle for a body with limbs formed by stitching through the stuffed work. Her hat is also knitted.

The many lands and peoples of Africa have originated a great variety of dolls including this tiny "Sierra Leone Mother and Baby" (7). Standing on a pedestal, she is decked out in beads, authentic costume, and headdress; the little bundle tucked into her back pouch represents her baby.

From the Andean Altiplano comes a felt "Peruvian Girl" (8), with painted face, attired in the characteristic shawl and bowler hat worn there since Inca days.

Germany offers a dirndl-skirted, felt "Gretel" (9) modeled after an authentic German *Puppe*, or doll, discovered there. Her affecting face is formed by molding damp felt over another doll's china head. Impregnated with glue, the stiffened felt is then slipped off, stitched, and stuffed.

From the Southwestern United States comes an exquisite "Navaho Woman" (10). Her beaded and sequined jewelry and the full-skirted turquoise velvet costume exemplify the style worn by Navaho women for more than a hundred years.

117

Navaho Woman

Materials

¼ yard (22.9 cm) of 36"-wide (.91-m)
   light-tan close-weave cotton fabric
½ yard (45.7 cm) of 39"-wide (.99-m)
   turquoise velvet
½ yard (45.7 cm) of 36"-wide (.91-m)
   printed cotton fabric
Scraps of red cotton
Small scraps of firm cardboard
A 6" (15.2-cm) square of pink cotton
   fabric
Sewing thread: to match all fabrics
Polyester fiber for stuffing
A scrap of ⅟₁₆"-thick (1.5-mm) brown
   leather or leatherlike vinyl
Seed beads: 100 red, 60 white, and 60
   turquoise
A beading needle
Two ⅝₁₆" × 1¼" (8-mm × 3.2-cm) strips
   of aluminum, cut from a can
Acrylic paint: black, red, and white
A very fine brush
1 yard (.91 m) of continuous-length
   uncurled black mohair
Cellophane tape
A few scraps of paper
A 7" (17.8-cm) length of natural or tan
   yarn
3 yards (2.74 m) red baby rickrack
¼ yard (22.9 cm) of ⅝"-wide (16-mm)
   embroidered metallic gold ribbon
60 transparent or silver sequins, ¼" (6
   mm) in diameter

The doll's body and bodice

1. Cutting the Fabric. Enlarge the patterns to the scale indicated, and cut them out, following the directions on page 155. Using the patterns, cut the fabric listed below and transfer all the appropriate pattern markings onto the pieces. From folded tan cotton cut two bodies, two arms, and two legs. From folded turquoise velvet cut two sleeves and one bodice. Also cut a 4¼" × 34"-long (10.8-cm × .86-m) rectangle for the upper skirt and a 4½" × 64"-long (11.4-cm × 1.63-m) strip for the lower skirt. Make sure the nap of the velvet runs from the top to the bottom of every section. Piece the skirt section, if necessary. From printed cotton fabric cut one upper petticoat and one lower petticoat the same sizes as the upper and lower skirts. Again, piece them, if necessary. From scraps of red cotton cut two shoe tops, and from tan fabric cut two shoe soles; also cut two sole pieces from cardboard. From pink cotton fabric cut one pants piece.

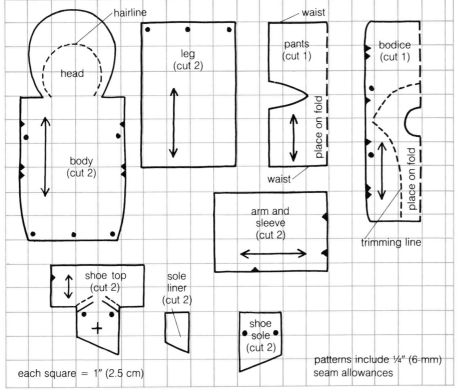

hairline

head

body
(cut 2)

leg
(cut 2)

waist

pants
(cut 1)

place on fold

waist

bodice
(cut 1)

place on fold

trimming line

arm and
sleeve
(cut 2)

shoe top
(cut 2)

sole
liner
(cut 2)

shoe
sole
(cut 2)

each square = 1" (2.5 cm)

patterns include ¼" (6-mm)
seam allowances

2. The Body and Bodice. Sew the two **body** sections together, wrong sides out, above the edges of the shoulders and around the head. Clip the seam allowances at the neck, and press them open.

The bodice. Stay-stitch around the neck edge of the bodice to prevent stretching. Turn the body right side out and place the bodice wrong side down over it, aligning the edges. Baste the bodice to the body, matching the notches and dots. Stitch the bottom edges of the bodice to the body.

3. The Arms and Sleeves. Baste the sleeves to the arms, right sides up, matching the notches and dots. Sew the ends of the sleeves and arms to the sides of the bodice and body, right sides together, between the dots. Clip the bodice at the ends of the seams, and fasten the threads. Sew the lower edges of the sleeves and arms together. Clip the seam allowances at the inner corner. Turn the body right side out, bringing the head carefully through the neck opening in the bodice. Stuff the head until it is very firm with polyester fiber, using a blunt instrument to pack the stuffing until the head is smooth and round. Then stuff the body until it is firm. Turn under the lower edges of the body ¼″ (6 mm), and whipstitch the opening closed. Stuff the arms, but not as firmly as the body, rounding out the shoulders to make them attractive. Make an inverted pleat at the seam near the lower edge of each sleeve to fit the arm, and stitch it in place.

4. The Legs. Fold each leg in half lengthwise, and sew the upper end between the dots and the long edges closed. Press the seam allowances open with your fingers. Turn the legs right side out, and sew a row of gathering stitches ¼″ (6 mm) from the lower edges of each one.

Stuff the legs until firm. Draw up the gathers tightly and fasten the threads. With the leg seams turned inward, whipstitch the legs to the lower edge of the body between the dots.

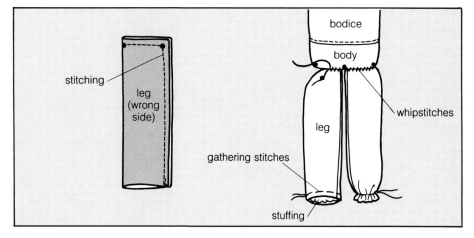

The features and hair

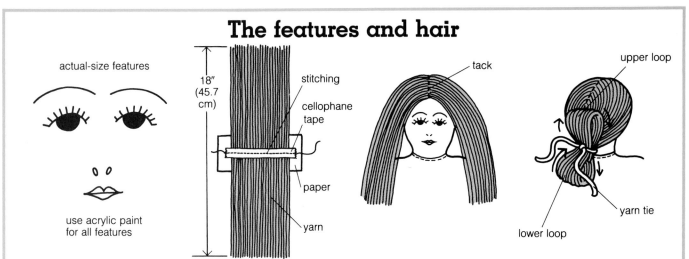

actual-size features

use acrylic paint
for all features

18" (45.7 cm)

stitching
cellophane tape
paper
yarn

tack

upper loop
yarn tie
lower loop

1. The Features. Trace the actual-size pattern for the features on tracing or tissue paper with a soft pencil. Turn the paper over and retrace the features, transferring them onto the front of the head, with the center of the eyebrows ⅝" (16 mm) below the hairline. Using the tip of the brush, paint the mouth and the nostrils with red acrylic paint, the eyes and eyebrows with black. Allow the paint to dry, then add a dab of white at each side of the eyeballs.

2. The Hair. Cut the black mohair into 18" (45.7-cm) lengths. Place the strands side by side, aligning the ends and spreading the strands so that they measure 5" (12.7 cm) across at the center.

Place a strip of cellophane tape across the mohair at the center. Slip a 3" × 7" (7.6 × 17.8-cm) piece of paper under the mohair and tape as shown. Stitch through the center of

the tape, mohair, and paper with red thread, using fine stitching (about fifteen stitches to the inch—2.5 cm). Tie the ends of the thread, and carefully tear away the paper and the tape. Lay the hair across the head so the stitching line forms a part down the middle of the head and the hairline begins at the pattern marking. Tack the hair to the head with matching sewing thread.

Tie all of the hair securely at the back of the neck with a 7" (17.8-cm) length of light-tan or natural yarn, smoothing it along the hairline at the front. Turn the hair up 1" (2.5 cm) below the tied section; turn the ends under 2" (5 cm) above the first turn and press the hair against the doll's head. Tie it across the center with the same piece of yarn, forming a loop below and above the tie. Wrap the yarn between the hair loops again; knot it securely. Trim the ends of the tie.

5. The Hands. Trace the actual-size pattern for the hand on tracing or tissue paper with a soft pencil. Turn the paper over and retrace the hand, transferring the pattern onto brown leather or vinyl; then turn the paper over again to trace the other hand. Cut the hands. Cut along the markings to make the fingers.

The jewelry. To make the rings and bracelets, use a beading needle with doubled thread that matches the hand. Start from under the lower end of the little fingers with knotted thread. Pick up a turquoise seed bead on the top of the hand, and push the needle back to the underside close to the first hole. Repeat to attach beads to the next two fingers, and then bring the needle up ¼" (6 mm) from the lower end of the thumb, as shown. String four white, three red, and then four more white beads on the thread to make a bracelet, and insert the needle at the opposite side of the hand from the top side to the underside, as shown. Fasten the thread securely. Repeat for the other hand.

Sew a row of gathering stitches ¼" (6 mm) from the lower edge of each sleeve. Insert a hand into each sleeve, top side up and thumb side in, so the seam of the sleeve is under the hand. Gather the fabric tightly along the thread, wind the thread around the gathers, and fasten it securely. Whipstitch the upper edge of each hand to the gathers.

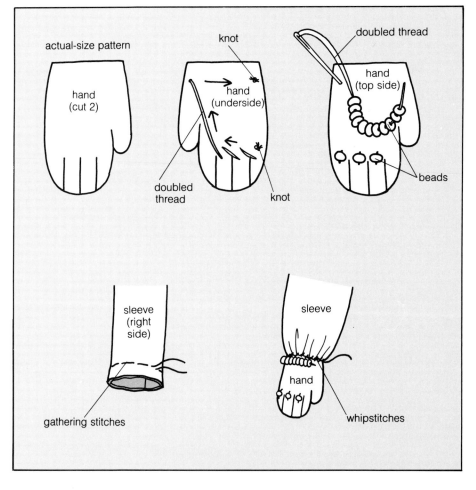

actual-size pattern

hand (cut 2)

knot
doubled thread
hand (underside)
doubled thread
knot

doubled thread
hand (top side)
beads

sleeve (right side)
gathering stitches

sleeve
hand
whipstitches

The doll's other clothes

1. The Shoes. Sew the soles to the shoe tops, right sides together, between the dots. Trim the seam allowances at the corners, and turn the shoes right side out. Clip the tops diagonally ¼″ (6 mm) at the inner corners along the solid lines transferred from the pattern. Make pleats in the tops, bringing the solid lines to the dotted lines. Tack the pleats ¼″ (6 mm) from the edges. Fold the ends of the top of each shoe together wrong side out, and stitch them along the edges to make a center-back seam. Press the seam allowances open, and turn the top right side out. Insert a piece of cardboard stiffening into each shoe, and stuff the toe section in front of the pleats with polyester fiber. Turn in the free edges of the soles, and slipstitch the soles and tops together along the edges. Turn in one edge of the back opening, and slipstitch it closed. Turn in the upper edges of the tops, put the shoes on the doll, and tack the tops to the legs.

2. The Pants. Stitch ¼″ (6 mm) from the edges around the leg openings; clip the curves almost to the stitching. Turn the fabric under along the stitching, press, and stitch along the folded edges.

Fold the pants in half, waist edges together and wrong side out. Seam the side edges and press the seam allowances open. Sew a row of gathering stitches ¼″ (6 mm) from the waist edge. Put the pants on the doll, gather the fabric tightly around the waist, and secure the thread. Sew the upper edge to the doll just below the bodice.

3. The Petticoat. Sew gathering stitches ¼″ (6 mm) from the upper edges of each petticoat section. Turn under ½″ (13 mm) on the lower edge of the upper section and press. Gather the top of the lower section to fit under the bottom of the upper section, adjusting the gathers evenly. Pin, then stitch them together. Make a ¼″ (6-mm) double hem on the bottom edge. Slip the petticoat on the doll, gather the fabric to fit the waist, and secure the gathering thread. Stitch the top of the petticoat to the body.

4. The Skirt. Sew a row of gathering stitches ¼″ (6 mm) from the upper edge of the top and lower skirt sections. Gather the upper edge of the lower section evenly to fit the bottom of the upper section. Pin them, wrong sides together, and stitch. Stitch a row of red baby rickrack on the right side over the seam. Turn under ¼″ (6 mm) on the bottom edge of the skirt. Stitch a row of rickrack along the bottom edge of the skirt on the right side. Slip the skirt over the petticoat, gather the fabric evenly around the waist, and secure the thread. Sew the top of the skirt to the doll along the bottom of the bodice.

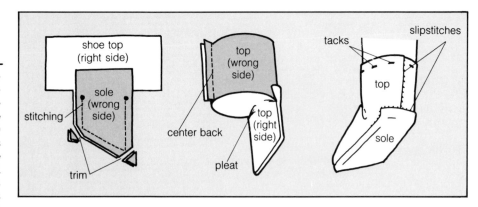

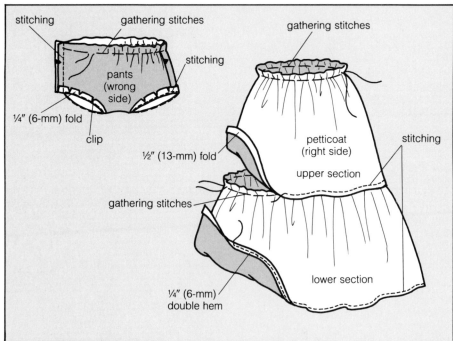

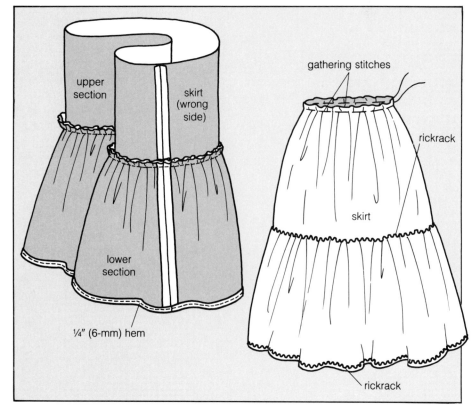

The finishing touches

1. The Sash. Wrap the gold-embroidered ribbon around the waist, overlapping the ends at one side. Turn under one end and sew the ribbon together with slipstitches.

2. The Trimming. Using doubled matching thread in a beading needle, sew the sequins in place, each topped with a red seed bead, ⅛″ (3 mm) apart along the center of the sleeves, and along the trimming lines on the bodice, the neck edge of the bodice, and down the center front to 1″ (2.5 cm) above the sash.

3. The Necklace. Attach a doubled thread to the edge of the neck on one side. String varicolored seed beads on the thread to a length of 9″ (22.9 cm), and then secure the thread next to the beginning knot, making a long loop of beads. Repeat at the other side of the neck. Tack the bead loop securely to the center front of the bodice just below the last center sequin, allowing the lower parts of the loops to hang free.

4. The Earrings. String three red seed beads, twelve turquoise beads, three red beads, twelve turquoise beads, and three red beads, in that order, on doubled thread; secure the ends at the hairline to one side of the head, between the eye and nose levels, forming a loop earring. Repeat for the other earring.

5. The Hair Decorations. Insert a beading needle with a doubled thread through the hair and bring it out ¾″ (19 mm) to one side of the center part at the hair line. String four white beads, three red beads, and four white beads, in that order, on the thread, and secure it straight back from the hairline in the hair. Add another string of beads ¾″ (19 mm) to the side of the first, and repeat on the other side of the head, making a total of four bead strings, as shown.

6. The Shoe Decorations. String two white beads, one turquoise bead, and two white beads, in that order, on a doubled thread; secure the ends of the thread over one line of the cross marked on the shoe. Sew four white beads on the other line of the cross, two on each side of the center.

7. The Bracelets. Cut two ⁵⁄₁₆″ × 1¼″ (8-mm × 3.2-cm) aluminum strips for bracelets. Bend one around each wrist above the bead bracelet, to cover the stitches.

Bend the doll's arms down, and tack the wrists securely to the sash at the doll's sides.

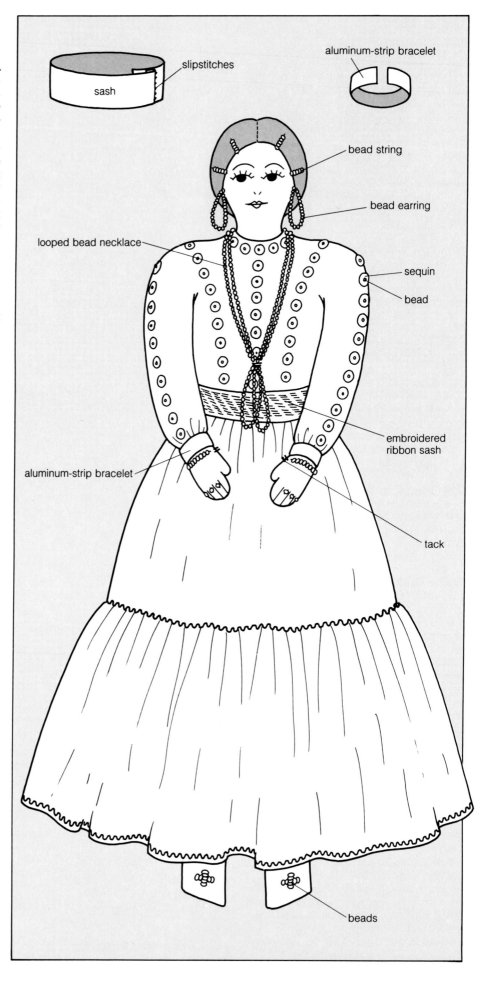

East Indian Stick Dolls

Materials

White glue
Polyester fiber for stuffing
½″-diameter (13-mm) wooden dowels: four 12″ (30.5-cm) lengths, two 5″ (12.7-cm) lengths, and a small scrap for noses
A 6″ × 12″ (15.2 × 30.5-cm) piece of bright-pink cotton fabric
¼ yard (22.9 cm) yellow cotton fabric
Sewing thread: to match all fabrics
A 6″ × 18″ (15.2 × 45.7-cm) piece of white cotton fabric

Embroidery floss: black and red
A 1″ × 9″ (2.5 × 22.9-cm) strip of blue cotton fabric
A 1½″ × 22″ (3.8 × 55.9-cm) strip of light-green cotton fabric
A 1″ × 22″ (2.5 × 55.9-cm) strip of dark-green cotton fabric
An 8″ × 22″ (20.3 × 55.9-cm) piece of semisheer yellow cotton fabric
A 6″ (15.2-cm) square of black cotton fabric
Two ³⁄₁₆″-diameter (5-mm) pink beads

The doll's bodies and clothes

1. The Hands and Feet. For each doll, glue a small amount of polyester fiber to one end of two 12″-long (30.5-cm) dowels to form the feet, and at both ends of one 5″-long (12.7-cm) dowel to form the hands. Place a 1″ (2.5-cm) square of bright-pink fabric over each padded end, and then glue the edges of the fabric to the dowel.

2. The Arms and Legs. Cut strips of yellow cotton fabric 1″ (2.5 cm) wide across the width of the fabric; press under ¼″ (6 mm) of fabric on one long edge of each strip. Beginning at the foot end of each long dowel, wrap the fabric strips around the dowel with the turned edge toward the foot, so that the cut edge does not show. Continue wrapping the fabric around the dowel for 9″ (22.9 cm). Hold the end of the strip in place with a dot of glue or a few stitches. Wrap the entire length of the 5″ (12.7-cm) dowel in the same way, turning under the remaining cut edges of the fabric at the end. Slipstitch the end of the fabric firmly in place.

3. The Features. For each doll, cut a 6″ (15.2-cm) square of white fabric. Trace the actual-size patterns for the faces given here on tracing or tissue paper with a soft pencil. Turn the paper over and retrace the features on the center of the white fabric square, with the dotted line 3″ (7.6 cm) from the top edge. Using

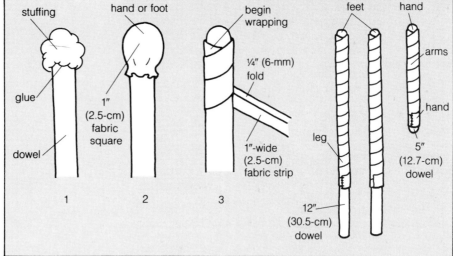

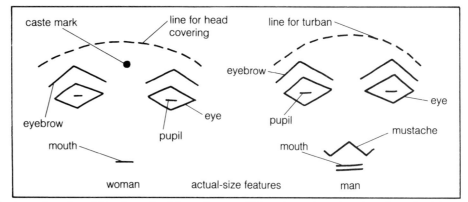

two strands of black embroidery floss, make the eyes, eyebrows, and the man's mustache with outline stitches.

Using two strands of red embroidery floss, embroider the mouths and the woman's caste mark.

4. The Heads. Hold two of the legs together, foot end down, to begin making the head for each doll. For the **man,** wrap polyester stuffing around the ends and the top 3″ (7.6 cm) of the dowels. For the **woman,** wrap polyester stuffing around the top 2″ (5 cm) of the dowels. For each head, cut a ¾″-long (19-mm) slice from the scrap of dowel with a utility knife to make the nose. Glue the nose flat against the center of the head, about ¾″ (19 mm) from the top end of the padding. Place each fabric face over the appropriate set of padded dowels, with the eyes on either side of the nose and the mouth (and the man's mustache) just below it. Fold and pleat the sides of the fabric around the back of the head, tucking down the fabric from the top of the head, then folding one side back over the other at the center back so that no cut edges show. Slipstitch this last fold in place along the center back.

5. The Torsos. For each doll, cut a piece of white fabric, 2½″ × 4½″ (6.4 × 11.4 cm), and turn under ¼″ (6 mm) on the two long sides and on one end. Starting with the unfinished end, wrap a piece of fabric tightly around each body, ½″ (13 mm) below the mouth for the man, and ⅞″ (22 mm) below the mouth for the woman. Lap the folded end on top at the center back, and slipstitch it in place.

For each doll, cut 1″ × 4½″ (2.5 × 11.4-cm) fabric strips as follows: two bright pink, two yellow, and one blue. Turn under ¼″ (6 mm) along one long side of each strip. Starting ⅛″ (3 mm) above the top edge of the torso, wrap a pink strip around each doll, with the folded edge at the top, so that no cut edges show. Turn under the free end at the center back, and pin it down. Then place a yellow strip around the body in the same manner, overlapping the bottom edge of the pink strip by ¼″ (6 mm). Attach the blue strip, another bright-pink strip, and the remaining yellow strip in the same way. Slipstitch all the strips together along the center back.

Tack the arms to the back side of the body so that their tops are about ½″ (13 mm) below the top of the stripes.

6. The Woman's Dress. Make the **bodice** by placing two small balls of polyester on the center of a 1½″ × 4½″ (3.8 × 11.4-cm) piece of light-green fabric. Fold the fabric lengthwise into thirds over the stuffing. With the seam side toward the body, wrap the fabric around the torso just below the arms, centering the stuffing at the front to form the bosom. Turn one end of the fabric under and place it over the other end at the center back; slipstitch the fold in place.

The skirt. Place the dark-green fabric strip right side down over the wrong side of the sheer yellow cotton fabric, aligning the long edges, and stitch them together, leaving a ¼″ (6-mm) seam allowance. Turn and press the dark-green

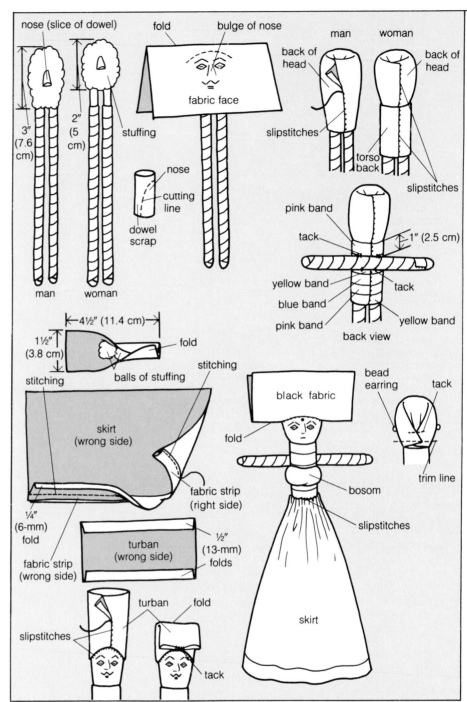

strip to the right side of the skirt. Press under ¼″ (6 mm) along the top edge of the green strip, and stitch along the edge of the fold to join the strip and the skirt. Fold the skirt in half, wrong side out, aligning the 8″ (20.3-cm) edges, and sew them together, leaving a ¼″ (6-mm) seam allowance. Turn ¼″ (6 mm) of fabric at the top of the skirt to the wrong side, and make a row of gathering stitches through both thicknesses of fabric by hand. Turn the skirt right side out and put it on the doll. Gather the top edge to fit around the lower edge of the torso, and slipstitch the skirt in place.

7. The Woman's Head Covering. Fold the 6″ (15.2-cm) square of black fabric in half, center the folded edge along the line shown in the features pattern, and slipstitch the fabric to the head along the

line. Pleat the fabric at the back to fit the head and tack it in place. Trim the ends even across the bottom. Sew a bead to each side of the head just in front of the head covering at eye level.

8. The Man's Turban. Cut a 4″ × 6″ (10.2 × 15.2-cm) piece of bright-pink fabric, and fold ½″ (13 mm) to the wrong side along both long edges. Beginning and ending at the center front, slipstitch one edge of the turban, right side out, around the head, following the line shown on the features pattern in front. Fold the free end under at the center front, lap it over the other end, and slipstitch it in place. Fold the top of the turban straight down in front, even with the bottom edge, and tack the center on the line shown on the features pattern.

124

Swiss Grandma

Materials

An 8″ × 14″ (20.3 × 35.6-cm) piece of off-white muslin
A 32″ (81.3-cm) length of heavy wire that can be twisted by hand
A 2″ (5-cm) square of white cardboard
Polyester fiber for stuffing
A 5″ × 7″ (12.7 × 17.8-cm) piece of beige nylon stocking
An 8″ (20.3-cm) square of blue knit fabric
Two 2″-square (5-cm) scraps of dark-blue and gray felt
White glue
Sewing thread: to match fabrics
A 6″ × 9″ (15.2 × 22.9-cm) piece of dark-green printed fabric
A 5″ × 14″ (12.7 × 35.6-cm) piece of white floral printed fabric
A 14″ (35.6-cm) length of ⅜″-wide (9.5-mm) lace
A 5″ × 7″ (12.7 × 17.8-cm) piece of red-and-white plaid fabric

An 8″ (20.3-cm) piece of ⅝″-wide (16-mm) lace
A 10″ (25.4-cm) length of yellow bias-fold tape
Heavy white thread and a large needle
Acrylic paint: black, green, and white
A small paintbrush
Felt-tip markers: black, red
A 6″ (15.2-cm) length of thin wire
White synthetic hair
A 5″ (12.7-cm) length of ¼″-wide (6-mm) gold ribbon
A 5½″ × 5½″ × 7¾″ (14 × 14 × 19.7-cm) triangle of red printed fabric
A 7″ × 7″ × 10″ (17.8 × 17.8 × 25.4-cm) triangle of purple-and-white polka-dot fabric
A 3½″-long (8.9-cm) piece of a tree branch, 1½″ (3.8 cm) in diameter
Two 2½″-long (6.4-cm) doll-size knitting needles made from blunted hat pins or nails
A ½″ (13-mm) ball of light-weight yarn

The doll's body

1. The Body. Cut a 4″ × 5½″ (10.2 × 14-cm) piece of muslin and fold it in half, aligning the shorter edges. Stitch along one end and the open side. Turn the body right side out through the open end, and stuff it firmly with polyester fiber. Turn the open edges under ¼″ (6 mm) and slipstitch them together.

2. The Arms. To make each arm, cut a 6″ (15.2-cm) length of wire, bend it in half, and twist the two halves together. Cut a 10″-long (25.4-cm), 1″-wide (2.5-cm) bias strip of muslin. Fold it in half lengthwise and, with the folded end of the muslin strip toward the bent end of the wire, wrap the muslin around the wire, beginning ½″ (13 mm) from the bent end, overlapping each wrap ¼″ (6 mm). Stitch the fabric together ½″ (13 mm) from the end of each arm to hold it in place.

3. The Hands. Trace the actual-size pattern given on tissue or tracing paper with a soft pencil. Turn the paper over on white cardboard and retrace the pattern twice. Cut out the hands. Cover the rounded end of each hand with a thin layer of polyester fiber, then stretch a circle of nylon stocking 1″ (2.5 cm) in diameter over the cardboard. Slip the bent end of the wire at the end of the arm into the hand along the cardboard; slipstitch the top edge of the stocking to the lower edge of the arm covering.

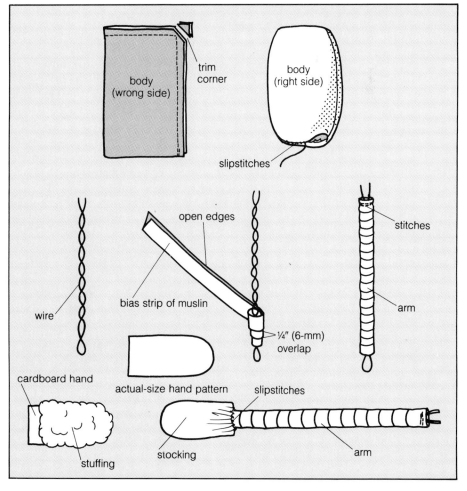

body (wrong side)

trim corner

body (right side)

slipstitches

wire

open edges

bias strip of muslin

¼″ (6-mm) overlap

stitches

arm

cardboard hand

stuffing

actual-size hand pattern

stocking

slipstitches

arm

The head, features, and hair

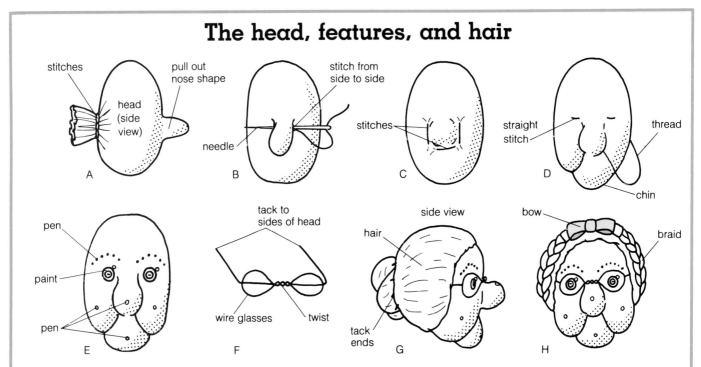

1. **The Head.** Wrap a small, firm ball of polyester fiber stuffing in a 5"-square (12.7-cm) piece of nylon stocking. Twist the stocking edges together and stitch them securely with a large needle and heavy white thread; with the thumb and forefinger, twist and pull out a nose shape on the smooth front side of the head just below the center (A). Stitch through the nose two or three times near the top (B); then stitch along each side and lower edge of the nose, running the needle entirely through the head to the back with each stitch and pulling the thread taut to make a deep depression in the face (C). Bring the needle out to the front of the face at one lower corner of the nose and wrap the thread diagonally around to the back of the head, pulling tightly to divide the cheek from the chin. Stitch through the head to the other corner of the nose and repeat (D).

2. **The Eyes.** Mark the positions for the eyes with a soft pencil: ¼" (6 mm) above each top side of the nose and ½" (13 mm) apart. Using black thread, make a tiny stitch starting and ending at the back of the head for each eye (D).

Paint a ¼" (6 mm) circle with black acrylic paint around the eye stitches. Put a dot of white paint in the center and to the left side of the black circle. Make a green dot in the center and to the right of each eye. Make an arching row of dots with a black felt-tip pen ⅛" (3 mm) above each eye for the eyebrows and a dot on each cheek and the chin for warts. Make a spot with a red felt-tip pen on the top end of the nose (E).

3. **The Glasses.** To make the glasses, form a 1" (2.5-cm) figure eight at the center of a 6" (15.2-cm) length of thin wire, and twist it at the center three times (F). Shape the glasses to the head with the loops circling the eyes and tack the ends to the sides of the head.

4. **The Hair.** Wrap synthetic hair around the top and sides of the head, stitching it in place as you go. Twist the ends together at the back to make a knot, and tack it to the head (G). Make a ¼"-wide (6-mm), 3"-long (7.6-cm) braid out of synthetic hair, and tack it on top of the head about ⅛" (3 mm) above the hairline. Tie the ¼"-wide (6-mm) gold ribbon into a bow and tack it to the center of the braid at the top of the head (H).

4. **The Legs.** To make each leg, cut a 9½" (24.2-cm) length of wire, bend it in half, and twist the halves together. To make the foot, fold ½" (13 mm) of the wire at the bent end so that it is at right angles to the rest of the leg. Cut a 1½"-wide (3.8-cm), 8"-long (20.3-cm) bias strip of blue knit fabric. Fold it in half lengthwise and, beginning ½" (13 mm) from the fold in the wire, wrap the legs as for the arms, stitching the upper end of the fabric to hold it in place.

5. **The Slippers.** Trace the actual-size patterns shown here on tracing or tissue paper. Using dressmaker's carbon and a tracing wheel, trace two slipper bottoms on dark-blue felt and two tops on gray felt. Cut out the pieces, align a top along the wide edge of each bottom and sew the edges together with white zigzag stitching or whipstitches. Glue the feet in place inside the slippers.

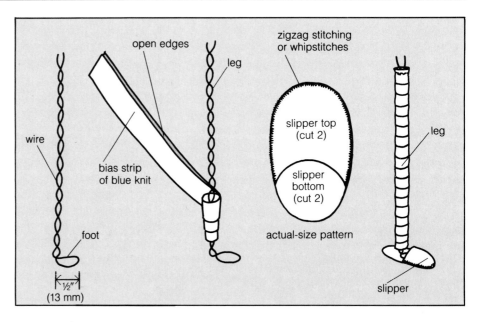

6. Attaching the Arms and Legs. Insert the inside end of the arms into the upper sides of the body, piercing the muslin with the wire ends. Whipstitch the arm wrappings to the body to hold the arms in place. Similarly, insert the top end of the legs into the lower edge of the body ½″ (13 mm) from the sides and sew the wrappings to the body.

The doll's clothes

1. The Blouse and Skirt. Make a pattern for the **blouse** on tissue or tracing paper from the diagram given. Cut one blouse piece from dark-green print, placing the center line on the fold of the fabric. Fold the blouse fabric in half, wrong side out, along the shoulder line and stitch the underarm seams. Clip the seam allowance at the corners under the arms. Turn under ¼″ (6 mm) at the ends of the sleeves and make a row of gathering stitches by hand along each edge. Turn the blouse right side out, and slip it on the body. Gather each sleeve over the edge of the hands and slipstitch the sleeve to the fabric on the hands.

The skirt. Turn under ¼″ (6 mm) of fabric along the bottom 14″-long (35.6-cm) edge of the white floral print, and stitch a band of ⅜″-wide (9.5-mm) lace along the edge of the fold on the right side of the fabric. Align the short sides, wrong side out, and stitch them together. Turn under ¼″ (6 mm) of fabric along the top of the skirt and sew it down with a row of gathering stitches. Turn the skirt right side out, and slip it on the doll over the lower edge of the blouse. Pull the gathering thread tightly around the body and secure it. Arrange the gathers evenly, and slipstitch the skirt to the body through the blouse.

2. The Apron. Turn under and stitch a ¼″ (6-mm) double hem along one 7″ (17.8-cm) edge and both 5″ (12.7-cm) edges of the red-and-white plaid apron fabric. Turn under the ends of the strip of ⅝″-wide (16-mm) lace, and stitch it to the right side of the apron along and even with the bottom edge. Make a row of gathering stitches along the top edge of the apron and gather the fabric to a length of 3″ (7.6 cm). Lap a 10″ (25.4-cm) length of yellow bias-fold tape ¼″ (6 mm) over the top edge of the apron and stitch along the bottom edges of the tape to attach it to the apron. Put the apron on the doll, and knot the sash at back.

3. Finishing the Doll. To attach the **head**, sew the lower edge securely to the center top of the blouse and body.

The shawl and scarf. Turn under and stitch a ¼″ (6-mm) hem along the long edges of the purple-and-white polka-dot and the red-print fabric triangles. Wrap the purple triangle, hem edge forward, over the woman's shoulders, around the front, and back under her arms, and knot the ends at the center of the back.

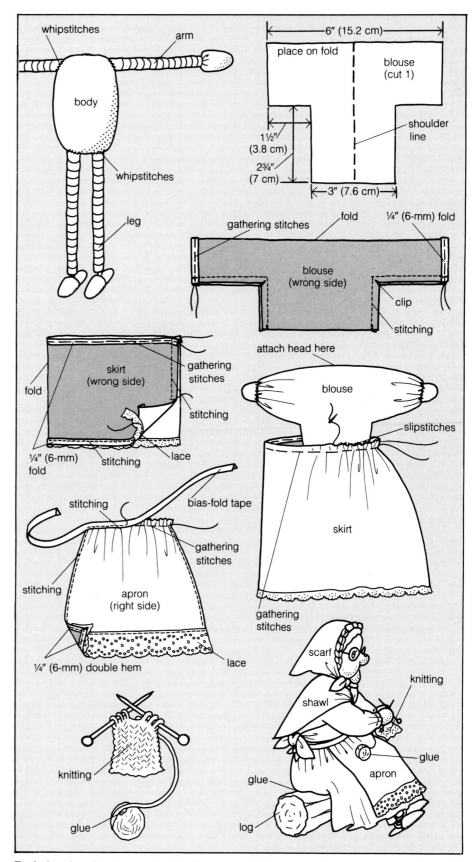

Tack the shawl to the waist. Tie the red triangle around the head and knot it under the chin.

The log. Cut off one side of the tree branch so that it lies flat. Bend the legs of the doll into a sitting position and glue her to the log.

The knitting. Using two doll-sized knitting needles, cast on about 10 stitches with lightweight yarn. Knit a 1″-long (2.5-cm) piece in the garter stitch (knit every row), stopping in the center of a row. Put a spot of glue on the ball of yarn to prevent unwinding. Tack each needle to the lower edges of a sleeve so Grandma seems to be knitting.

The doll's body

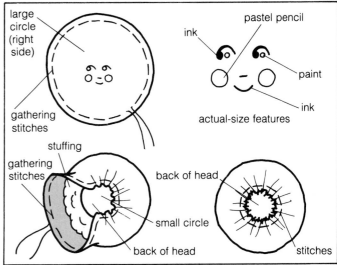

1. The Head. Cut a 2¾"-diameter (7-cm) circle and a 1" (2.5-cm) circle from the rust-colored cotton scrap. Trace the actual-size pattern for the eyes, nose, and mouth on tissue or tracing paper with a soft pencil. Turn the paper over and retrace the features, transferring them onto the right side of the large circle, with the eyes centered vertically and horizontally. Color the eyes, nose, and mouth with a black felt-tip pen. With a paintbrush, make a small dot of white paint in the center of each eye to the right of the black dot. Lightly color the cheeks with the burnt-orange pastel pencil in the areas indicated.

Make a row of gathering stitches along the edge of the large circle. Place a ball of polyester fiber stuffing on the wrong side of the face and place the small circle on top of the stuffing. Gather the large circle over the small circle and sew the circles securely together, adjusting the fabric and the stuffing so that the head is round and very firm and the face is centered on one side of the head.

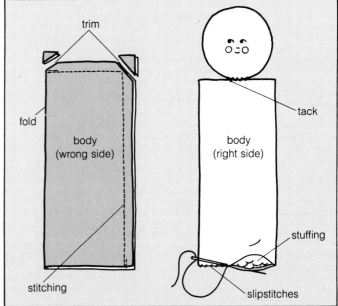

2. The Torso. Fold the red cotton fabric in half lengthwise, wrong side out, and stitch the long side and one short side closed, leaving a ¼" (6-mm) seam allowance. Trim the closed corners. Turn the body right side out and stuff it firmly with polyester fiber. Turn under ¼" (6 mm) of fabric along the open edges and slipstitch them together. Center the bottom of the head at the other end of the torso and tack it in place.

Peruvian Girl

Materials

A 4" × 6" (10.2 × 15.2-cm) piece of rust-colored cotton
A fine-point black felt-tip pen
White acrylic paint
A small paintbrush
A burnt-orange pastel pencil
Sewing thread: rust, black, and white
Polyester fiber for stuffing
A 3" × 3½" (7.6 × 8.9-cm) piece of red cotton fabric
A scrap of rust felt
A scrap of cardboard
Two 4½" (11.4-cm) lengths of wire
White glue
4 or 5 yards (3.6 or 4.6 m)

black knitting worsted
A 4¾" × 12" (12.1 × 30.5-cm) piece of white crinoline
A 1" × 12" (2.5 × 30.5-cm) strip of yellow felt
A 1" × 12" (2.5 × 30.5-cm) strip of orange felt
A 2¾" × 12" (7 × 30.5-cm) piece of blue felt
1 yard (.91 m) burnt-orange yarn
A scrap of coarse-weave cotton fabric with varicolored random-width stripes
A 2½" (6.4-cm) square of white felt

The doll's clothes

1. The Feet and Legs. Trace the actual-size pattern given here for the foot on tissue or tracing paper. Use the pattern to cut two feet from rust felt and two feet (the soles) from cardboard.

Cut the 9" (22.9-cm) length of wire in half. Bend ½" (13 mm) at one end of each piece of wire to form a right angle. Push a wire through the dot on each felt foot section. Cover the top of each cardboard sole with white glue, and attach the cardboard to the bottom of the felt pieces, with the ends of the wires between them as shown.

Cut two 1" × 4" (2.5 × 10.2-cm) pieces of rust-colored cotton for the legs. Press under ¼" (6 mm) on both short (1" or 2.5-cm) ends of each piece. Fold each leg in half lengthwise, right sides together, and stitch the open side closed, making a ¼" (6-mm) seam allowance. Trim the seam and turn the leg right side out. Slip the legs down over the wire. Glue the bottom of the fabric leg to the top of the foot. Insert the wires protruding from the tops of the legs into the lower edge of the body ¼" (6 mm) from the side of the body, and whipstitch the fabric tops of the legs securely to the body.

2. The Skirt and Underskirts. Cut the piece of white crinoline into one 2½" × 12" (6.4 × 30.5-cm) strip and one 2¼" × 12" (5.7 × 30.5-cm) strip to make the underskirts. Place the yellow felt strip along the bottom edge of the wider strip, overlapping it ½" (13 mm), and stitch them together. Sew the orange felt strip to the narrower strip of crinoline in the same manner. Work one row of herringbone stitches with burnt-orange yarn just in from one long edge of the blue felt piece for the skirt. One at a time, fold the skirt and the underskirts in half, end to end and right sides together; stitch the short edges together, leaving a scant ¼" (6-mm) seam allowance. Turn each one right side out. Place one skirt over the other: the yellow-trimmed underskirt over the orange-trimmed underskirt and the blue skirt on top, aligning the top edges of all three. With a doubled thread, sew a row of gathering stitches by hand through all three thicknesses along the top edges. Slip the skirts on the doll, gather the top edges to fit the center of the body, and secure the thread. Sew the skirts to the body at the waist.

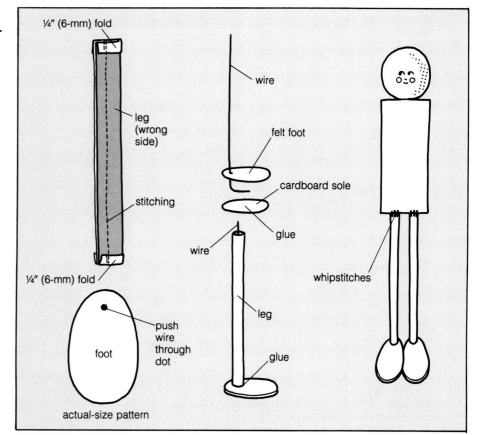

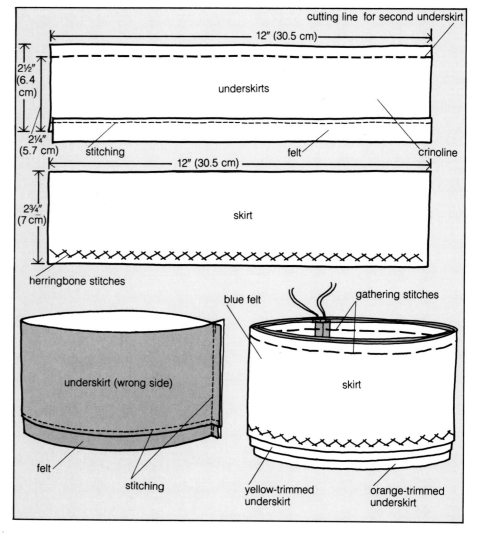

3. The Hair. Starting at the bottom of the back of the neck, begin looping black yarn back and forth across the head, all the way to each side and all the way to the top, anchoring it with stitches at each side as you go. Clip the yarn. Cut ten 8″ (20.3-cm) lengths of black yarn. Lay them across the head from side to side, in parallel fashion, beginning ⅜″ (9.5 mm) above the eyes, and continuing back about 1″ (2.5 cm); anchor them at the center with backstitches. Smooth the hair over the sides of the head, and tack it to the head in a bunch even with the mouth. Divide the hair into three sections on each side, and make a braid about 1¼″ (3.2 cm) long. Tie the end of each braid with a length of orange yarn, and trim the ends to ½″ (13 mm). Trim the ends of the yarn ties to ¼″ (6 mm).

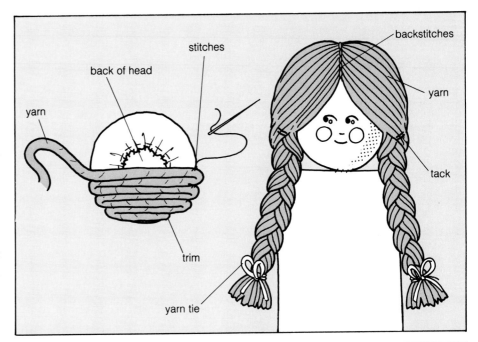

4. The Shawl and Hat. To make the **shawl,** cut a 3¼″ × 9½″ (8.3 × 24.2-cm) bias strip from the coarse-weave cotton fabric. Trim the short sides at an angle to make the shorter of the long edges 7½″ (19.1 cm), as shown in the drawing. Pull one or two threads along the longer edge to form a fringe, turn under ½″ (13 mm) along the shortened edge, and wrap the shawl around the doll's shoulders with the turned edge up; cross the ends of the shawl and tack them in place.

The hat. Cut a 2¼″-diameter (5.7-cm) circle from white felt. Make a row of gathering stitches ¼″ (6 mm) from the edge. Gather the stitches to make a hat with a slightly ruffled brim and secure the thread. Tack the hat to the head. Tie a 4″ (10.2-cm) length of black yarn around the hat for a band, and tack the yarn to the hat.

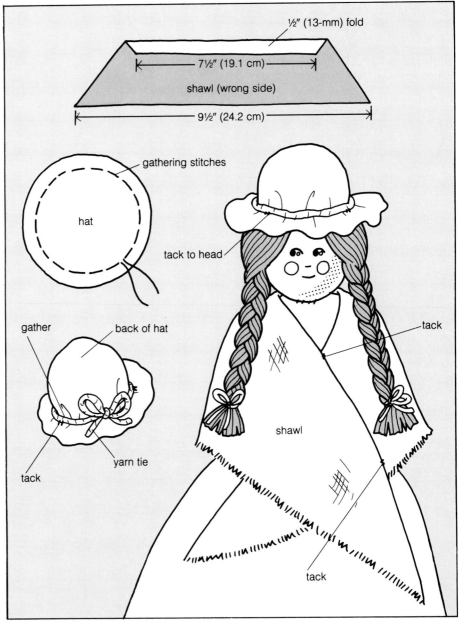

130

A Colleen from Kildare

Materials

Knitting worsted:
approximately 35 yards
(32 m) each of dark brown,
burnt orange, loden green,
natural (off-white), and
oatmeal
1 pair size 5 knitting needles,
or whatever size gives

correct gauge
Polyester fiber for stuffing
Heavy-duty thread to match
yarn: burnt orange, loden
green, and oatmeal
Gauge: 8 stitches = 2″
(5 cm); 6 rows = 1″
(2.5 cm)

The doll's body

1. The Body. Using dark-brown yarn, cast on 30 stitches, and work *Rows 1-4* in the stockinette stitch (knit 1 row, purl 1 row). (Use the stockinette stitch throughout unless otherwise directed.) *Rows 5-6:* Cut the yarn, and tie on burnt orange. *Rows 7-25:* Use loden green. *Rows 26-27:* Use burnt orange. *Rows 28-29:* Use natural. *Rows 30-31:* Use burnt orange. *Rows 32-33:* Use natural. *Rows 34-35:* Use burnt orange. *Rows 36-37:* Use natural. *Rows 38-39:* Use burnt orange. *Rows 40-41:* Use natural. *Rows 42-50:* Use oatmeal. *Row 51:* Knit 1 and knit 2 together across (there will be 20 stitches on the needle). *Row 52:* Purl across. *Row 53:* Knit 1 and knit 2 together six times, then knit 2 (14 stitches). *Row 54:* Purl across. *Row 55:* Knit 2 together across (7 stitches). Cut the oatmeal yarn, leaving a 12″ (30.5-cm) end.

Finishing the body. Thread an embroidery needle with the 12″ (30.5-cm) end of the oatmeal yarn. Carefully slip the seven remaining stitches off the knitting onto another knitting needle. Beginning with the outside stitch that is not attached to the

end of the oatmeal yarn, thread the yarn end through the seven stitches with the embroidery needle, and pull it tightly to close the top of the head. Using the same strand of oatmeal yarn, sew the head together down the center back. Change to burnt-orange yarn, and sew together the striped chest section. Then sew the legs and feet together with the appropriate yarns, leaving the seam open across the bottom of the doll.

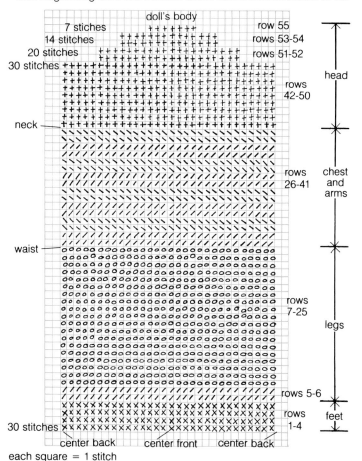

each square = 1 stitch

+ oatmeal
\ natural
/ burnt orange
o loden green
x dark brown

The features and hair

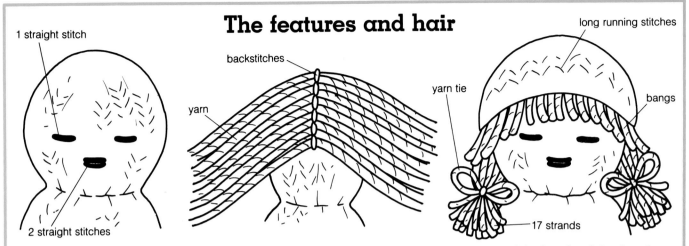

1 straight stitch

2 straight stitches

backstitches

yarn

long running stitches

yarn tie

bangs

17 strands

neckline

side fold
(for arms)

stitches for arms

waistline

stitches for legs

1. The Features. Using dark-brown yarn and an embroidery needle for the features and starting and stopping at the back of the head, make a straight stitch for each eye, and two parallel straight stitches for the mouth, as shown.

2. The Hair. Cut twenty-five 9" (22.9-cm) lengths of burnt-orange yarn. Lay each strand of hair across the top of the head from side to side with the strands close together, and stitch them along the center of the head with backstitches. Tie the back seventeen strands of hair on each side of the head into ponytails with a bow of loden-green yarn at the neckline level. Leave the remaining front strands loose for bangs. Put the hat on the head and baste it in place with loden-green thread, using long running stitches. Trim the bangs to frame the face.

2. The Doll's Hat. Cast on 28 stitches, and work the hat in the stockinette stitch (chart, page 131). *Rows 1-3:* Use loden green. *Row 4:* Use burnt orange. *Row 5:* Use natural (off-white). *Rows 6-7:* Use loden green. *Row 8:* Use natural. *Row 9:* Use burnt orange. *Row 10:* Use loden green. *Row 11:* Knit 2 together and knit 1 seven times, knit 2 together twice (18 stitches). *Row 12:* Purl across. *Row 13:* Knit 1 and knit 2 together across (12 stitches). *Row 14:* Purl across. *Row 15:* Knit 2 together across (6 stitches). Cut the yarn, leaving a 10" (25.4-cm) end.

Finishing the hat. Thread an embroidery needle with the 10" (25.4-cm) end of loden-green yarn, and close the top of the hat as you did the top of the head. With the same strand of yarn, sew the side opening of the hat together, being careful to match the stripes.

3. Stuffing the Doll. Starting and ending at the center-back seam, make a row of running stitches around the neckline with doubled oatmeal thread, leaving both ends of the yarn long. Stuff the head firmly with polyester fiber. Gather the neckline along the yarn until the neck is about 1½" (3.8 cm) in diameter. Knot and tie the threads, and pull them to the wrong side.

Outline the arms as follows: With the center-back seam and center-front line together, mark with contrasting thread the four vertical rows of stitches on each side of the chest (two rows from the front, two from the back on each side). With burnt-orange thread, stitch the front and back together, running down the "ditches" between the arm and chest rows from the first orange stripe below the neckline to the waistline, using backstitches or close running stitches. Knot the thread securely and pull it to the wrong side. Repeat this procedure for the other arm.

Stuff the chest and the legs; the stuffing need not be very firm. Sew the bottom of the feet closed from one side to the other with dark-brown yarn.

Make the legs as follows: Separate the stuffing below the waist evenly on each side, or leg. Beginning four rows below the waist with loden-green yarn, stitch the center-back (seam) and center-front lines together, ending the stitches at the stripe of burnt orange.

Czech Couple

Materials

1/8 yard (11.4 cm) dark-natural
  or light-natural linen
Pastel pencils: charcoal, pink
Sewing thread: to match all fabrics
Polyester fiber for stuffing
10/1 denier linen thread
  (available in weaving-supply
  stores) or Knit-cro-sheen, to
  match the natural linen
No. 5 red pearl cotton
A 4" × 11" (10.2 × 27.9-cm)
  piece of lightweight cardboard
A 13" × 16" (33.1 × 40.6-cm)
  piece of navy-and-white
  polka-dot fabric
An 8" × 13" (20.3 × 33.1-cm)
  piece of white cotton fabric
A 7" (17.8-cm) square of
  white linen
A 14" (35.6-cm) length of
  white twine
2 sheets of medium-weight
  8½" × 11" (21.6 × 27.9-cm)
  paper

The dolls' bodies

1. Cutting the Fabric. Enlarge the patterns to the scale indicated and cut them out, following the directions on page 155. Using the patterns, cut the following from folded natural linen: four bodies, eight legs, and eight arms.

2. The Bodies. For each doll, stitch two body pieces right sides together, leaving the bottom and areas between dots open. Clip the seam allowances on the curves, turn the body right side out.

The arms. Stitch two arm sections right sides together for each arm, leaving the straight end open. Clip the seam allowances along the curves and at the corner of the thumb. Turn each arm right side out, and stuff it firmly with polyester fiber, but leave it somewhat flat near the opening. Insert the arms ¼" (6 mm) into the side openings of the body, thumbs up, with the body seam allowances turned in, and pin through all the layers. Stitch the arms in place along the edges of the bodies. Stuff the bodies firmly.

The legs. Stitch two leg sections right sides together for each leg, leaving the straight end open. Clip the seam allowances along the curves, and turn the leg right side out. Stuff as for the arms, leaving the upper end somewhat flat. Fold ¼" (6 mm) of fabric under along the lower edge of each body. Aligning the center-front and -back seams at the top of each leg, insert the legs about ¼" (6 mm) into the lower edge of the body, and pin. Stitch the legs in place.

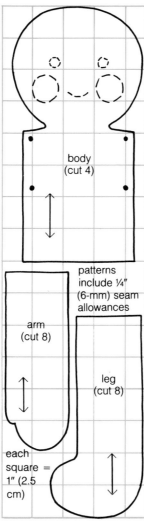

body
(cut 4)

patterns
include ¼"
(6-mm) seam
allowances

arm
(cut 8)

leg
(cut 8)

each
square =
1" (2.5
cm)

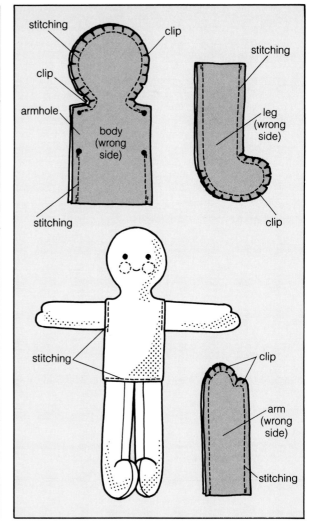

stitching

clip

clip

stitching

armhole

body
(wrong
side)

leg
(wrong
side)

clip

stitching

stitching

clip

arm
(wrong
side)

stitching

The features and hair

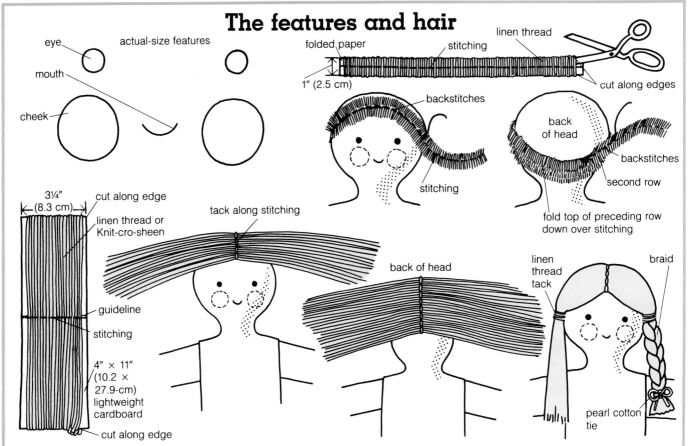

1. The Features. Trace the actual-size patterns for the features on tracing or tissue paper with a soft pencil. Turn the paper over and retrace the features, transferring them onto the faces. Following the patterns, draw the eyes and mouth with the charcoal pastel pencil, and make rosy cheeks with the pink pastel pencil.

2. The Girl's Hair. Draw a line across the 4″ × 11″ (10.2 × 27.9-cm) cardboard piece centered between the two short ends. Wind linen thread or Knit-cro-sheen lengthwise around the cardboard 300 times, with the threads close together in an evenly distributed 3¼″-wide (8.3-cm) bundle. Stitch carefully across the threads, using the centered line as a guide. Cut the threads along both edges of the cardboard, then gently tear the cardboard away.

Place the hair across the head from side to side so that the line of stitching starts ¾″ (19 mm) below the center of the head seam and goes over the top of the head, ending at the center back. Tack the hair to the head along the line of stitching, and smooth the hair to the sides. With a needle and linen thread or Knit-cro-sheen, tack the hair to the

sides of the head. Divide each side of the hair into three equal sections and make braids 1½″ (3.9 cm) long. Tie the ends of the braids with red pearl cotton, and trim the ends of the braids even ½″ (13 mm) below the ties.

3. The Boy's Hair. Cut five 2″ × 11″ (5 × 27.9-cm) strips from the sheets of paper, and fold each strip in half lengthwise. Wrap linen thread or Knit-cro-sheen crosswise around each folded strip from one end to the other, with the threads very close together. Stitch lengthwise along the center of each strip of paper, through the linen threads. Cut the loops of thread along each long edge of the paper, and gently tear the paper away.

Attach the first strip of hair around the head with backstitches, as shown in the drawing, starting along the hairline on the forehead ½″ (13 mm) below the head seam. Fold the ends of hair above the line of stitching down over the stitching, and attach the next strip of hair ¼″ (6 mm) above the first. Continue attaching strips of hair in concentric rows, ¼″ (6 mm) apart, around the head, spiraling inward until the center back of the head is covered.

The dolls' clothes

1. Cutting the Fabric. Enlarge the patterns to the scale indicated, and cut them out, following the directions on page 155. Using the patterns, cut the girl's dress from navy-and-white polka-dot fabric folded twice, placing the shoulder and center edges along the folds. Cut the boy's shirt from white cotton fabric, placing the shoulder and center edges along the folds. For the boy's pants, cut the white linen square in half to make two pieces, each measuring 3½″ × 7″ (8.8 × 17.5 cm).

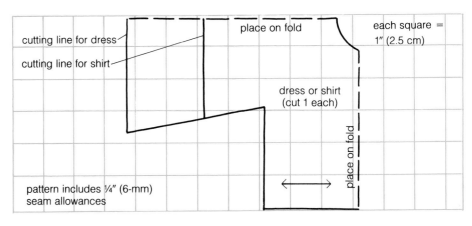

2. The Dress and Shirt. Stitch around the neck edge of the dress and shirt a scant ¼″ (6 mm) from the edge. Clip the seam allowances every ¾″ (19 mm) around the neck, and press them to the wrong side. Then stitch ⅛″ (3 mm) from the edge of the neck, along the fold.

Turn under ¼″ (6 mm) along the ends of the sleeves, then fold another ¼″ (6 mm) to the wrong side, and stitch the hem in place. With the wrong sides out, align the underarm and side edges, and stitch the seams. Clip to the corner of the underarm, press the seam allowances open, and turn the dress or shirt right side out. Make a ¼″ (6-mm) double hem along the bottom of the garment as you did for the sleeves.

Finishing the dress and shirt. Work large buttonhole stitches, about ¼″ (6 mm) deep and 3/16″ (5 mm) apart, around the neck edge with red pearl cotton.

The tie. To make the tie, cut two 40″ (101.6-cm) lengths of pearl cotton; hold them parallel, and knot them together at both ends. Hold one end and twist the other end until the tie starts to buckle. Hold the knotted ends together and let the halves twist around each other. Knot all the threads together 1″ (2.6 cm) from each end, and cut the looped end open. Thread the tie under every other buttonhole stitch along the neck edge, beginning and ending at the center front.

Slip the shirt on the boy and the dress on the girl, pull the ties snug, and make bows with the ends of the ties.

3. The Boy's Pants. Make a ¼″ (6-mm) fringe at the lower end of each pant leg by pulling out the horizontal threads, one at a time. Fold each pants section in half lengthwise, wrong side out, and seam it starting at the fringed bottom end and ending 3″ (7.6 cm) from the top edge. Clip the seam allowances at the ends of the two openings, and then press them open.

Turn the pants sections right side out; align the seams and free edges above them, and stitch the pants sections together, forming the crotch seam. Clip the seam allowances at the crotch, and press them open. Turn under ¾″ (19 mm) of fabric along the top edge of the pants and stitch a hem. Slip the pants on the boy over the shirt, and make pleated folds around the waist to fit the doll's body. Knot both ends of the twine, then tie it around the waist, making a bow at the front to hold the pants in place.

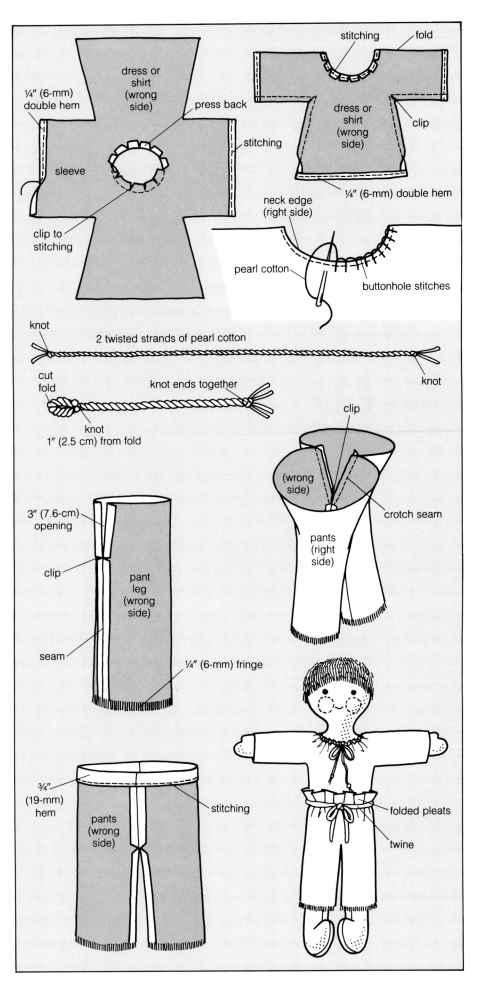

135

Gretel

Materials

A doll's head, about 4½" to 5" (11.4 to 12.7 cm) long from the base of the neck to the top of the head
Petroleum jelly
Wheat paste (available in hardware stores)
Two 10" (25.4-cm) squares of thin cotton-knit fabric
½ yard (45.7 cm) pale-orange or cream-colored felt
White glue
Acrylic paints: white, blue, red, black, and light brown
2 paintbrushes: one for apply the glue, the other very fine with stiff bristles for painting the features
Sewing thread: to match the fabrics, felt, and hair
Polyester fiber for stuffing
An 8.8-ounce (250-gram) cone of light-yellow linen thread, size 4 (available in weaving supply stores)
A 5" × 7" (12.7 × 17.8-cm) piece of heavy paper
A 3" × 20" (7.6 × 50.8-cm) piece of cardboard
⅜ yard (34.3 cm) white cotton fabric
⅜ yard (34.3 cm) red felt
A 9" × 18" (22.9 × 45.7-cm) piece of black felt
¾ yard (68.7 cm) ⅛"-wide (3-mm) elastic
1 yard (91.4 cm) of 1"-wide (2.5-cm) white lace
5 snaps
Light-blue embroidery floss
A 7" (17.8-cm) length of ½"-wide (13-mm) white lace
1 hook and eye
¼ yard (22.9 cm) of ⅞"-wide (22-mm) red embroidered trimming
Five ⁷⁄₁₆"-diameter (11-mm) silver or black embossed decorative buttons

The doll's head

1. Molding the Head. Choose a ceramic or bisque doll's head with well-defined features and no hair, to use as a mold for the felt head. (Inexpensive new dolls are available in toy shops, and used dolls can be found for reasonable prices in thrift shops.) The felt face will not pick up all the detail of the face being used as a mold, and will tend to have smoother features. A doll with a small button nose is not suitable. A plastic head can also be used, but plastic is more likely to be gouged when the felt mask is pried off. Begin work on the head at least four days before you plan to complete the doll, which will allow time for the head to dry between steps. Meanwhile, you can start constructing the doll's body and clothes if you wish.

Coat the front half of the mold head thickly with petroleum jelly. Mix three tablespoons of wheat paste with water so that it has the consistency of thin cream. Dip a 10" (25.4-cm) square of cotton knit fabric into the paste, and let the excess run off. Brush off any excess paste with your fingers. Drape the wet fabric over the doll's face so the lengthwise grain runs along the axis from the top of the head to the neck.

Beginning at the nose, smooth the fabric over the face and the front of the head. Press the fabric into the eye sockets and the indentations around the nose and mouth. Slit the fabric at the base of the neck and stretch it upward and outward from the chin and neck area to eliminate any wrinkles.

You may have to cut the edges along the neck and the top of the head, forming darts in the fabric to keep it smooth. Cut along the base of the darts to remove the excess fabric. The edges of the slits should just meet. Trim off any excess fabric around the head, and make sure the fabric is still in place around the eyes, nose, and mouth. Carefully move the head to a safe place and let it dry completely; this will take between twelve and twenty-four hours, depending on the humidity.

When the fabric has dried, cut a 10" (25.4-cm) square of pale orange or cream-colored felt, and soak it in a bowl of warm water for a few minutes. Mix about one tablespoon (14.5 ml) each of white glue and water in a cup. Brush a thin, even coating of the glue over the knit fabric on the head. Then squeeze the excess moisture from the felt and place it over the knit fabric, stretching and smoothing the felt over the face as you did the fabric.

Trim off the excess felt around the head, as you did for the knit fabric, and slit it at the base of the neck. Before removing gathers or darts of excess fabric from the top and sides of the head, be sure to first stretch the felt firmly back over the head. The few small puckers remaining will be covered by the hair.

When the felt is in place, brush another thin, even coating of glue all over it. Return the head to the safe place. When the felt is thoroughly dry, care-

Making the head

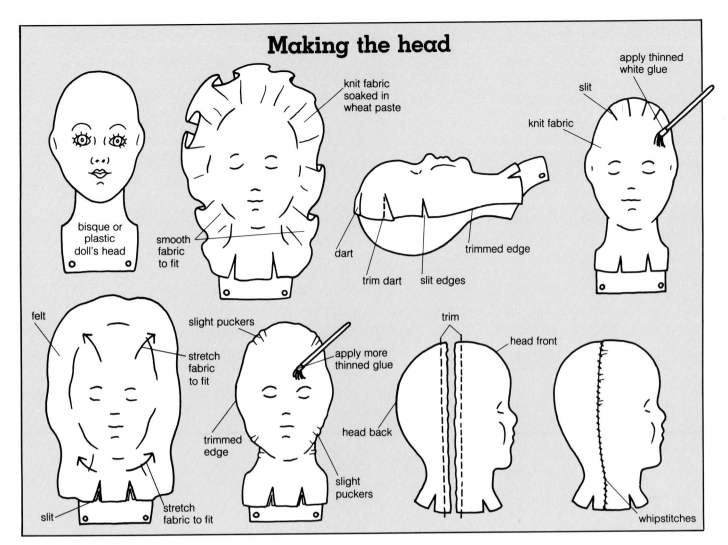

fully loosen the molded face by inserting a blunt table knife under the knit fabric layer and gently working it loose from the form. Coat the inside of the head with glue for added stiffness, and put it aside to dry.

Wash the mold head to remove the petroleum jelly and wheat paste. Then, make the back of the head, following the same basic procedure described for the front of the head.

2. Joining the Head Pieces. Trim the two molded halves of the head so they will fit together, using the original head as a guide. The seam should be just behind the ears. With a fine needle and dou-

bled thread, whipstitch the halves of the head together, beginning at the top center. Work carefully; the felt may be brittle. Stuff the head and neck area with polyester fiber until firm. Trim the neck so it extends about 1¼" (3.2 cm) below the jaw lines. Put the head aside until the body has been finished.

The doll's body

1. Cutting the Body Fabric. Enlarge the body patterns to the scale indicated and cut them out, following the directions on page 155. Using the patterns, cut the body front and back and the top; two body sides; two foot soles; four arms; and four legs—all from pale-orange or cream-colored felt. Transfer the markings indicated on the patterns to the fabric pieces.

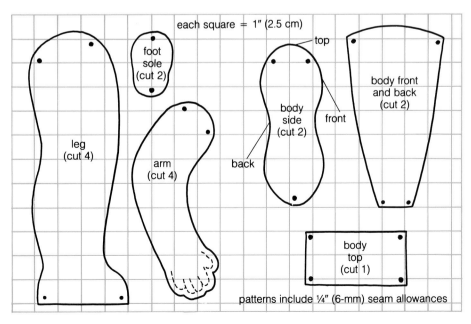

2. The Body. Align the top edges of the body front and back pieces with the sides of the body top, right sides together, and join them. Stitch the bottom edges of the front and back together. Press open the seam allowances. Matching the dots, pin the sides to the body; clip into the seam allowance 1/8" (3 mm) along the edge of the front and back as needed to fit the curves. Stitch the seams, leaving a 2½" (6.4-cm) opening at the back of one side. Turn the body right side out, stuff it with polyester fiber until firm, and slipstitch it closed.

3. The Arms and Legs. Align the edges of the **arm** pieces right sides together, and join them, leaving an opening between the dots at the top end; follow the outline of the hand, not the lines between the fingers. Trim the seam allowances around the fingers, and clip them around the fingers and in the inner curves of the arm. Turn the arm right side out. Repeat for the other arm.

Stuff both arms firmly, but use less stuffing in the hands so that they remain somewhat flat. Turn under the seam allowance along the open edge of each arm, and slipstitch closed. To make the fingers, sew three equidistant lines of tiny backstitches at the end of each hand (indicated by the pattern markings) through both thicknesses of fabric.

The legs. Align the edges of two leg pieces right sides together, and join them, leaving openings between the dots at the top and bottom. Clip the seam allowances at the inner curves, and press them open. Pin the back of a foot sole to the back of the leg, right sides together, matching the dots. Clip the seam allowance on the leg edge as needed to fit the curve of the sole as you pin them together. Stitch the edges together. Turn the leg right side out and stuff it firmly. Turn the seam allowance under at the top end of the leg, and slipstitch the opening closed. Repeat to make the other leg.

4. Attaching the Arms, Legs, and Head. Place each **arm** along the side of the body so the tops of the arm and body are aligned and the thumb is pointed

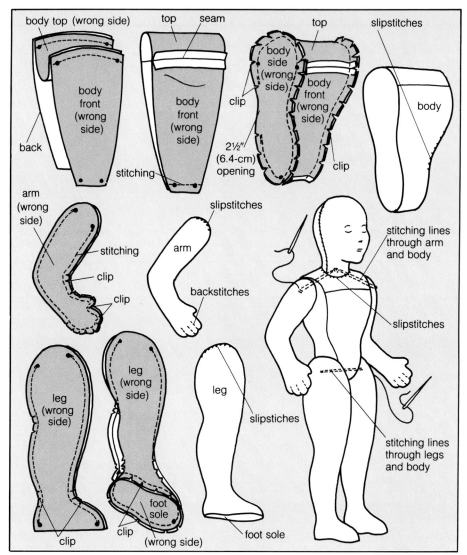

forward. With a long needle and doubled thread, sew through the center of the arms ½" (13 mm) below the top seam, then diagonally up through the body to the center of the top. Stitch back and forth between each arm and the top of the body several times to hold the arm securely. Knot the thread.

The legs. Position a leg at each side of the lower body, with the foot facing forward. Again with a long needle and doubled thread, sew through the cen-

ters of the legs and the body, about ¾" (19 mm) below the top of the legs and ¾" (19 mm) above the bottom of the body. Sew back and forth through both legs several times to join the legs securely to the body. Knot the thread.

The head. Bend under about ½" (13 mm) around the bottom edge of the head, shaping the edge to fit the curve of the body. Slipstitch the head to the body at the top center, sewing completely around the edge of the neck.

The doll's clothes

1. Cutting the Fabric. Enlarge the patterns for the clothes to the scale indicated and cut them out, following the directions on page 155. Then cut the clothes from the fabrics given below, using the patterns or the dimensions listed. Transfer any pattern markings to the appropriate fabric pieces.

From folded white cotton fabric cut one blouse front and two blouse backs; also cut a 1" × 15" (2.5 × 38-cm) bias strip for the blouse, an 8" × 9" (20.3 × 22.9-cm) piece for the apron, and a 4½" × 21" (11.4 × 53-cm) rectangle for the

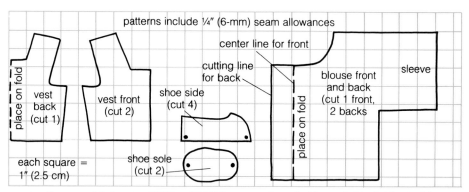

pants. From red felt cut a 10¼" × 27" (26 × 68.6-cm) section for the skirt and a 1½" × 11" (3.8 × 27.9-cm) piece for the

waistband. From folded black felt cut one vest back two vest fronts, four shoe sides, and two shoe soles.

The features and hair

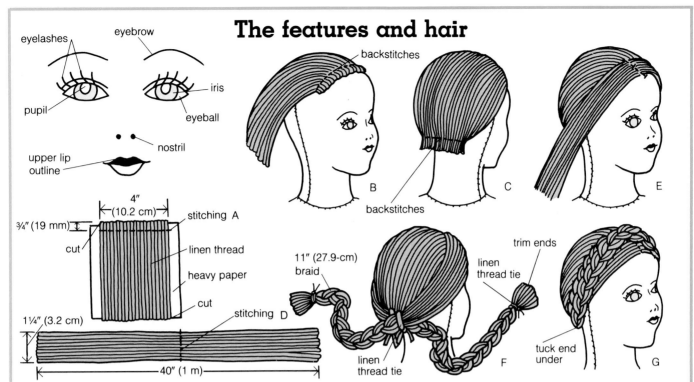

1. The Features. Lightly pencil the features on the face, following the drawing. Paint the eyeballs white, irises blue, and pupils black, letting each color dry before using the next. Make a thin light-brown line for each eyelid, then paint the lashes. Make thin light-brown lines for the brows. Mix red and white to paint the lips and nostrils pale pink. Lightly rub a small amount of pale-pink shading on the cheeks with your finger. Outline the top of the lips with a darker shade of pink.

2. The Hair. The center-front hairline should be about 1″ (2.5 cm) above the eyebrow line and the back hairline about 1″ (2.5 cm) above the chin line. Measure the distance over the center of the head between the front and back hairlines; then cut a piece of heavy paper 1½″ (3.8 cm) shorter than this distance by about 5″ (12.7 cm) wide. Wind yellow linen thread around the paper about 200 times to make a bundle about 4″ (10.2 cm) wide of tightly spaced loops across the 5″ (12.7-cm) side of the paper. Stitch through the thread and the paper ¾″ (19 mm) from one end. Cut through the thread along both edges of the paper, and gently tear the paper away from the stitching (A).

Center the hair on the head with the stitching 1½″ (3.8 cm) behind the front hairline; attach the front of the hair to the head with large backstitches along the row of stitching

(B). Arrange the hair over the top of the head, and attach it to the back of the head securely with long backstitches 1″ (2.5 cm) above the back hairline. Trim the bottom ends of the hair about ½″ (13 mm) below the stitching (C).

To make braids, wrap linen thread around a 20″ (50.8-cm) piece of cardboard eighty times. Hold the strands together at one end of the cardboard and cut the thread along the other. Compress the thread at the center so that it is about 1¼″ (3.2 cm) wide, and stitch across it (D). Cut four 8″ (20.3-cm) lengths of thread for ties. With straight pins, anchor the hair through the stitching to the center front of the head at the hairline, overlapping the front ends of the other hair (E). Working first on one side, then the other, drape the hair around the head and tie the strands of each side separately at the center back. Place one side above the other, and pin both to the head, covering the bottom ends of the other hair. Braid each side for about 11″ (27.9 cm). Tie the ends with matching thread, and trim the ends 1″ (2.5 cm) from the ties (F). Bring the braids over the top of the head, crossing them at the center front and tucking the ends under the opposite braid. With a needle and doubled thread, secure the braids to the head, through the hair underneath, and to each other (G). (This doll's hair should never be treated roughly.)

2. The Pants. Turn under ¼″ (6 mm) of fabric twice on each long edge of the pants section, and stitch along the edge of the inner fold to make a casing at the top and a hem at the bottom. Use a small safety pin or bodkin to thread a 9″ (22.9-cm) length of elastic through the casing. Tack the ends of the elastic at both ends of the casing. Fold the pants in half right sides together, align the short edges, and join them. Turn the pants right side out, and centering the seam down the front, tack the front hem to the back for ¼″ (6 mm) on both sides of the seam for leg openings.

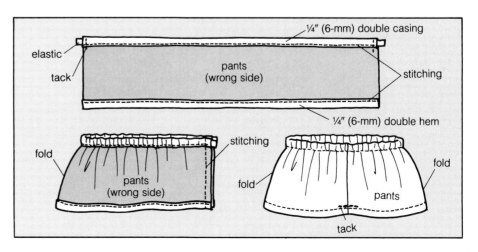

3. The Blouse. Make a ½″ (13-mm) double hem along the center edge of each back section. With right sides together, stitch the backs to the front along the shoulder edges, and press the seam allowances open (A). Place the right side of the white bias strip along the wrong side of the neck edge so that ½″ (13 mm) of the strip extends beyond the neck opening. Stitch them together close to the neck edge. Fold the bias strip over the seam allowances to the right side, and turn under a scant ¼″ (6 mm) of fabric along the free edge. Turn the ends of the strip in even with the edges of the back opening, and stitch around the neck along the lower edge of the bias strip to make a casing. Make a ¼″ (6-mm) double hem along the end of each sleeve, stitching along the inner edge of the hem to form a casing. Make a narrow rolled hem at both ends of a 16″ (40.6-cm) length of 1″-wide (2.5-cm) lace, and sew the lace to the neck casing as close as possible to the edge. Insert a 7″ (17.8-cm) length of elastic in the casing and tack the ends at the ends of the casing. Sew an 8″ (20.3-cm) length of 1″-wide (2.5-cm) lace to the edge of each sleeve casing. Insert a 3½″ (8.9-cm) length of elastic in each sleeve casing, and tack the ends at the ends of the casing (B). Align the underarm and side edges, right sides together, and join them. Clip the seam allowances at the inner corners, and press them open. Make a ¼″ (6-mm) double hem along the bottom of the blouse (C). Sew snaps to the top edges of the neck binding and 3″ (7.6 cm) down the back opening.

4. The Apron. Draw light pencil lines ¾″ (19 mm) apart lengthwise along the wrong side of the apron, beginning 1″ (2.5 cm) from one side. From the wrong side, make rows of alternating long and short running stitches along the pencil lines with blue embroidery floss so that the larger stitches are on the right side of the fabric. Make a double ¼″ (6-mm) hem along both 9″ (22.9-cm) sides and along the bottom edge. Sew the ½″-wide (13-mm) lace to the apron just above the bottom edge. Make a row of gathering stitches ¼″ (6 mm) from the top edge of the apron, and gather to a width of 3¾″ (9.5 cm). Put the apron aside.

5. The Skirt. Align the short ends of the skirt fabric right sides together, and join them, leaving 2″ (5 cm) open at the top edge. Turn under a ½″ (13-mm) hem along the lower edge, and stitch the hem in place. Make a row of gathering stitches along the top edge of the skirt by hand. Gather the top of the skirt evenly to match the length of the waistband. Place the waistband, right side down, against the wrong side of the skirt, and align the top edges. Stitch them together ½″ (13 mm) from the top.

With the skirt seam centered at the back, baste the apron to the center front of the skirt with the top edges even. Fold

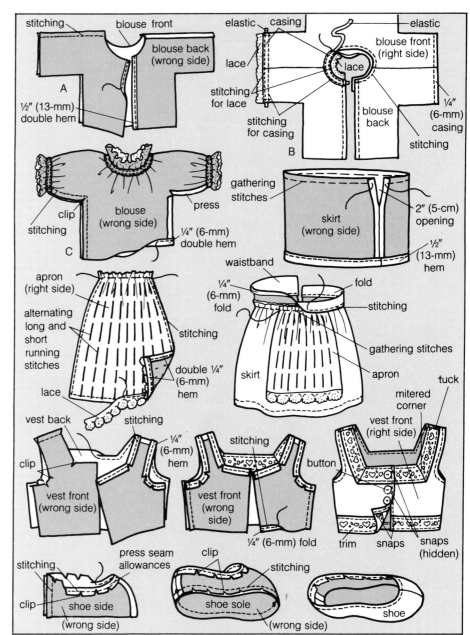

the waistband over the top edge of the skirt and apron, turn under ¼″ (6 mm) along the edge, and pin. Then stitch along the ends and the lower edge of the waistband, through the apron and skirt. Put the blouse and skirt on the doll, overlap the ends of the waistband so that the skirt is snug, and join the ends of the waistband with a hook and eye.

6. The Vest. With right sides together, stitch the vest front pieces to the back at the shoulders. Fold ¼″ (6 mm) of fabric to the wrong side along the neck and armhole edges, clipping into the seam allowance at the corners and along the curves. Stitch the folds in place. Turn the vest right side out. Pin, then stitch the decorative trim to the neck edges, mitering the corners and making tucks in it at the shoulder seams.

With right sides together, stitch the back to the front pieces at the sides. Turn up ¼″ (6 mm) of fabric along the bottom edge of the vest, and stitch. Place a strip of trim along the bottom edge of the vest

and stitch it in place around all four sides. Turn under ¼″ (6 mm) of felt and trim along both front edges and stitch in place. Lap the right side over the left; sew three snaps, evenly spaced from top to bottom, so that the vest fits snugly. Sew five buttons evenly spaced along the outside edge of the right side.

7. The Shoes. For each shoe, stitch two shoe sides together along the front and back ends with the right sides together. Press the seam allowances open. Press ¼″ (6 mm) of fabric along the top edge of the shoe toward the wrong side, clipping ⅛″ (3 mm) into the seam allowance along the curves; stitch the fold in place. With the right sides together, pin the sole to the sides, aligning the edges and matching the dots. Clip the edge of the sides ⅛″ (3 mm), if necessary, to fit the curves of the sole. Stitch the sole and sides together and turn the shoe right side out. Slip the shoes on the doll, and tack them to the feet at two or three places around the top edges.

The doll's body

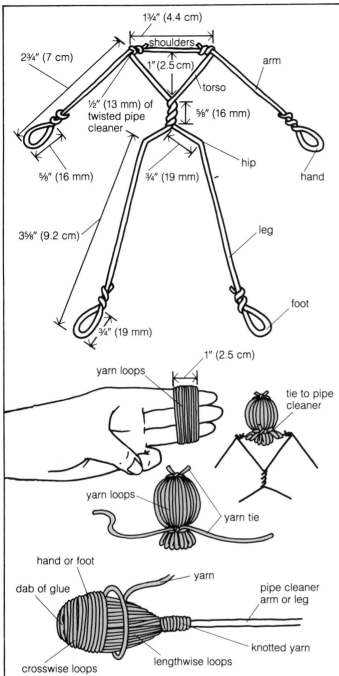

Greek Yarn Doll

Materials

Three 9″-long (22.9-cm) white
  pipe cleaners
Three 12-yard (10.9-m) skeins
  of needlepoint or crewel
  yarn, 1 each: flesh-colored,
  white, and navy
Embroidery floss: gold, dark
  blue, coral, and black

Polyester fiber for stuffing
A 10″ × 14″ (25.4 × 35.6-cm)
  piece of muslin
Sewing thread: to match the
  fabric and ribbon
A 6″ (15.2-cm) length of ⅝″-
  wide (16-mm) coral
  ribbon

1. The Skeleton. Bend one of the 9″-long (22.9-cm) pipe cleaners to form the shoulders, arms, and hands as follows: Make a flat 1¾″-long (4.4-cm) shoulder section at the center of the pipe cleaner. Bend each end down and out at an angle for 2¾″ (7 cm) to form the arms and make ⅝″-long (16-mm) loops at the ends of the arms for the hands. Twist each end of the pipe cleaner around the arm to anchor it.

Attach a pipe cleaner at the bend of each shoulder by twisting about ½″ (13 mm) at one end around the shoulder. Bend the two pipe cleaners down to meet 1″ (2.5 cm) below the midpoint of the shoulder, forming a triangle for the torso, and twist the ends around each other for ⅝″ (16 mm) to create the waist. Separate the pipe cleaners below the waist, and bend them out ¾″ (19 mm) to the sides to form the hips. Then bend them down and slightly outward for 3⅝″ (9.2 cm) to make the legs. Make a 1″-long (2.5-cm) loop at the end of each leg, and twist the end of each pipe cleaner around the leg to secure it.

2. The Head. Wrap 4 to 5 yards (3.6 to 4.5 m) of flesh-colored yarn around three fingers, keeping the bundle about 1″ (2.5 cm) wide. Tie the bundle tightly through the loops at the top with another piece of yarn, and slip it off your fingers. Keeping the front and back surfaces of the loops smooth, make a tie around the outside of the loops approximately 1″ (2.5 cm) down from the top tie to form the neck, and leave long ends on the tie. Using the long ends, tie the neck securely to the top center of the shoulders.

3. Wrapping the Hands and Feet. To wrap each hand, tie one end of the flesh-colored yarn to the twisted end of the pipe cleaner at the wrist. Wrap the hand lengthwise first. Then put a drop of glue on the end of the hand, and continue wrapping around the pipe cleaner from side to side until the twists at the wrists are completely covered. The finished hand should measure about ¼″ (6 mm) across. Wrap the feet in the same manner with gold embroidery floss. Cover the pipe cleaner completely and evenly to the end of the twist at each ankle.

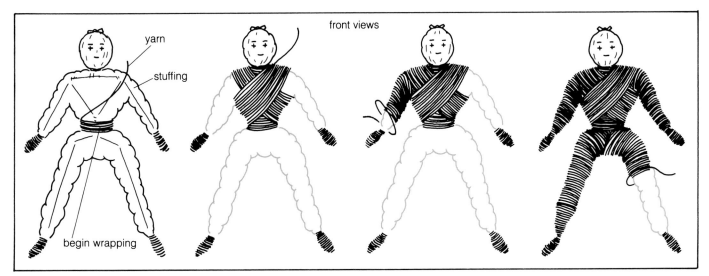

front views

yarn

stuffing

begin wrapping

4. Padding and Wrapping the Body. Using polyester fiber, **pad the skeleton** to fill out the torso, arms, and legs. The bulk of the padding should be across the shoulders and the hip line. Take care to match the thickness of the padding evenly on both sides.

    Wrapping the body. With a single continuous strand of white yarn, wrap the body as shown. Begin by tying the yarn around the waist. Then wrap the waist with closely spaced loops until it is completely covered. Wind the yarn across the chest and around the neck. Wrap the neck. Wind the yarn diagonally around one shoulder and the op-

posite side, until the shoulder, back, and side are covered. Then wrap the yarn on the opposite diagonal to cover the rest of the torso. Finally, wrap the arms and legs. Tie the yarn securely before cutting the end.

5. The Features. Stitch the face with coral embroidery floss for the mouth, black for the brows, and a blue horizontal stitch crossed with a black vertical stitch at the middle for each eye. Use small, straight stitches, as shown. Make the mouth ⅜" (9.5 mm) above the bottom of the head, the eyes ¼" (6 mm) above the mouth and ¼" (6 mm) apart, and the eyebrows ¹⁄₁₆" (1.5 mm) above the eyes.

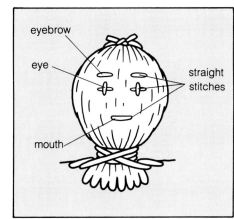

eyebrow

eye

mouth

straight stitches

The doll's clothes

1. The Tassel Hat. Wrap two 1-yard (.91-m) lengths of dark-blue embroidery floss and a 1-yard (.91-m) length of gold floss around three fingers, as you did for the head. Slip a 10" (25.4-cm) length of blue floss through the bundle of loops and use it to tie a knot around them; leave the ends of the floss intact. Slip the loops off your fingers. Thread a needle with the two ends of blue floss and draw them through the top of the head, leaving a ⅝" (16-mm) length of floss holding the loop tassel. Insert the two ends of floss back through the end of the tassel, knot them and then wrap and knot them around the tassel ⅜" (9.5-mm) down from the top. Cut the bottom ends of the loops and comb the strands together.

    Stitch a circular ½"-diameter (13-mm) hat on top of the head with backstitches of coral embroidery floss that spiral out from the center. Leave the strand that holds the tassel free.

2. The Shoe Tassels and Hose. Make two tassels with navy yarn, using the same technique as you did for the hat but wrapping the yarn around only one finger. Each tassel should be approximately ½" to ⅝" (13 mm to 16 mm) in finished length. Tie a tassel around each ankle, and bend the feet up at

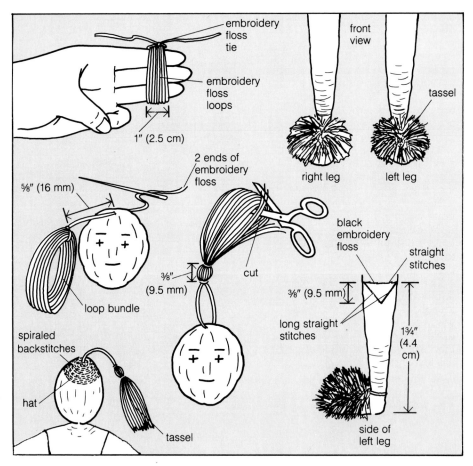

embroidery floss tie

embroidery floss loops

1" (2.5 cm)

front view

tassel

right leg

left leg

2 ends of embroidery floss

⅝" (16 mm)

loop bundle

cut

⅜" (9.5 mm)

black embroidery floss

straight stitches

⅜" (9.5 mm)

long straight stitches

1¾" (4.4 cm)

spiraled backstitches

hat

tassel

side of left leg

right angles to the legs. The tassels should cover the top of the feet.

To simulate hose, make a line of long stitches around the leg 1¾" (4.4 cm) above the foot, using black embroidery floss. Using long straight stitches, sew a ⅜"-deep (9.5-mm) 5⁄16"-wide (8-mm) V on the outside of each leg below and touching the horizontal line.

3. The Sleeves, Skirt, Vest, and Sash. From the 10" × 14" (25.4 × 35.6-cm) piece of muslin cut two 2¾" × 3¾" (7 × 9.5-cm) rectangles for the **sleeves.** Turn up and stitch a ¼" (6-mm) hem on one end of each sleeve, and make two rows of gathering stitches at the other end, leaving 3"-long (7.6-cm) thread ends. Stitch the upper and lower edges of each sleeve together. Turn the sleeves right side out, and slip one on each arm, gathered end first and seam at the bottom. Gather the top of each sleeve tightly around the doll at the shoulder. Knot the ends of the gathering thread close to the gathers, then slip them through a needle and use them to slip-stitch the sleeve to the doll's body.

The skirt. Cut eight gores for the skirt 2⅝" (6.7 cm) long, 1¾" (4.4 cm) across the top, and 2¼" (5.7 cm) across the bottom. Stitch the gores together along the side edges, leaving ¼" (6-mm) seam allowances. Press the seam allowances open. Turn up and stitch a ¼" (6-mm) hem along the wider (bottom) edge of the skirt. Stitch two rows of gathering stitches around the top edge of the skirt.

Turn the skirt right side out and slip it on the doll. Gather the top of the skirt evenly and tightly around the doll's waist, along the gathering threads. Slip-stitch the top of the skirt to the doll's body.

The vest. Wrap the vest on the body using navy yarn. First wrap the yarn around one arm at the shoulder and tie it. Continue wrapping, covering the gathering stitches on the sleeve and wrapping as much of the shoulder as possible toward the neck. Pass the yarn diagonally across the back and wrap the other shoulder in the same fashion.

Then wrap the yarn in a figure 8 pattern around the arms and across the back of the body only—until the vest looks adequate. Secure the yarn, and tack the loops around the shoulders in place.

The sash. Wrap the coral ribbon tightly around the waist, covering the top of the skirt and the bottom of the vest. Overlap the ends at the back, turn under the edge of the outside end, and then stitch it to the other end. Slipstitch the top and bottom edges of the ribbon in place on the skirt and the vest.

Sierra Leone Mother and Baby

Materials

A 9" (22.9-cm) square of dark-brown fabric

Sewing thread: dark brown, white, black, and red

A 2" (5-cm) square of cardboard

Polyester fiber for stuffing

⅛ yard (11.4 cm) dark-pink and white printed fabric

A 2" × 5" (5 × 12.7-cm) scrap of white lace

½ yard (45.7 cm) of black yarn

Eight tiny white beads

The doll's body and clothes

1. Cutting the Fabric. Enlarge the patterns to the scale indicated and cut them out, following the directions on page 155. Using the patterns, cut two body pieces, two baby pieces, and one fabric base from dark-brown fabric. Cut the smaller base piece from cardboard. Trace the actual-size features shown opposite on the right side of one body piece with a pencil and dressmaker's carbon.

2. Sewing the Body. Stitch the edges of the body sections, right sides together, leaving the straight end open. Clip the seam allowances along the curves of the head, and turn the body right side out. Stuff the body with polyester fiber so that it is firm and round. Make a row of gathering stitches with a needle and thread along the edge of the fabric base. Center the cardboard base on the fabric base, gather the fabric over the cardboard, and knot the threads.

Turn under ½" (13 mm) of fabric along the open end of the body, and pin it to the center of the base over the gathers. Slipstitch the body to the base.

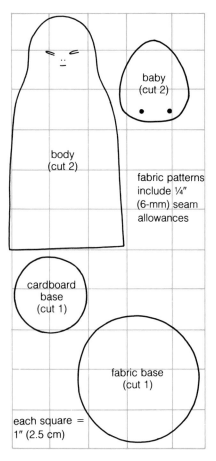

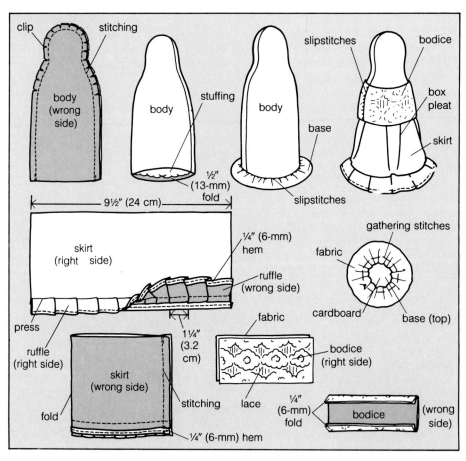

144

3. The Skirt. Cut a 3" × 9½" (7.6 × 24-cm) piece from the dark-pink and white printed fabric for the skirt and a 1" × 14" (2.5 × 35.6-cm) piece for the pleated ruffle. Press under ¼" (6 mm) of fabric along one long edge of each piece, and stitch along the folds. With the right sides together, pin the unfinished edge of the ruffle ¼" (6-mm) in from the stitched bottom edge of the skirt, making a ¼"-deep (6 mm) pleat every 1¼" (3.2 cm). Stitch the pleated ruffle to the skirt ½" (13 mm) from the bottom edge of the skirt, and press the ruffle down over the seam. Fold the skirt in half, wrong side out, align the side edges, and stitch them. Turn the skirt right side out, and slip it on the doll so the ruffle is even with the base. Make four box pleats around the top of the skirt to fit the skirt to the body; stitch the top to the body.

4. The Bodice. Cut a 1¾" × 5" (4.4 × 12.7-cm) piece from the printed fabric and one from the lace, to make the bodice. Place the lace over the fabric, and use the two as one piece. Press under ¼" (6 mm) along each long edge of the bodice. Beginning at one side, wrap the bodice around the doll, over-lapping the top edge of the skirt by ¼" (6 mm). Turn under ¼" (6 mm) at the end of the bodice strip, and slipstitch it in place over the body seam at one side.

5. The Arms and Sleeves. To make the **arms,** cut two 1¼" × 3" (3.2 × 7.6-cm) pieces from dark-brown fabric. Fold each piece in half lengthwise, and stitch it across one short end and along the open side. Turn the arms right side out with the help of a long blunt object. Stuff both arms with polyester fiber, and then tack the open end of an arm to each side of the bodice top.

The sleeves. Cut two 2½" (6.4-cm) squares for the sleeves from the printed

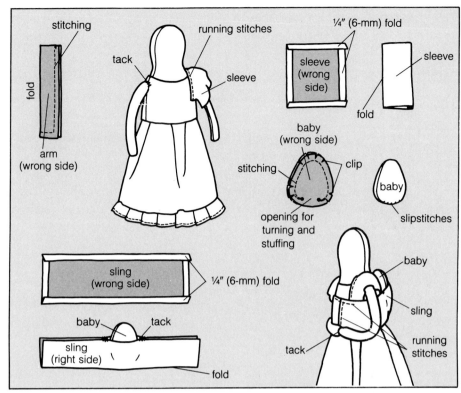

fabric. Press under ¼" (6 mm) of fabric around all four edges of each square, then fold the squares in half, right side out. Place sleeve in a U shape over each arm with the fold out, and stitch it in place through both edges to the bodice with tiny running stitches.

6. The Baby and Sling. Align the **baby** pieces, right sides together, and stitch around the edges, leaving a small opening on the bottom between the dots. Clip the seam allowances along the curves, and turn the baby right side out. Stuff the baby so that it is somewhat flat, and slipstitch the opening closed.

The sling. Cut a 2½" × 6" (6.4 × 15.2 cm) piece from the printed fabric. Press under ¼" (6 mm) on all four edges, then press the piece in half lengthwise, right side out. Place the baby upright inside the fold at the center of the sling. Tack the top edges of the sling together at the sides of the baby. Place the sling and baby on the doll's back, with the top edge of the sling ½" (13 mm) below the top of the bodice. Wrap the end of the sling around the doll's waist to the center front, and sew the edges together with tiny running stitches. Sew the top edge of the sling to the front of the bodice. Tack the hands to the lower edge of the sling at the center front.

The features, hair, and kerchief

1. The Features and Hair. Make the **features** as follows: Make lazy-daisy stitches for the eyes with white thread, and fill them in with a few black straight stitches. Make two tiny straight stitches with red thread for the nose, and a few red straight stitches for the mouth.

The hair. Lay eight to ten 2½"-long (6.4-cm) strands of black yarn across the head from side to side. Sew them to the center of the head with backstitches covering ¼" (6 mm) of the area on both sides of the head seam. Smooth the hair to the sides, and tack it to the sides of the head about ½" (13 mm) below the center stitching.

2. The Kerchief and Earrings. To make the **kerchief,** cut a 3½" × 3½" × 5" (8.9 × 8.9 × 12.7-cm) triangle from the printed fabric. Press under ¼" (6 mm) of fabric along the longest edge. Place the triangle over the head, with the folded edge just above the eyes, and tie it around the head, kerchief-style. Then tack it in place at the back.

The earrings. To make each earring, thread four white beads on a knotted piece of white thread. Tack the top of the beads to one side of the head about ⅛" (3 mm) lower than eye level.

Chinese Man

Materials

A 20″ × 6″ (50.8 × 15.2-cm) piece of medium-weight muslin

A 10″ × 14″ (25.4 × 35.6-cm) piece of blue cotton

Small scraps of heavyweight interfacing

Sewing thread: beige and blue

Polyester fiber for stuffing

Embroidery floss: red and black

A 15″ (38.1-cm) length of blue soutache braid

A 5″ (12.7-cm) length of round elastic

White glue

The doll's body

1. Cutting the Fabric. Enlarge the patterns to the scale indicated and cut them out, following the directions on page 155. Using the patterns, cut the following pieces, and transfer all appropriate markings onto them. From folded muslin, cut one head front, one head back, one body front, one body back, four arms, four legs, and two shoe soles. From folded blue cotton, cut one jacket, one front flap, one collar, two pants pieces, and two shoe sides. From interfacing, cut two shoe sides and two shoe soles.

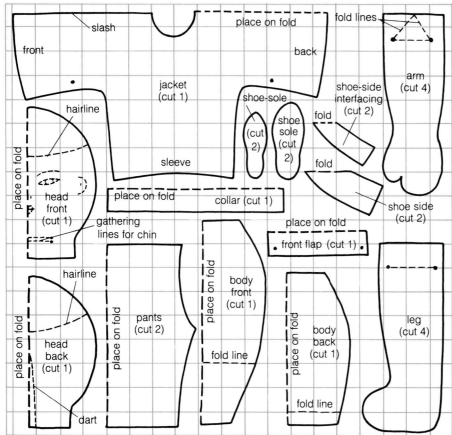

each square = ½″ (13 mm)

patterns include ¼″ (6-mm) seam allowances unless otherwise specified in the instructions

2. The Head and Body. With the sewing machine set for fifteen to twenty stitches to the inch (2.5 cm), stitch the body and head seams twice to prevent them from ripping.

The head. Stitch the dart in the back head section. Make two rows of gathering stitches along the gathering lines on the front head section. With the right sides together, stitch the head front to the head back around the edges, leaving the bottom of the neck open. Trim the seam allowances to ⅛″ (3 mm), and clip them on the inner neck curves, then turn the head right side out.

Stuff the head with polyester fiber until it is very firm. Pull in the gathering stitches to make the chin, then push more stuffing into the head with a blunt pencil point. Knot the ends of the gathering stitches.

The body. Fold and pin ¼″ (6 mm) of fabric to the wrong side along the neck edges on the front and back body sections. Stitch the body back to the body front, right sides together, along the side edges down to the fold line. Trim the seam allowances to ⅛″ (3 mm), and clip them at the ends of the fold lines across the lower part of the body sections. Turn the body right side out.

Attaching the head to the body. Insert the neck in the body, matching the side seams. Pin the head in place, covering the gathering stitches around the base of the neck with the folded edge of the body opening. Partly stuff the body, then whipstitch the head in place. Add more stuffing to the body until it is packed firmly. Fold under the edges of the flap on the body front. Pin the flap over the body back, and whipstitch.

3. The Arms and Legs. Stitch two **arm** sections, right sides together, around the edges, leaving the shoulder end open. Stitch slowly around the hand, being careful along the small curves. Trim the seam allowances to ⅛″ (3 mm) and clip almost to the seam line between the thumb and the other fingers. Repeat for the other arm. Turn the arms right side out, using the blunt end of a toothpick to push out the hand and thumb.

To stuff the arms, wind small amounts of polyester fiber around a toothpick, then push the stuffing gradually into the hand and thumb until they are firm. Stuff the arm to within ½″ (13 mm) of the end, then fold the top of the arm to a point, as shown in the drawing. The arms should be 2¾″ (7 cm) long from the end of the hand to the top of the stuffing. Pin an arm to each side of the body, with the point of the arm on the side seam of the body ¼″ (6 mm) below the neck seam. Sew the arms to the body, using three or four long stitches every ¼″ (6 mm).

The legs. Stitch two leg pieces right sides together, leaving the top end open. Trim the seam allowances to ⅛″ (3

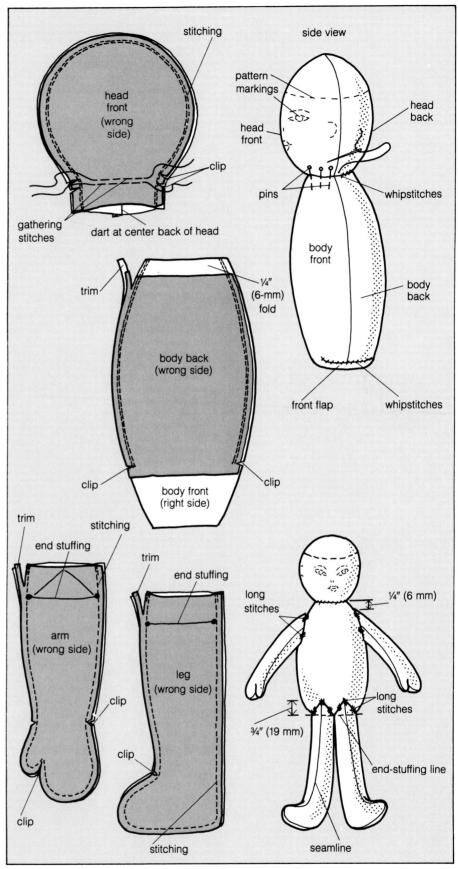

mm), then turn, and push out the foot with a blunt pencil point. Stuff the legs firmly up to the pattern marking.

Fold the open ends of the legs to a point aligning the front and back seams as you did with the arms. The legs

should be 3″ (7.6 cm) long from the foot to the top of the stuffing. Pin the legs to the body front between the dots marked on the pattern. Sew the legs in place, using three or four long stitches every ¼″ (6 mm).

The features and hair

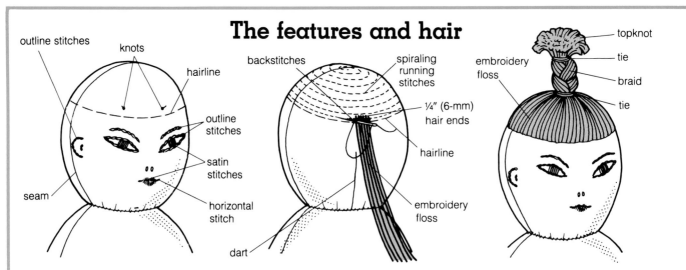

1. The Features. Embroider the features with one strand of embroidery floss and a fine needle. Insert the needle and end the thread above the hairline, so that the knots will not show after the hair has been added.

The mouth. First embroider the upper lip and then the lower lip, using red floss and vertical satin stitches. The bottom of the lower lip should be ½″ (13 mm) from the neck edge. Take care to keep the outline even. Make a ¹⁄₁₆″-long (5-mm) horizontal stitch at each corner of the mouth.

The other features. Use black embroidery floss for all the other features and outline stitches to embroider all but the pupils of the eyes and the nostrils. Use vertical satin stitches for the eyeballs and two very small vertical stitches ⅛″ (3 mm) apart for the nostrils.

2. The Hair. Starting ⅛″ (3 mm) above the hairline, sew a line of running stitches that spirals to the top of the head, pulling the thread tight as you go, to smooth the head.

Cut about a hundred single strands of 3½″-long (8.9-cm) black embroidery floss. Lay the strands close together vertically against the head, a few at a time, with the top of each strand ¼″ (6 mm) above the hairline. Sew a backstitch over each strand at the hairline so that the needle comes out slightly beyond the next strand. Make another backstitch, pushing the needle in at the point where it first came through. After all the strands have been sewed in place, backstitch around the hairline again to ensure that all the strands of hair are very secure.

Pull all the hair to the top of the head smoothly, gathering it at the center. Wrap a long piece of red floss around the hair two or three times and tie it tight. Divide the hair into three equal parts and braid it for about ½″ (13 mm), including the ends of the red floss. Wrap and tie the end of the pigtail with red floss. Trim the ends of the hair even, so they measure about ⅜″ (9.5 mm) from the outer tie.

The doll's clothes

1. The Jacket. Slash the center front open. Turn under and stitch ⅛″ (3-mm) hems at the ends of the sleeves. With the right sides together, stitch both sleeves under the arms from the sleeve edge to the dot. Clip the seam allowances at the curves. Stitch ⅛″ (3-mm) hems along both sides of the front opening, the bottom edges of the jacket, and the side slits. Turn the jacket right side out.

The front flap. Fold under ⅛″ (3 mm) on the short ends of the front flap piece, then fold the flap in half lengthwise, right side out, encasing the folded ends. Pin the front flap to the wrong side of the right front opening of the jacket between the dots on the flap so that the folded edge of the flap extends ³⁄₁₆″ (5 mm) out from the edge of the opening. Stitch the flap in place.

The collar. Fold under ⅛″ (3 mm) on the short ends of the collar, then fold it in half lengthwise, encasing the folded ends, as for the front flap. Pin the two unfinished edges of the collar to the neck edge, right sides together, and stitch it in place. Trim the seam allowances, and press the collar away from the jacket so that it stands up.

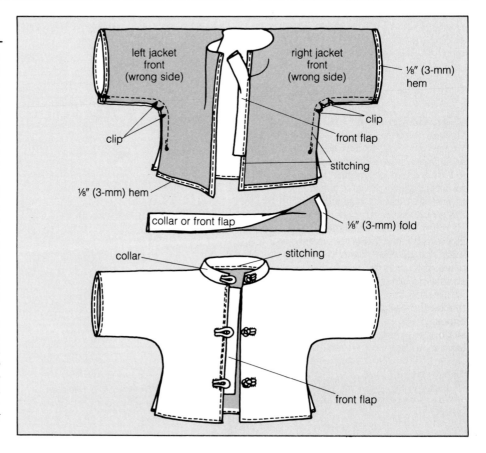

2. The Closures. Cut three 5″ (12.7-cm) lengths of soutache braid to make Chinese ball buttons. Pin each length at its center to a piece of cardboard, and loop the ends of the braid as shown in the drawing. Gently pull the knot tight, shaping it into a ball. Cut the ends to ½″ (13 mm), then fold the ends under ¼″ (6 mm). Sew the ends of the knots to the left side of the jacket, spacing them 1″ (2.5 cm) apart, starting on the collar.

Cut three 1¾″ (4.4-cm) lengths from the remaining soutache braid. Form each one into a loop, turn under ¼″ (6 mm) on each end, and tack the ends to the loop. Sew it in place on the right side of the jacket and the collar, making sure that the loop fits its corresponding knot.

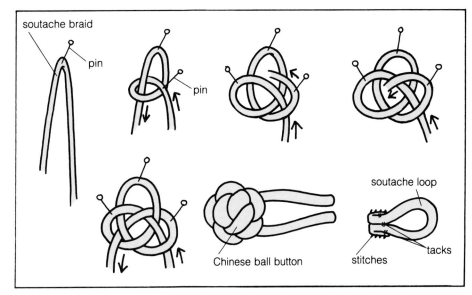

3. The Pants. Stitch a ⅛″ (3-mm) hem along the bottom of the leg on both pants pieces. Align the front and back of the pants right sides together, and stitch the edges together from the waist to the top of the legs, forming the crotch seam. Align the front and back of the crotch seam and the inner edges of the legs. Stitch the inner leg seams. Trim the seam allowances to ⅛″ (3 mm). Fold the waist edge under a scant ¼″ (6 mm), and stitch it close to the inner edge to form a casing, leaving a ½″-long (13-mm) opening. Insert a 5″ (12.7-cm) length of round elastic cord through the casing. Try the pants on the doll, inside out, and tie the elastic in a small knot so the pants fit snugly. Take the pants off, trim the ends of the knot, and stitch the opening closed. Turn the pants right side out and slip them on the doll.

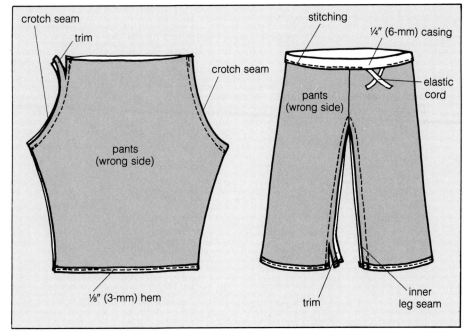

4. The Shoes. Dilute about ½ teaspoon (2.5 ml) of white glue with a few drops of water. Brush the shoe sole interfacings with diluted glue, then place one on the top of each muslin shoe sole. Glue the muslin edges down over the interfacings. Glue the shoe side interfacings to the shoe sides in the same manner, clipping the muslin at the pattern marking and gluing the edges down over the interfacing. Press the shoe pieces under a weight until the glue dries. Fold each shoe side, and stitch the back seams. Whipstitch the edge of each shoe sole to the bottom edge of a shoe top. Put the shoes on the doll, and make a few stitches through the heel of the shoe into the foot to hold the shoes on.

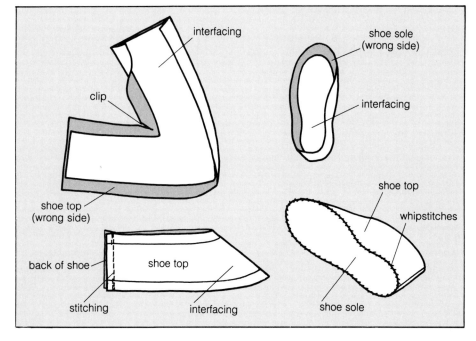

149

Appendix

All about faces

A doll's face can be made to reflect a character in a child's book or a fairy story, to look like a cartoon or comic character, to resemble a famous personality or historical figure, or even to impersonate a friend or member of your family.

Whatever the character and expression you would like to create, you must carefully plan the shape and proportion of the doll's face and use appropriate techniques to make them to produce the desired effect.

Every mark, no matter how small, affects a doll's expression. Even the weight of a line can change its look. Straight lines usually indicate severity and age, as does an oval-shaped face, while curved lines and a round face and features suggest youth. Try drawing different faces on paper or cutting shapes from fabric and arranging them on the doll's face before deciding which is right.

To avoid a deformed look, pay careful attention to the placement of the doll's features. For example, on an adult or older child doll the eyes should be placed halfway down from the top of the head to the chin, with the eyebrows just above them. For a baby or a small child, place the eyebrows at the midpoint of the head, with the eyes a little below them. Placing the eyebrows far above the eyes gives a quizzical look.

Doll faces are symmetrical. The easiest way to make a perfectly symmetrical face is to draw one side of the face on tissue or tracing paper, fold the face in half along the center, and trace the features on the other side of the paper. Add freckles across the nose and cheek in random fashion, if desired. A nonsymmetrical face, one with a crooked smile, for example, tends to suggest a comic character.

A good way to transfer the face onto flat fabric is to place the fabric over your design, place both on a lightbox or against a window during daylight hours, and copy the face with a pencil or markers.

The eyes. Eyes can be made in any shape from a straight line or a circle to a very elaborate, realistic design, and their expression can be changed by varying the amount of space between them. Omit the eyebrows and eyelashes to simplify the face. If you wish to make glasses for a doll, use thin wire or metallic trims, or embroider them onto the face.

The nose. The nose can be normal size on a historically correct doll, oversized on a comic doll, or omitted entirely on a simple baby doll.

Here are some ways to add or make three-dimensional noses. If the doll's head has a center-front seam, the head can be shaped to bulge out where the nose would be. Or a small circle of fabric can be stuffed, gathered, and sewed to the face. Another variation is to stitch three small triangles of felt or fabric together along the two sides, stuff the resulting pyramid, and sew it to the face for a nose. A two-dimensional nose can be a straight or a curved line or simply a pair of dots representing the nostrils.

The ears. Dolls' ears are often omitted, especially if the hair covers that part of the head. If you do make ears, place them on the sides of the head at a level between the eyes and the bottom of the nose.

The mouth. Place the mouth halfway between the eyes and the edge of the chin. A mouth can be a thin line, a small heart, a large lopsided grin, a frown, a smile, or any number of other shapes, but in general male dolls tend to have simpler mouths than their female counterparts.

Colors. Choose a color palette for the doll's features that will reinforce its personality. Pastel features suggest a dainty or a dreamy mood. Bright colors suggest a cheerful or an amusing face. Dark, strong colors are appropriate for an older face or a more sophisticated look. An older girl or woman doll might wear lipstick, rouge, or eye makeup.

Harmonize the colors used for the features with the color of the skin, and make sure to choose appropriate colors for the features of a particular ethnic group or nationality. Also, take into consideration the hair color or the colors of the clothes you plan to use. For example, a doll with copper-colored hair might look better with coral rather than bright red lips, and a doll with a blue dress would look well with eyes of the same blue in a different shade.

Working the features. In most cases, the face can be worked either before or after the head is sewed and stuffed, but if you wish to use an embroidery hoop for the machine or hand embroidery, work the features before the head is sewed together. Then sew the head carefully so that the features remain centered. This method will also allow you to discard the face if it is not satisfactory.

If you work the features after the head is sewed, the doll will really seem to come alive in your hands, and you will place the features more accurately. You will also be able to sculpt the face slightly by pulling the thread tightly at particular points as you sew the features in place.

Drawn or painted features. Drawing and painting are probably the easiest and quickest methods to use for making a doll's features. However, a face with a great deal of detail, such as an elaborately painted eye, requires time and patience to execute effectively.

Paint works best on relatively smooth fabrics; it is not suitable for hand-knitted, crocheted, or yarn dolls. If you choose to paint, use either textile paints, which can be heat-set with an iron or a clothes dryer, or acrylic paints mixed with a small amount of detergent liquid to make them flow on more easily. Draw the features lightly with a pencil or transfer them from a pattern before painting. A small brush with stiff bristles made for acrylic paints is the easiest tool to use.

Felt-tip markers are also very easy to use for drawing a face quickly, and they come in a wide selection of colors. Permanent markers are a must for any washable doll or one that might get wet. However, permanent ink will sometimes bleed into fabric, so test the marker on a scrap of fabric first. Water-based markers, on the other hand, usually do not bleed and are therefore easier to control, but they are obviously not suitable for a doll that will be washed.

Charcoal pencils and pastel pencils are effective for drawing the features on a doll that will not receive rough treatment. Spraying the finished face with a fixative will give it some protection but will not make it durable. Lipstick, crayons, pastels, colored chalk, and pastel pencils are perfect for making rosy cheeks and freckles, and for adding a touch of eyeshadow to a fashionable lady doll. If the pencil marks fade, they can be touched up from time to time.

Embroidery. Making a doll's face with embroidery stitches may take a little more time to execute, but the results will last. Embroidery is the best method to use on hand-knitted, crocheted, and yarn dolls, and it works well on almost any fabric. The materials used in embroidering—embroidery floss, pearl cotton, and crewel yarns—are readily available and easy to use. Experiment with other types of thread, yarn, and string as well to create different textures and colors.

If you stitch the face after the doll is stuffed, begin and end the thread at the back of the head or pull it to the back of the head after each stitch to create a slightly sculptured face.

An interesting face can also be quickly achieved with machine zigzag stitching or other embroidery stitches before the doll's head is sewed together. For a somewhat three-dimensional face, use two layers of fabric with

Expressions

cheerful

sad

happy

sleepy

laughing

angry

girl

boy

man

woman

baby

old person

quilt batting between them, and embroider the features by hand or machine.

Appliqué. Features cut from fabric or felt and appliquéd to a doll's face are effective, especially when the shapes are simple in design. Woven and knitted fabric pieces must usually be hemmed if they are to be sewed on by hand, since the unfinished edges will ravel with use. Felt is perhaps the best choice for appliqué, since the edges require no finishing.

Fabric features can be appliqued by hand with slipstitches, running stitches, or an embroidery stitch, or they can be attached by machine with zigzag or embroidery stitching.

To simplify the sewing process, cut the pieces from iron-on fabric mending tape or cut fusible webbing to back the fabric shapes; then secure them in place with an iron and sew around the edges.

Alternatively, instead of sewing the features

in place, you can attach them with special fabric glue or white glue, although this method is less satisfactory for dolls that will receive hard use.

Use buttons, beads, sequins, and trimmings for part of the features to give a special sparkle to the face.

In some instances, it is possible to appliqué a whole face to the head or body of a doll. This is an excellent method for repairing an old worn-out face.

The following designs for faces and features can be rendered in a number of ways. They may be painted or drawn on, if the face fabric is relatively smooth, or they may be achieved with a variety of stitches. In general, use straight stitches for short, straight lines, outline stitches for outlines, and satin stitches to fill open areas. Large areas can also be cut from felt or other fabric and then appliquéd or glued in place. For additional designs, refer back to the projects in the book. Any of the techniques shown earlier can be adapted in many ways for other dolls.

Eyes

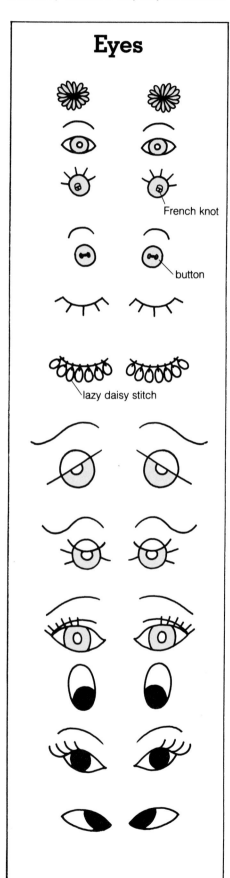

Noses

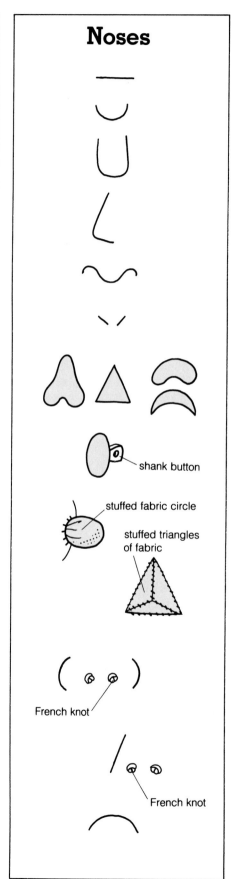

Mouths

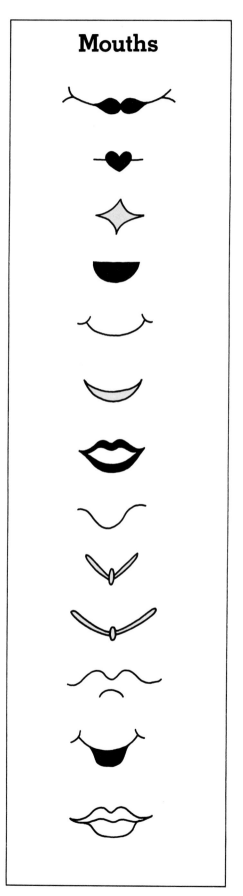

All about hair

A doll's hair, like that of a person, is one of its most characteristic features. When you plan your doll's hair, choose materials and styles that will emphasize the doll's personality. For example, a cute topknot or a fringe of feminine finger curls would be just right for a girl in a lacy dress, while a rough-and-tumble boy needs a mop of unruly hair. If your doll represents an ethnic group, nationality, or particular historical period, spend some time researching the appropriate hairstyles, to give the doll an authentic look.

Yarn and thread, the most common materials used for doll hair, come in an endless variety of colors, textures, and sizes. Knitting worsteds and rug yarns make good, basic hair, sturdy enough for a small child's doll. Those made of acrylic fibers have the advantage of being washable. Mohair yarn yields a fluffy, fuzzy texture while handspun yarns and kinky bouclés create scraggly, bushy hair. Cotton yarn and some twine are smooth and very soft to the touch, whereas pearl cotton and embroidery floss make fine, shiny, realistic tresses. Also,

do not overlook nylon cord, jute, linen yarn, silk thread, and the many colorful cotton crocheting threads. If your yarn basket does not have just what you need, visit yarn and craft stores to find the material with color and texture that best suits your doll's personality.

For a realistic look, the thickness and texture of the hair should match the size and look of the doll. Thick, rough, and bulky yarns make good hair for large dolls with a simple hairstyle. Thin yarns, such as Persian, embroidery floss, or heavy sewing threads can be used on a large doll to achieve a very accurate representation of real hair, but you will need a great number of such strands to cover the head.

For a small doll, thin yarns and threads must be used if you want to show a great deal of detail. However, if your approach to dollmaking is whimsical or if you are making a cartoon-like doll, you can disregard realistic scale altogether. Try attaching a few tufts of thick yarn in a cluster to the head, or wrap and secure a simple coil of bulky yarn around the head of a small doll.

Complete hair shapes can also be cut from fake fur, felt, or fabric, and then appliquéd to the head. Interesting three-dimensional bouffant hairstyles and buns can be shaped from

stuffed fabric and sewed in place. Velvet, terry cloth and satin each adds its own special texture as well. Synthetic doll hair (available from doll-supply companies), inexpensive human hair switches and beards (available from theatrical-supply or costume shops), unspun wool, and even bits of cotton wool or polyester fiber can also be arranged on a doll's head and stitched in place. As an alternative for certain dolls, try painting, drawing, or embroidering hair on the head with the same materials and techniques used to make the features (pages 150-152). Unusual hair textures can be created with satin stitches, long and short stitches, French knots, chain stitching, and other embroidery stitches made from any of the yarns described earlier. For a finishing touch, decorate your doll's hair with feathers, beads, clips, ribbons, or artificial flowers to match or accent its clothes.

The drawings and instructions that follow provide some basic techniques for attaching yarn and thread hair to a fabric doll's head, and for arranging the hair in attractive styles. Be sure to refer back to the projects in the book for many other techniques and styles, all of which can be adapted to different dolls and varied by using different materials.

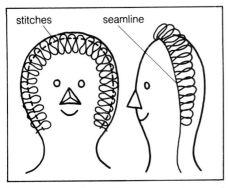

In-seam looped hair. To use a single row of strands or loops of yarn for hair, stitch the row to the right side of the head front piece, along the seam line. Then join the front and back pieces of the head with the right sides together, leaving an opening at the bottom to turn the head right side out.

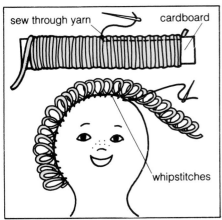

Surface looped hair. Another way to attach a single row of loops is to wrap the yarn around a strip of cardboard 1″ (2.5 cm) to 3″ (7.6 cm) wide. Stitch the loops together along one side, and carefully slide them off the cardboard. Attach the loops across the top of the head by sewing over the first row of stitches with whipstitches. In fact, if you wish, the whole head may be covered in this manner.

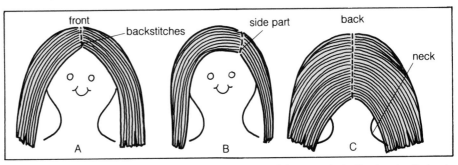

Long, thick hair. To make longer hair attached along a part, wrap yarn lengthwise around a piece of cardboard that is the same length as the finished hair. Cut the strands along one end of the cardboard. Place a few strands at a time in parallel rows across the center front of the head, beginning above the face (A). With a needle and matching yarn or thread, tack the center of the strands to the head with backstitches. For a side part, center the hair over the head, but tack the strands along the side of the head (B). For straight hair or pulled-back styles, end the backstitches about halfway down the back of the head (C). For styles pulled to the side, end the stitches just above the bottom of the back of the head.

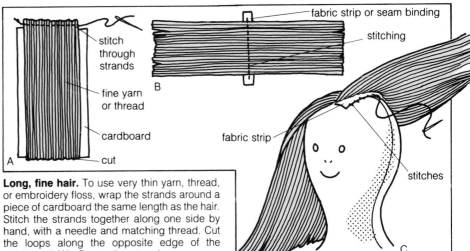

Long, fine hair. To use very thin yarn, thread, or embroidery floss, wrap the strands around a piece of cardboard the same length as the hair. Stitch the strands together along one side by hand, with a needle and matching thread. Cut the loops along the opposite edge of the cardboard (A). Center the strands over a narrow strip of fabric or seam binding cut to the length of the part, and stitch them together by hand or machine (B). Place the strip of fabric or seam binding across the center of the head from front to back and sew its edges to the head (C). To make the hair fall straight, apply a thin layer of glue to the head and smooth the

hair over the glue so that the underneath strands are held in place to cover the head, or smooth the hair over the head and tack some or all of the strands invisibly to the head around the sides and the back with matching sewing thread.

Ponytails. To make ponytails at the sides of a doll's head, smooth the hair to each side of the head, and tie the strands together with ribbon or yarn. Tack the underside of the ties to the head, and trim the ends even.

Braids. To make braids, smooth the hair to the sides of the head, and divide each side into three equal parts. Braid the strands, tie the ends with pieces of yarn or ribbon, and trim them even.

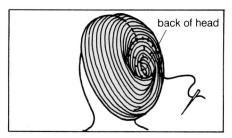

French twist or back knot. To shape a French twist or back knot, drape the strands of yarn around the head to the center back. Wrap all the hair in one direction vertically to make a French twist, or in a flat circle to make a knot, and stitch the hair to the head to hold it.

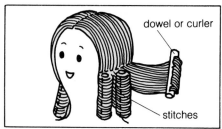

Finger curls. To make finger curls, use tiny curlers, toothpicks, small dowels, or any other cylindrical objects and one of the following techniques to form the curls. You will have to experiment to find the best method.

Wrap the hair around a curler, and stitch through the yarn to hold it in place. Some soft, fine yarns and threads can be curled with a setting solution, and do not need stitching. To make the setting solution, dissolve 1 cup (240 ml) of sugar in ½ cup (120 ml) of boiling water. Let the solution cool slightly. Then dip the hair into the mixture, set it on the curlers, and let it dry. Remove the curlers carefully. Some light-weight wool yarns can simply be wrapped around curlers and set with a steam iron, but do not touch the wool hair with the iron.

Layered hair. To make a shag or layered hairstyle, wrap yarn around pieces of cardboard of different lengths; cut along one edge as shown in making long, fine hair. Attach the longest layer to the head first (using back-stitches), continue with each successively shorter layer, attaching the strands to the head in the same way across the center of the head.

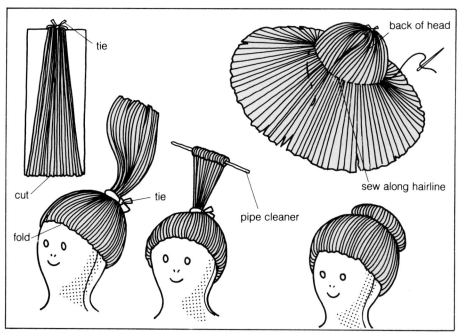

Pulled-back hairstyle. To make a pulled-back hairstyle, make two strips of hair, following the instructions for fine or coarse long hair. Attach the center of one strip of hair along the front hairline so that half the yarn hangs down over the back of the head. Attach the other strip over

Long hair attached around hairline. To make long hair to be attached around the hairline, wrap very long pieces of yarn around a piece of cardboard that is twice the length of the distance from the hairline to the center of the head plus the length needed to make a ponytail or bun. Tie the yarn together at one edge of the cardboard and cut along the other edge. Tack the tied end of the yarn to the center of the doll's head, and arrange the hair evenly around the head. Sew the hair in place along the hairline with matching thread. Fold the hair back over the stitching and pull it up into a **ponytail** over the center of the head. Tie the ponytail with yarn or ribbon.

To make a **topknot or bun,** curl the ends of the ponytail around a pipe cleaner; anchor the hair in place with stitches. Tuck the ends of the pipe cleaner out of sight.

the first one, along the center of the head, just behind the front hairline so the hair falls along the sides of the head. Pull the front section back over the rest of the hair, tie it into a bunch with ribbon or yarn, and tack the bow to the head.

Transferring designs and markings

Dressmaker's carbon. Trace the design from the pattern on tracing or tissue paper. Place dressmaker's carbon between the design and the wrong side of the fabric, and trace over the design with a pencil or tracing wheel. This method can be used on any fabric and should be used for all deep-pile or loose-weave fabrics such as fake fur and knits. To make lighter markings on a close-weave fabric, use the paper and pencil method that follows.

Paper and pencil. For symmetric designs to be used on a smooth fabric, trace the design from the pattern on tracing or tissue paper with a soft pencil. Turn the paper over and retrace the design, transferring it to the fabric. If the design is asymmetric, go over the lines with the same pencil on the underside of the tracing or tissue paper and do not turn the paper before placing it on the fabric. For dark fabrics, use a light-colored pencil.

Lightbox or window. Trace the design with a heavy pencil or pen on tracing or tissue paper. Place the fabric over the paper against a window during daylight hours or on a lightbox. Using a pencil, trace the design on the fabric. This method can also be used to paint or draw a face or design directly on the fabric with marking pens, acrylic paints, pastel pencils, or other marking devices.

Transfer pens and papers. Other types of transfer pens and papers are available at art supply or fabric and craft supply shops. Use them, following the manufacturer's instructions.

Enlarging patterns

Several methods used for enlarging patterns are described below. Choose the one that best suits your needs.

Creating an enlarged grid. Use a piece of tracing or wrapping paper large enough to accommodate the final design. Starting with a perfect right angle of the paper at one corner, duplicate the number of squares indicated on the original pattern grid, spacing the lines ½" (13 mm), 1" (2.5 cm), 2" (5 cm), etc., apart according to the scale indicated on the original. Copy the pattern square by square, first marking dots on the grid where the pattern lines intersect it. Then sketch in the lines between the dots, and include any other pattern markings. Cut out the enlarged patterns.

Using grid paper. Instead of drawing a grid, you can save time by using a sheet of blue graph (quadrille) paper, which is available in several forms. One type has ten squares to the inch (2.5 cm) with a heavier line marking every inch. Another has ¼" (6-mm) squares; draw a heavy line where necessary to mark the dimension you need. Sewing supply stores sometimes carry special grid paper for enlarging

patterns or dressmaker's pattern paper with marks an inch (2.5 cm) apart that can be connected to form a grid.

Master grid. If you are going to make a number of patterns using the same scale grid, it saves time to make a master grid on heavy paper or grid paper. Tape a layer of tissue or tracing paper over the grid, and draw the pattern as you would on the grid itself. When the pattern is complete, remove the tracing and save the grid for use with another pattern.

Photostat. The patterns in this book can be photostatted to the scale given with the pattern. However, this process is somewhat expensive. Check the classified directory of your telephone book for a photostat service in your area.

Pantagraph. A pantagraph is a reasonably priced mechanical device, available in art supply stores, for reducing or enlarging drawings. Follow the directions that come with the pantagraph for use.

Enlarging or reducing a doll's size. To make a doll that is a different size from the one given, divide the desired height by the total number of squares included in the height of the pattern. Be sure to consider all the pieces—head, body, arms, and legs as well as all the clothing. Try to make the distance between the lines of the grid a round number of a commonly used fraction such as ½" (13 mm), ¾" (19 mm), 1½" (3.8 cm), etc. Draw the grid and enlarge or reduce the pattern, following the instructions given above.

Hand and machine sewing stitches

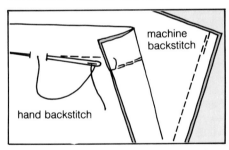

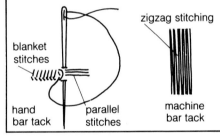

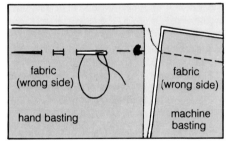

Backstitch. *By hand:* Push the needle up from the underside of the fabric and insert it ¹⁄₁₆" (1.5 mm) to ⅛" (3 mm) behind the point where the thread emerged. Bring the needle out again the same distance in front of the first stitch. Repeat. This stitch is particularly strong and useful for anchoring fabric and other materials in place.

By machine: Stitch backwards at the beginning or end of a seam to reinforce it.

Bar tack. *By hand:* Make two or three close, parallel stitches the length the bar tack is to be, and cover them with closely spaced blanket stitches that catch the fabric underneath.

By machine: Make a row of medium to wide zigzag stitching set close together (twenty stitches to the inch—2.5 cm—or whatever the instructions for your machine direct) to hold two pieces of fabric securely or to reinforce an area.

Basting. Make long running stitches (¼" or longer by hand, or six per inch—2.5 cm) on a machine to hold two or more layers of fabric together temporarily until they are permanently stitched. Leave a long end or ends on the thread so that it can be easily pulled out.

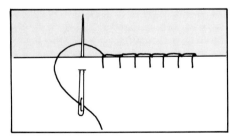

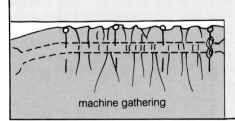

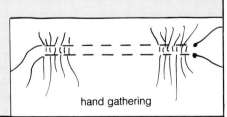

Buttonhole stitch. Bring the thread out from underneath the fabric about ¼" (6 mm) from the edge, keeping the thread under the point of the needle. Repeat at even intervals. Use the stitch to finish edges or to make buttonholes or eyelets.

Gathering stitches. *By hand:* Make one or two parallel rows of small, ⅛"- to ¼"-long (3- to 6-mm) running stitches, knotting one end of the thread and leaving the other end free for gathering.

By machine: Make one row or two parallel

rows of long running stitches (on most machines, about six stitches per inch—2.5 cm). Pull the thread ends on the top side of the fabric to gather it.

155

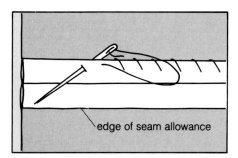

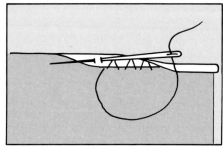

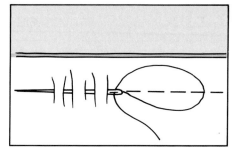

Overcast stitch. Make even diagonal stitches over an edge of fabric to finish it and prevent raveling.

Rolled hem. Fold the edge of fabric under ¼″ (6 mm) or less. Hiding the knot under the fold, take a tiny stitch in the fabric on the underside of the hem, then take a tiny stitch in the fabric just below the edge of the hem. Repeat for an inch, then draw up the stitches to roll the hem.

Running stitch. Weave the point of the needle in and out of the fabric two or three times and pull the thread through, keeping the stitches small and even. Used primarily for joining fabrics, basting, and gathering.

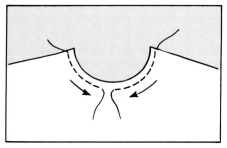

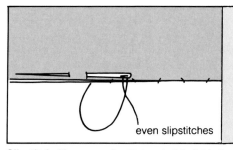

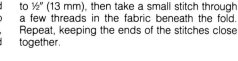

Stay stitching. Make a row of machine stitching (ten to twelve stitches per inch—2.5 cm) just inside a seam line to prevent it from stretching out of shape during handling and sewing. Stay stitching is most important along curved edges, and on a neckline it is done from the shoulder edges to the center of the neck on each piece.

Slipstitch. Use even slipstitches to join folded edges of fabric. Make ⅛″- to ¼″-long (3-mm to 6-mm) stitches along the edge of each fold, alternating from one fold to the other and spacing the stitches close together.

Use uneven slipstitches to make an invisible hem or to attach a trim. Slip the needle through the underside of the folded edge for ¼″ (6 mm)

to ½″ (13 mm), then take a small stitch through a few threads in the fabric beneath the fold. Repeat, keeping the ends of the stitches close together.

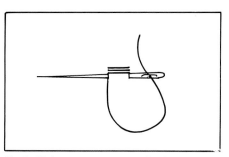

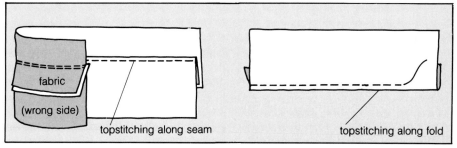

Tack. Make one or more small stitches in the same spot to hold fabric, trim, or yarn in place.

Topstitching. For decorative effect or to hold two pieces of fabric together, make a row of straight stitches on the right side of the fabric along a seam or line along the edge of a fold.

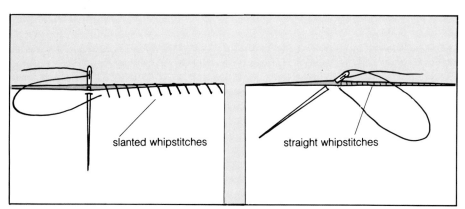

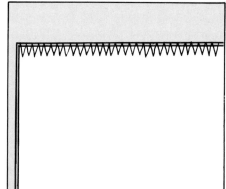

Whipstitch. Insert the needle at right angles and close to the edge of the fabric to be joined to produce slanted stitches.

To produce straight stitches perpendicular to the edges of the fabric, make an overhand stitch by inserting the needle through the fabric on a slant.

Zigzag stitching. Machine-stitch in a zigzag pattern to join two pieces of fabric, finish a seam allowance, stitch on an appliqué, do decorative embroidery, or topstitch.

Embroidery stitches

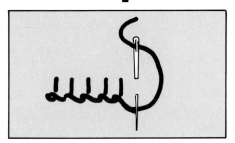

Blanket stitch. Make parallel vertical stitches of equal length along an edge or fold of the fabric, keeping the loop of thread under the point of the needle to make each stitch. Use for a decorative finish or border.

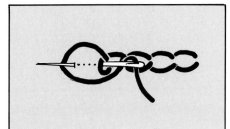

Chain stitch. Bring the thread out on the line where the stitch will be. Insert the needle where the thread came out and make a short stitch along the line, keeping the thread under the needle. This makes a loop, which should lie flat. Repeat, keeping stitches the same length.

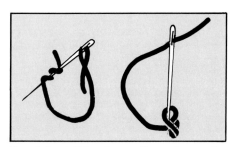

French knot. Bring the needle out from under the fabric, wind the thread around the point of the needle two or three times or more (depending on the size of the knot desired). Insert the needle close to where it came out but not in the same hole. Keeping tension on the thread with one hand, pull the needle to the wrong side with the other hand to form a knot.

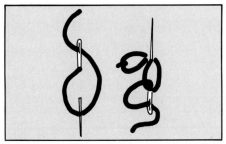

Lazy daisy stitch. Bring the needle out from under the fabric. Insert the needle in the fabric next to where it just emerged and make a stitch that is the length desired, keeping the thread under the needle in the same manner as for the chain stitch. Insert the needle just outside the far end of the resulting loop of thread and make a small stitch over the end of the loop. Bring the needle out where the next stitch will begin.

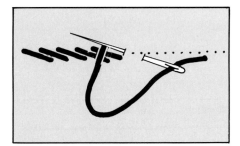

Outline, or stem, stitch. Working backward along the line of a design, make stitches of equal length, keeping the thread on the same side of the needle—either to the left or right of it—and bringing the needle out each time where the preceding stitch started.

Satin stitch. This stitch, intended to fill in an area solidly, is formed by making long straight stitches side by side and close together.

Straight stitches. Bring the needle up through the fabric at one end of a line in a design and insert it back down at the other end of the line.

Needlepoint

Starting and ending yarn. When making the first stitch on the canvas, leave a 1″ to 2″ (2.5- to 5-cm) tail of yarn on the wrong side; hold the end of the yarn flat against the canvas, and work the first few stitches over it. When ending a strand of yarn, bring the needle and yarn to the back of the canvas. Insert the yarn under the last few stitches, then cut the end off.

Half-cross stitch worked horizontally. Starting at the upper left, work each row of stitching from left to right, turning the canvas at the end of each row. To form each stitch, bring the needle out at the end of the row of canvas to be worked. Insert it in the diagonally adjacent hole of the row above, and bring it out in the hole directly below. Repeat, forming diagonal stitches across the canvas. Turn the canvas around 180 degrees, and work the next row in the same manner.

Half-cross stitch worked vertically. Start at the lower right-hand corner of the canvas to be covered. To make each stitch, bring the needle out in the row to be stitched, insert it in the diagonally adjacent hole above and to the right, and bring it out in the adjacent hole to the left. Repeat, working diagonal stitches up the canvas. At the end of each row, finish the last stitch leaving the needle on the back of the canvas. Turn the canvas around 180 degrees and work the next row in the same manner.

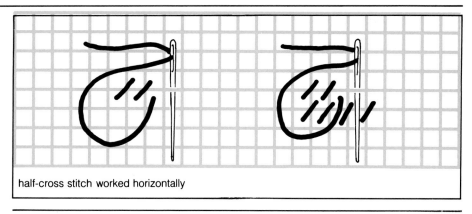

half-cross stitch worked horizontally

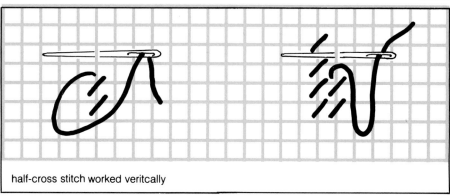

half-cross stitch worked veritcally

Knit and crochet

Gauge. The gauge in knitting or crocheting is the number of stitches and rows per inch (or per 2.5 cm) knitted or crocheted with a specified size needle or hook and yarn. Make a swatch at least 2″ (5 cm) square, block it, and measure it. If there are more stitches than the gauge calls for, you are working too tightly and must change to larger needles or a larger hook. If there are fewer stitches, you are working too closely and need smaller needles or a smaller hook. It does not matter what size needles or hook you use as long as the gauge is correct. **Note:** Do not try to adjust the tension in your stitches to change the stitch size.

Joining a new yarn. Tie the new yarn to the old yarn close to the work, at the outer edge, if possible, where the end may be sewed into a seam. To join a new yarn within a row, knit or crochet with the new yarn, leaving 1½″-long (3.8-cm) ends on both the new and old yarns. Tie the ends together on the wrong side, and when the work is finished weave them into a matching section of the work with a yarn needle or crochet hook.

Changing colors. For multicolored pattern work, tie a new color around the color in use, close to the last stitch worked. Leave a 1½″-long (3.8-cm) end of yarn to weave in on the wrong side when you are finished. When working, bring the new color from under or around the previously used color to prevent a hole from forming. Carry the preceding color loosely on the wrong side.

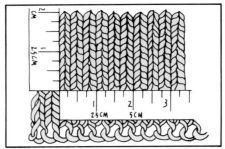

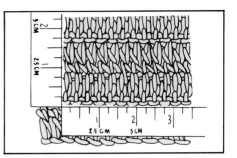

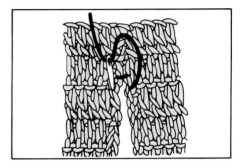

Fastening off. When one stitch or loop is left at the end of a piece of knitting or crocheting, cut the yarn about 3″ (7.6 cm) away from the loop, pull the end of yarn through the last loop, and weave the end into the work with a tapestry needle or crochet hook.

Sewing seams. Hold the edges of the work together, right sides out, and use a tapestry needle and matching yarn to sew them to-gether. Bring the needle up through the first stitch on the end of one edge. Insert the needle down through the first stitch on the opposite edge. Repeat at even intervals, working from side to side and matching rows and patterns.

Weaving in ends. With a yarn needle or crochet hook, run the loose ends of yarn under several stitches on the wrong side of the work. Trim the ends.

Knit

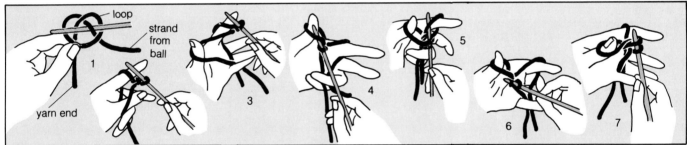

Casting on stitches. 1. Start to cast on stitches with an end of yarn long enough to allow 1″ (2.5 cm) per stitch for heavy yarn and ½″ (13 mm) for lightweight yarn for each stitch to be cast on. For example, if you are casting on 24 stitches using lightweight yarn, you will need an end that is 12″ (30.5 cm) long. To make a slipknot, form a loop in the yarn near the end, lay the loop back over the yarn, and pull the yarn through the loop with a knitting needle.

2. Hold the needle with the slipknot in one hand, then draw up the two ends of yarn and hold them securely between the ring finger and little finger of the other hand. For right-handers, slip the forefinger and the thumb of the left hand between the strands, with the strand from the ball at the back.

3. Bring the thumb up and spread the fingers.
4. Put the needle under the outer strand on the thumb.
5. Pick up the strand on the forefinger.
6. Pull it through the loop on the thumb.
7. Let the loop slip from the thumb.
8. Tighten the stitch. Pick up the end strand (front) with your thumb, and repeat for as many stitches as you need.

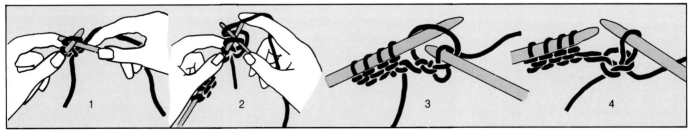

To knit. 1. Hold the knitting needle for the cast-on stitches in the left hand. Wrap the yarn around the little finger of the right hand, under the ring and middle fingers, and over the forefinger; hold the second knitting needle in the right hand. Insert the right needle into the front of the first stitch, and bring it up behind the other needle.

2. Wrap the yarn under the back and over the point of the right needle.

3. Draw the yarn through the stitch.
4. Slip the stitch from the left needle to the right one. Repeat steps 1 through 4 until all the stitches specified in the instructions have been knitted.

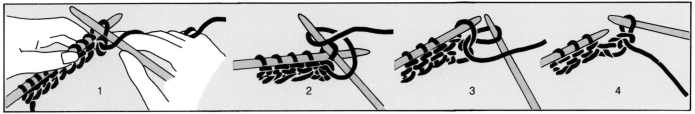

To purl. 1. Hold the needle with the stitches in the left hand, and hold the yarn in the right hand just as for knitting. Insert the point of the right needle into the back of the first stitch and bring it up in front of the left needle.
2. Wrap the yarn around the needle the same as for knitting—under and then over the point of the right needle.

3. Draw the yarn through the stitch, forming a new stitch on the right needle.
4. Slip the stitch from the left needle. Repeat steps 1 through 4.

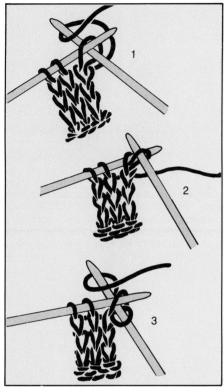

To increase. 1. Insert the right needle into the front of the first stitch on the left needle and bring it up behind the left needle.
2. Knit the stitch but do not remove it from the left needle.
3. Insert the right needle into the back of the same stitch and knit it again. Then remove the stitch from the left needle. There should be two loops on the right needle.

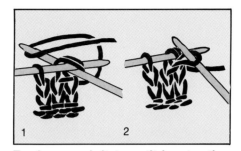

To decrease—knit two stitches together. This creates a stitch that slants to the right.
1. Insert the needle in the front of two stitches at the same time as for regular knitting. Knit the two together, bringing the yarn through both.
2. Slip the stitches off the needle together.

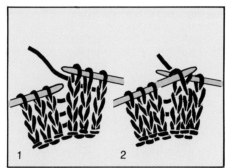

To decrease—slip, knit, pass slip stitch over knit stitch. This method creates a stitch that slants to the left.
1. Slip one stitch from the left needle onto the right needle, then knit one stitch.
2. Pass the slipped stitch over the knit stitch by lifting it back onto the left needle from behind the right needle.

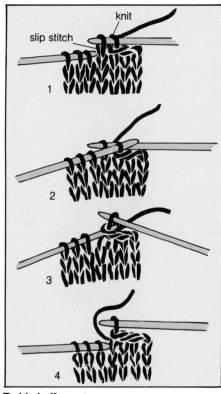

To bind off
1. Knit or purl two stitches, depending on the instructions
2. Insert the left needle into the first of the two stitches.
3. Pull the first stitch over the second stitch back onto the left needle.
4. One stitch will remain on the right needle. Knit or purl another stitch, then repeat from step 2. Bind off loosely to match the elasticity of the garment.

Crochet

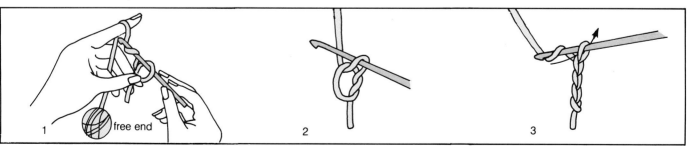

Chain stitch. All crochet starts with a chain.
1 and 2. To begin, wrap the yarn over the index finger and between the ring and fourth fingers of the left hand, and hold the crochet hook as you would a pencil in the right hand. Make a slipknot on the hook about 6" (15.2 cm) from the end of the yarn as follows: Loop the free end of the yarn over and around the hook, as shown. To make a chain, wrap the other end of the yarn over and around the hook, behind the loop, and draw the yarn through the loop.
3. Repeat until you have the number of chain stitches required. One loop always remains on the hook. Hold the work with the left thumb and third finger near the stitch you are making.

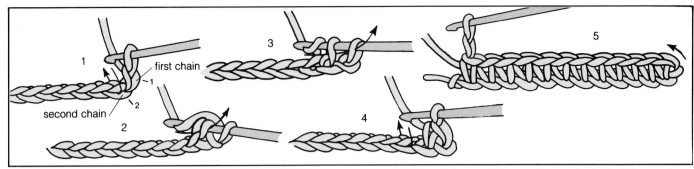

Single crochet. 1. To work the first row of single crochet in a foundation chain, insert the hook from the front under the top two strands of the second chain from the hook.
2. Bring the yarn forward over the top of the hook and catch it with the hook. This is called "yarn over" or "thread over."
3. Draw the yarn through the stitch so that there are two loops on the hook, and yarn over again.
4. Draw the yarn through the two loops so that one loop remains on the hook. This completes one single crochet. To continue, single crochet through each stitch across the row.
5. Chain one to turn and start a new row; begin in the first stitch of the previous row.

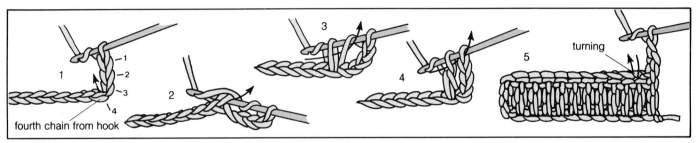

Double crochet. 1. To work the first row of double crochet in a foundation chain, yarn over, and insert the hook from the front under the top two strands of the fourth stitch from the hook.
2. Yarn over, and draw the yarn through the stitch, making three loops on the hook.
3. Yarn over, and draw the yarn through two of the loops, so that two loops remain on the hook.
4. Yarn over, and draw the yarn through the two loops so that one loop remains on the hook, as in drawing 1. This completes one double crochet.
5. To continue, double crochet in every stitch. At the end of a row, chain three and turn. The chain three counts as the first double crochet in the next row. Make the next double crochet in the second stitch .

Triple crochet. 1. To work triple crochet in a foundation chain, yarn over twice, and insert the hook from the front under the two top strands of the fifth stitch from the hook.
2. Yarn over, and draw the yarn through the stitch to make four loops on the hook.
3. Yarn over, and draw the yarn through two of the loops so that three loops remain on the hook.
4. Yarn over, and draw the yarn through two of the loops so that two loops remain on the hook.
5. Yarn over, and draw the yarn through both loops so that one loop remains on the hook. This completes one triple crochet. To continue, triple crochet in every stitch across the row.
6. At the end of the row, chain four and turn. To continue in triple crochet, insert the hook in the second stitch.

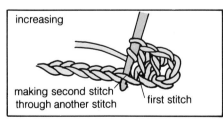

To increase. Make two stitches in one stitch of the previous row. Each time you do this, you add an extra stitch to the row.

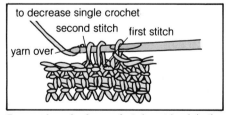

Decreasing single crochet. Insert hook in the next stitch of the previous row and draw yarn through to make a second loop. Repeat in the next stitch to make three loops. Yarn over; draw the yarn through all three loops.

Slipstitch (left). Use to join two pieces of crochet where an invisible stitch is required. Insert the hook from the front through the two top strands of a stitch. Yarn over, and draw the yarn through the stitch and the loop on the hook.

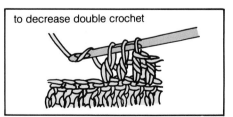

Decreasing double crochet. Yarn over, and insert the crochet hook in the next stitch of the previous row. Draw the yarn through the stitch to make a third loop on the hook. Yarn over, and draw the yarn through two of the loops. Yarn over again, and insert the hook in the next stitch of the previous row to make three loops on the hook. Yarn over, and draw the yarn through two of the loops, making three loops on the hook. Yarn over, and draw the yarn through all three loops on the hook.